SHORT ROUTE BRIDGE AT ST. MARYS

Williams, Photographer

A History of Pleasants County, West Virginia

Robert L. Pemberton

HERITAGE BOOKS
2008

HERITAGE BOOKS
AN IMPRINT OF HERITAGE BOOKS, INC.

Books, CDs, and more—Worldwide

For our listing of thousands of titles see our website
at
www.HeritageBooks.com

Published 2008 by
HERITAGE BOOKS, INC.
Publishing Division
100 Railroad Ave. #104
Westminster, Maryland 21157

Copyright © 1929 Robert L. Pemberton

All rights reserved. No part of this book may be reproduced or transmitted in any form or by any means, electronic or mechanical, including photocopying, recording or by any information storage and retrieval system without written permission from the author, except for the inclusion of brief quotations in a review.

International Standard Book Numbers
Paperbound: 978-0-7884-1207-3
Clothbound: 978-0-7884-7601

PREFACE

In writing the history of Pleasants county a great difficulty was that of winnowing out traditions and getting absolute facts. The unwritten history of any locality abounds with extraordinary legends which, in the course of time, have become accepted as literally true, and this has happened even in the short space of time since the first settlement of this county. In looking over the work I find several passages which should have been expanded by giving more nearly complete details, but it was impossible to obtain them, and in some instances impracticable or foreign to the design of the book.

Yet, in spite of the difficulties, I have thoroughly enjoyed gathering the facts and putting them into what I trust is a readable shape. In performing this work I have gone into the official records of the county; much of interest has been derived from the letters and journal of Thomas Browse, recourse has been freely had to the files of the St. Marys Oracle, which are almost complete from the year 1881, and for about the same period of time I have been enabled to supply something from my own recollection.

The general plan of the book has been to trace the gradual advance that has been made from the life of the hardy pioneer to the present age of comparative affluence and comfort—an advance that has been very marked within the last forty years, and which is perhaps not so appreciated as it should be. Few of the present generation can realize the hardships their parents were forced to endure, the meager subsistence derived from farms in the days when the chief products were hoop-poles and tanbark, or the hand-to-mouth existence of the laborer who sought to rear a family on the pittance of a dollar a day. Yet I take this opportunity to observe that, despite the tremendous improvement in physical welfare, it is very doubtful that a greater degree of happiness exists today.

It has been my effort not only to bring about a better regard for the men and women who ventured into the winderness and prepared the way for the pleasure and ease of future generations, but also to give due credit to the founders and builders of the county and town. Wisdom and strength of character are displayed equally well in a small as in a large community. It is not the stage, but the actor, that commands admiration.

Robt. L. Pemberton
St. Marys, W. Va., March 9, 1929

INDEX OF CHAPTERS

CHAPTER I—GEOGRAPHICAL DESCRIPTION

Location and Area—Islands—Ohio River described—Bottom lands—Hills—Creeks—Burning Springs - Eureka Anticlinal—Oil Sands—Minerals—Climate—Farm Products—Population. Page 1

CHAPTER II—RIVAL DISCOVERIES AND CLAIMS

Tygart the Trapper—Isaac and Jacob LaRue—French Discovery—La Salle—La Belle Riviere—English Claims—Bienville's Expedition—The Lead Plates—Christopher Gist—Remains of Mound Builders—French and Indian War—Washington's Voyage—First Settlements—Border Warfare—Tragedies of the Ohio—Opening the Forests—Pioneers. Page 11

CHAPTER III—OUR FIRST SETTLERS

Genesis of Pleasants County—LaRues, Triplett, Riggs, Reynolds, Henderson—Journal of Lewis Summers—Chimney Bottom—Gorrell, Smith, Rolston and other families—Old State Road—Christian Schultz—Thomas Browse and his Journal—Alexander H. Creel—Vaucluse—Rumors of Railroad—Fighting for Glory—Floating Stores. Page 29

CHAPTER IV—MAKING A NEW COUNTY

First Discussion—Donations—The Vote—Organization

—Building the Court House—Licensing "Ordinaries"—First Courts—Elections and Politics—Mustering the Militia. Page 53

CHAPTER V—THE BEGINNING OF ST. MARYS

First Owners of Site—Survey Made—Creel's Vision—Plat of Town—Creel street—First Buildings—Road to Northwestern Pike—Teamsters—B. & O. Railroad—Town Incorporated. Page 62

CHAPTER VI—DURING THE CIVIL WAR

Sentiment divided—Vote of 1860—Secession Ordinance—Forming New State—Prisoners of War—Confederate Raid—Drafting Men—Bounties. Page 70

CHAPTER VII—EARLY INDUSTRIES

Squatters Cabins—Tanbark and Lumber—Rafting—Barrel Staves—Fossil Oil—Great Oil Strike, Hendershot Well—Transporting Oil—First Well Shot—Wells at Vaucluse—Coopering—Eureka-Belmont Field. Page 75

CHAPTER VIII—THE FIRST SCHOOLS

Schools described—School Districts—Official Oath in 1865—Salaries of Teachers—Tax List Washington District 1865—Old Time Teachers—The Town School and Teachers. Page 87

CHAPTER IX—THE COMING OF THE NEWSPAPER

The Watchword—County Postoffices—St. Marys in 1877—River Transportation—Leading Citizens Described—Literature—Apparel—Fishing—Prettyman's Observer.
Page 94

CHAPTER X—BUILDING THE RAILROAD

Steamboats—St. Marys in 1884—Surveys for Road—Great Flood of 1884—First Passenger Service.
Page 105

CHAPTER XI—STRIVING FOR IMPROVEMENT

The old Court House—M. P. Church—Sheep and Cattle—Silver Ore—Telephones—A Teachers Institute—S. Kinnaird—Barney Olmstead—Stores and Hotels—Belmont Founded—Campaign of 1888—Big Oil Wells at Eureka.
Page 114

CHAPTER XII—THE BELMONT OIL BOOM

La Grippe—The Kangaroo Ballet—Belmont and Eureka Hotels—The Tom Cat Well—Bicycles—Star Route Carriers—Gas in St. Marys—New Schoolhouse—Broad Run Field.
Page 137

CHAPTER XIII—THE OIL BOOM AT ST. MARYS

Willow Island Run and Calcutta—War with Spain—Newport Centennial—Billsville—Coldest Day—Saloons—Water Works—Hotel Commercial Fire—Belmont Schoolhouse—New M. E. Church South—Electric Railways—Fairplains Addition—Phonographs—Automobiles.
Page 161

CHAPTER XIV—INDUSTRIAL ENTERPRISES

Spindel Top—Good Roads—New M. E. Church—Church of Christ—License—Button Factory—Gas Prices—High School—Oil Refinery—Flood of 1913—Chautauquas—Agricultural Agents—Electric Plant—Glass Factories.
Page 181

CHAPTER XV—THE WORLD WAR

War Declared—Drafting—Vagrancy Act—Training Camps—Food Regulations—Mortalities—Peace—The Return—The American Legion.
Page 207

CHAPTER XVI—RECENT IMPROVEMENTS

Property Valuations—The Banks—Making Roads—The Short Route Bridge—New Court House—City Charter Enlarged—Political Parties.
Page 217

CHAPTER XVII—CITY CHARTER, COUNTY POLITICS

The Recent Charter—Political Parties Banned—Water Works—National Politics in County—Equal Successes—List of County Officials. Page 226

CHAPTER XVIII—NEWPORT

When Founded—New England Settlers—Temperance House—Old Mill—Schools—Churches. Page 237

CHAPTER XIX—RELIGIOUS ACTIVITIES

Pioneer Preachers—Formation of Early Societies—Friends or Quakers. Page 242

CHAPTER XX—THE OLDER FAMILIES

Page 252

A HISTORY OF PLEASANTS COUNTY

CHAPTER I

GEOGRAPHICAL DESCRIPTION

Pleasants county is in the northwestern part of West Virginia, extending about eighteen miles along the Ohio river, its general direction being that of the river, southwest. Its greatest length is from the mouth of Sheets run in the line of Tyler county to the mouth of Bull creek, about twenty and one-half miles; the average distance from the river to the line of Ritchie county is about seven miles, varying from nine miles at Hebron to five miles near the head of Schultz Fork of French creek.

On the east it is bounded by Tyler county and on the south by Ritchie and Wood counties—the three counties from which it was formed. On the northwest lies Washington county, Ohio. It is one of the smallest counties in the State, having an area of 130 square miles. Only the counties of Hancock, Brooke and Ohio are smaller.

The title of West Virginia embraces the Ohio river to the low water mark on the farther shore, consequently several of the beautiful islands of that stream belong to Pleasants county. The first of these, following the flow of the river, are Grape and Bat Islands, about three miles above the town of St. Marys. The narrow channel between these two islands has been partly filled with silt, so that now they form practically but one island, being separated only in high water. Grape Island received its name from the great tangle of grape vines found on it by the early settlers, and Bat Island, which is much smaller, was so called because it was infested by bats.

Barely half a mile farther down stream we come to Middle Island, getting its name from the fact that a large creek disgorges itself about midway of its length. It lies close to the West Virginia shore, being separated from it only by a narrow creek known as the Thoroughfare. Ordinarily water from the river flows the whole length of the Thoroughfare, but when Middle Island creek is swollen by heavy rains, its waters flow up around the head of the island as well as down towards its foot, converting it into a true delta. The city of St. Marys lies opposite to the lower half of this island.

Proceeding down the river, below the mouth of French creek, are the Three Brothers Islands, named in honor of the Briscoe brothers, who are said to have taken tomahawk claims on them about 1783. The First Brother Island lies close to the main shore at Belmont, and the separating channel has so filled in recent years that now it is really a part of the mainland. The writer remembers skating in this channel in February, 1879, but for several years corn has been grown where the water of the river then flowed.

The Second Brother Island, commonly known as Broadhead because of the wide sandy bar which almost blocks the river in low water, lies well out in midstream. The boat channel, as in the case of almost all the islands in the whole course of the river, is on the Ohio side, and in order to scour out that channel, making it deeper, the Federal Government built a dyke about thirty-five years ago extending from the main shore just below French creek to the head of the island, resulting in the dead water below the dam becoming rapidly filled with silt. These two islands probably originated from the detritus carried out of French creek.

The Third Brother Island, located also well out in the river, perhaps owes its existence to McElroy run, and

Willow Island, which nestles close to the shore about a mile below, is perhaps a creation of Cow creek.

All of these islands have very fertile soil and are not much affected by high water, except in case of extreme floods. Permanent residences have been built on three of them—Grape, Middle and Broadhead Islands. They are especially adapted to growing peaches and small fruits, while the yield of corn is unexcelled.

The width of the Ohio varies greatly. At Bens Run it measures 1,320 feet between the low water marks on either shore, and at St. Marys the width is 1,056 feet. There are proportionately greater variations in the depth of the channel. At Bens Run the depth at low water is 2.3 feet; just above Grape Island it is 19 feet; about midway of Middle Island it is shallowest, being a little less than two feet; at St. Marys it gets down to 20 feet, and at Vaucluse to 23 feet. According to old rivermen, however, the low water marks set by government surveyors are not always to be relied upon, and one instance has been related to the effect that men rowing a skiff were compelled to look upward to see the established low water mark. This has led to occasional disputes as to the actual height of a flood.

Since the completion of the dams and locks built by the Federal Government steamboats have been enabled to navigate the river at all times excepting when prevented by very heavy ice. Before the dams were built, the depth was greatly affected by long continued drouths, so that only very small flat-bottomed boats could get over the shoals. At Grape Island and at Middle Island wagons have been driven from shore to shore.

The river has a fall of about six inches to the mile, giving it a slow current. It is subject, especially in early Spring, to sudden freshets, when its speed is increased to five or six miles an hour. These rises are usually due to thaws, melting snow and rain about the headwaters of the Allegheny or Monongahela rivers. As the Allegheny rises in northern Pennsylvania and flows through a part of New York, while the Monongahela rises in the interior of West Virginia, it is fortunately seldom that both of those streams pour out their over-swollen waters at the same time. However, that happened in February, 1884, producing the largest flood known up to that time in the Ohio Valley. The flood of March, 1913, which affected the valley only south of Wheeling, was the result of rain alone falling over the entire State of Ohio.

Formerly the river was replete with all kinds of freshwater fish, affording a good livelihood for many fishermen, as then there were no restrictions as to the amount of the catch or as to the means employed. The water was usually very clear and there were long stretches of sand or gravel beaches, backed by willows and balsam poplars or tacamahacs. Of late years, however, great quantities of poisonous acids, refuse from the manufactories, drain into it, making the water quite green and killing immense quantities of fish. At one time we recall seeing it literally white from one shore to the other with the upturned bodies of slain fish, and the smell of their decaying bodies was noticeable at a considerable distance.

The raising of the water level by the dams has entirely covered the white beaches. The average level of the pool formed by the dam is about 580 feet above sea level. or about eight feet above low water, so that a comparatively slight rise in the river will cover the dams. A rise of thirty feet sends the water over the lowest bottoms. But the floods carry down great quantities of silt, thus continually renewing the fertility of the low lands and gradually building them higher. At times the depth of this deposit on land that was covered by quiet backwater has been from two to four inches. But most of the bottom land in this county is above the highest flood known, and only a small portion is subject to overflow by an ordinary freshet.

This bottom land, or alluvial plain, extends the entire length of the county, a distance of eighteen miles, being broken only in two places by what are termed "narrows," where the river beats close to the foot of the hills. One of these is at Raven Rock and the other at Vaucluse. There are two or three terraces of these bottom lands, mostly composed of sand and gravel carried down from the upper waters towards the close of the glacial period.

The surface is usually composed of a rich humus, and in places there is an admixture of clay, rendering the land suitable for every kind of crop that can be grown in a temperate climate.

Back of the bottoms rise the hills, to the height of about 1100 feet above sea level, their several terraces showing evidences of the erosion that has been tearing them down through countless ages. Where the streams have cut deep channels in the ancient plateau, the several levels are easily traced on opposite sides of the valleys. For the most part the hills form long ridges, separating the streams, but in some places are unmistakable signs of cross currents and possibly of lakes, as might have been the case in the neighborhood of Arvilla, where there is a large area of low hills, the summits two or three hundred feet lower than the surrounding ridges.

The highest point in the county is on the old State Road ridge, which separates this county from Ritchie, near the head of Burnt Cabin Run. It is 1232 feet above sea level. The next highest point is 1207 feet high, near the residence of D. M. McCullough, a short distance west of Adlai postoffice

Though many of the hillsides are so steep as to be almost precipitous, yet the summits are gently rounded, affording excellent pasture and ideal sites for apple orchards. It is well known that the fruit grown on the hill tops has a much better flavor than that grown in the valleys.

The county is well supplied with streams. Excepting the Ohio river, the largest stream is Middle Island creek, which rises in the southeastern border of Doddridge county and flows through that county and Tyler before entering Pleasants near the village of Shiloh. Its length has been estimated variously between 150 and 200 miles, and it is designated as the longest creek in the world. Really its length and volume of water would entitle it to be ranked with the rivers, and, in fact, we have seen it stated that some of the first comers attempted to fasten upon it the name of Louisa river. The late Virgil A. Lewis, first State Historian of West Virginia, reports it as Be-yan-soss creek, a name given to it by the Indians, but whose meaning is unknown, while a map of about 1753 gives it as By-en-soss. When Washington voyaged down the Ohio in 1770 he says it was known as Bull's creek, from a trapper of that name who frequented it.

After entering this county its course is generally parallel to that of the Ohio, from which it is separated by Mount Carmel ridge. Originally the creek probably joined the river below Newport, the Mount Carmel ridge then terminating in the hill on the farther side of the river, opposite St. Marys. The river then flowed westward, through what is known as Ferguson's Valley, to Milltown, where it again turned to the south. So the river dug into the ridge on the north while the creek attacked it from the southeast, their combined efforts wearing it down until a new channel was made for the river and the hill became isolated. This theory seems plausible, and would perhaps account for the high bottom land on which the greater part of St. Marys is located, and it is strengthened by the fact that there is plenty of river gravel on the Kelley farm, it having been probably washed there when the river broke through the ridge barrier.

In the floods of 1884 and 1913 the waters of the river again flowed in their ancient channel through Ferguson's Valley, completely encircling the Newport hill.

The principal tributaries of Middle Island creek in this county are Sugar creek and McKim creek, both rising in Tyler county, the latter being much the larger stream.

French creek, Cow creek and Bull creek are the other chief streams, all rising in the dividing ridge between this county and Ritchie, fowing northwest and emptying into the Ohio. French creek, whose mouth is about three miles below St. Marys, is $12\frac{1}{2}$ miles long and has a fall of 345 feet. Cow creek, a little shorter with about the same fall, empties into the river about seven miles below St. Marys. Bull creek, which enters the river ten miles below St. Marys, is credited with being $13\frac{1}{2}$ miles long and with a fall of 265 feet. The last named stream separates this county from Wood. All these streams have narrow valleys, with very little bottom land.

The Burning Springs-Eureka anticlinal or fold crosses the western part of the county, entering just below Borland, then running north to Cow creek near the mouth of Pedro run, in which course it crosses Horseneck. From Cow creek it runs northeast to the Ohio river at the mouth of French creek. The anticlinal is an upward break in the strata of the earth, forming a ridge from which the otherwise level beds of rock and earth slope on either side. The summit of this ridge has been eroded, leaving some of the lower strata exposed. At various places along this anticlinal oil bearing rocks are found lying on the surface. In fact, it was on this fold that oil was first found in West Virginia, both at Burnings Springs in Wirt county and at Horseneck in Pleasants. This discovery led to the conclusion which has since been verified that oil in considerable quantities is very apt to be found on anticlinals. The large rocks piled in mass near the base of the hill on the farm of T. C. Hammett, near Eureka, are samples of this oil bearing stratum.

However, while oil has been found in greatest profusion along this fold of the earth's crust, it has also been discovered in every portion of Pleasants county in varying rocks, or sands, as they are technically called. On Horseneck run the first producing sand is found at a depth of from 100 to 300 feet, or at 700 to 500 feet above sea level. This sand, locally called the Horseneck, is considered identical with the First Cow Run sand, and is recorded in the Smith well at Belmont at 520 feet above sea level.

These oil sands are far from being uniform in thickness, and in some places either thin away or break off entirely, leaving no trace. This may account for the wide divergences often found in well records or logs, some acknowledging only two Cow Run sands, others three; some taking account of the first and second Salt sands, the Maxton, the Keener and the Big Injun, while others classify all these as of the Big Injun series. Each sand, however, has its distinct characteristics, easily distinguished by experienced drillers.

The Smith well log did not put the Horseneck in the Cow Run series, for he records that he came to the First

Cow Run sand 294 feet below the Horseneck, or 126 feet above sea level. The log of the Brockunier well in the same field does not mention the Horseneck or the First Cow Run, but states that the Second Cow Run sand was struck at 80 feet above sea level, and curiously enough the Second Cow Run sand is noted in the log of a well drilled on the Arn farm at Lytton as at exactly the same level. The Brockunier well was on the anticlinal while the Arn well was about ten miles east by north.

The record of the Cooper Hollow well near St. Marys shows the depths of some of the sands below sea level: First Salt sand, 7 feet below; Second Salt 357 feet; Maxton sand, 452 feet; Keener, 572 feet; Big Injun, 592 feet, and Berea, 1152 feet below. In the Arn well at Lytton the number of feet below sea level: First Salt, 180; Maxton, 640; Keener, 740, and Big Injun, 808. In the A. W. Gorrell well on Cave Run near Hebron, drilling from a little more than 800 feet above tide, the log gives the First Salt sand at 1166 feet; Maxton, 1673 feet; Keener, 1792 feet; Big Injun, 1816 feet; Berea, 2273 feet; Gordon, 2553 feet, and the Fifth sand, 2656 feet.

Most of the oil produced in Pleasants county comes from the Cow Run and Salt sands, and it is all of a notably high grade quality. Some maintain that there is yet a strong probability that the deeper sands, when exploited, will yield plentifully. Gas in varying quantities is found in all parts of the county, but chiefly in the southern part, around Schultz. Usually enough gas is found in the oil wells to furnish power for pumping them.

While coal underlies almost all the county, the beds are thin and cannot be worked to advantage except in a few instances. Some of fairly good quality has been produced from the hills about St. Marys, the veins being from twelve to sixteen inches thick. In the neighborhood of Borland two or three mines are still operated for local use, and the beds are from two to three feet thick.

There are no massive beds of limestone, yet shallow strata of three or four feet in thickness are found everywhere. It is very hard and so far as known contains no fossils. On Sled Fork of Cow creek is found a thin layer of black limestone crowded with white fossil shells, apparently minute clams or cockles. In the neighborhood of Belmont there is said to be a considerable showing of limestone of such quality that it could be burned, and a few years ago it was proposed to establish lime kilns there.

Sandstones, or freestones, of many grades are plentiful. In Tannery Hollow, below St. Marys, occur thick beds of Sewickley sandstone, of fine texture, the grains varying in color from gray to buff. This has been utilized for building purposes and also in late years for the manufacture of grindstones. On the ridge between Shawnee run and Middle Island creek is found a stone so soft that it can easily be cut with a heavy hoe, and is used in making concrete.

Good brick clay is plentiful, beds twelve to fifteen feet thick being found under the coal seams. And along the base of all the river hills is a good pottery clay, analysis showing more than 23 per cent of alumina and 70 per cent of silica.

In drilling oil wells sulphur water is occasionally encountered. One of these wells, said to have fine medicinal properties, is near the mouth of Broad run. At Borland is a sulphur and salt well of such acknowledged virtues that an hotel has been built to accommodate the many who resort there for the sake of their health. A few miles east of that is the Triplett mineral well, yielding about the same constituents, whose water had an extensive sale throughout the east about two score of years ago.

The climate is a fine average of the temperate zone. The temperature rarely gets above 90 in the summer or below zero in the winter. The average mean for February, the coldest month, is 29.2 degrees, and for July, the warmest month, 75.4 degrees. The mean annual temperature is 53.2 degrees. The average killing frosts occur on April 24 and October 16, giving about six months of growing weather. The snowfall averages 39.2 inches, and the rainfall average is 46.83 inches. The records show that we may depend on 100 days of clear sunshine every year.

The prevailing wind is from the southwest. Fortunately, this section seems to lie outside the paths of the great storms, for there is no record of anything more than what might be called a "stiff gale" occurring within the county.

The rich flavor of fruit grown on the hills has been mentioned, and in addition the same peculiarity is said to mark the hill-grown potatoes, especially when grown in the clay soil locally known as "white oak clay." This soil, when properly tilled, will withstand quite a long drouth, and a yield of 100 to 200 bushels of potatoes per acre can usually be depended on. The average yield of corn on hill land is 25 bushels, and of wheat about 20. On the river bottoms corn will produce from 40 to 80 bushels, and potatoes 200 bushels and more. These are staple crops, but the diversity of farm products as exhibited at the annual county fair is remarkable, and demonstrates that whatever can be grown in a temperate zone can be successfully produced here, so varied are the soils and their adaptability. The river and creek bottoms are peculiarly suited to early truck gardening, and their value for that purpose is greatly enhanced by good roads and near markets.

Another matter upon which emphasis should be placed is that blue grass, red top and clover are indigenous over the entire county. After a clearing has been effected no seeding for pasture has to be made. Visitors from the north and east have frequently commented with surprise that our hills remain green all through the winter. This indicates that it is an ideal section for cattle raising and dairying, and every hillside can produce unfailing springs of fine water.

It is recorded that the early settlers on the river bottoms raised their own cotton, but a crop could not always be depended on and the growing of flax was much easier. But we have seen fairly good cotton produced in a hillside garden, leading us to believe that with a proper selection of site and suitable cultivation even this crop could be made available.

The people are mainly of Anglo-Saxon descent, among whom may be properly classed the Scotch-Irish, who settled here about 1820. There are a few of French, Irish and German descent. Many of the early settlers came from Virginia, east of the mountains, and some from

Pennsylvania, descendants of Germans. A few negro slaves were held here before the Civil War, but while the general sentiment of the people has been against slavery, there has also been a marked antipathy to the negro element, and for years the county has been without a single negro resident.

CHAPTER II

RIVAL DISCOVERIES AND CLAIMS

Like the early ages of most lands, that of Pleasants county is shrouded in "the mists of antiquity," although the period is not so far distant but that men now living have seen and conversed with the early pioneers. But so rapid are the ravages of time upon the memory that very little is known of the first adventurers into this territory.

There is a tradition that a trapper named Tygart dwelt for a time on Middle Island about the year 1765, and there is no doubt that this region was frequented by white hunters and trappers at a much earlier period. In his tour of the Ohio Valley in 1770 and 1771 George Washington made a cursory examination of the lands along the river, noting the principal creeks and islands, the broad bottom lands and the heavily timbered hills. But the first permanent settlement was made by the brothers, Isaac and Jacob LaRue, Frenchmen who had been granted a large tract of land in reward for their services in the Revolutionary War.

Their estate extended from the shores of the Ohio, including Middle Island, to the head of Willow Island Run. In the year 1790 they built a cabin on Middle Island, and their tombstones are still standing in the little family graveyard near where their cabin stood. That was five years after the establishment of Fort Harmer at the mouth of the Muskingum, three years after the founding of Williamstown by Isaac Williams, and two years after the settlement at Marietta was made by sturdy sons of New England.

The entire land was a wilderness. The hills were covered with vast forests kept open by the continual browsing of buffaloes and deer. An old gentleman told us that so late as 1820, when he came here as a boy, there was scarcely any underbrush because of the deer that still browsed around their cabin. On the small streams colonies of beavers were often met with, and bears and panthers throve upon the abundance of their natural prey.

The aspect of the Ohio river itself has changed much since that time. In many places it has eaten its way hundreds of feet back from its former bounds, and its channel was then littered with half sunken logs and trees, which made navigation dangerous.

Only a few years previously the whole country had been wrested from the hands of the French, who were the discoverers of the Ohio and claimants of the entire watershed by right of that discovery. But nearly one hundred years had elapsed before any attempt was made to utilize the land they claimed.

In his interesting volume, "The Ohio River," Professor Hulbert of Marietta says:

"There is no question but that the brave LaSalle discovered La Belle Riviere of New France (the Allegheny and the Ohio) about 1670. He left no record that confirms this, but his later references to the Ohio are almost conclusive evidence that he descended that river probably to 'the Falls', as the Rapids of Louisville have been known since the dawn of history in the West. It was in the last year of the first half of the eighteenth century that the first European to leave record of it sailed the waters of the Ohio. This was Celeron de Bienville, a chevalier of the Order of St. Louis, commanding a detachment sent to La Belle Riviere by Marquis de la Galissoniere, commander of all New France and the country of Louisiana. The story of the advance from Montreal of this picturesque company of men, comprising a captain, eight subaltern officers, six cadets, an armorer, twenty men of the troops, one hundred and eighty Canadians and nearly thirty savages—equal number of Iroquois and Abenakes, is the very epitome of romance."

The French translated the Indian word Oyo into La Belle Riviere—the beautiful river. The first English who traveled upon it knew it only by its Indian name, and with slight change of spelling it has gone by that name ever since—the Ohio. So much for British pertinacity. The early Moravian settlers, who made it their duty to become familiar with the Indian languages, affirm that "oyo" means "very," and that the full name was "Oyopeck-han-ne," meaning "very white river." This name was given it because its surface was frequently troubled by southwestern winds which covered it with whitecaps.

But long before Celeron's voyage down the Ohio in 1749 the river was fairly well known to the Virginia colonists through the trappers and hunters who had penetrated beyond the mountains, and through the Iroquois Indians, who were friendly to the English.

By the treaty of Utrecht in 1715 the French had acknowledged the suzerainty of the English over the Iroquois, a great Indian nation that claimed possession by right of conquest of all the territory north of the Ohio River. This in itself would give to England preference in any dealing made with that Indian tribe, and well-established custom would inhibit any treaty made between the Iroquois and any other nation without the consent of England.

At Lancaster, Pennsylvania, in 1744, commissioners from the colonies of Pennsylvania and Virginia purchased from the Six Nations, an Indian federation of which the Iroquois nation was chief, the right to establish colonies within their territory. On the strength of this agreement, in 1747 the Ohio Company was formed and petitioned the king of England for a grant of 500,000 acres on "Romanetons and Buffalo Creek on the south side of the River Allegane, otherwise the Ohio, and betwixt the two creeks and Yellow Creek on the north side of the River, or in such parts of the west of said Mountains as shall be adjudged most proper by the Petitioners."

The condition was that the Ohio Company should establish one hundred families upon the lands within seven years. Members of this company in Virginia were Colonel Cresap, Colonel William Thornton, William Nimmo, Daniel Cresap, John Carlisle, Lawrence Washington, Augustus Washington, George Fairfax, Jacob Gyles, Nathaniel Chapman and James Woodrop.

In March, 1749, the petition was granted, limiting the land, however, to 200,000 acres, and in 1750 the company employed Christopher Gist of North Carolina to explore and report upon the most favorable site for a settlement.

In the meantime the French at Montreal had awakened to the imperiled condition of their claim to the entire valley of the Mississippi, including the Ohio, and in June, 1749, Celeron set forth with his martial company from Montreal to seal the French rights to the valley. From Lake Erie he made the portage to Lake Chautauqua, whence he floated down Conewango creek to the Allegheny, which he called the Ohio. At the mouth of the creek he buried a leaden plate on which had been engraved a declaration that the Ohio and all its tributaries, and all the lands on both sides of the river, belonged to the king of France and would be maintained by him. Similar plates were buried at the mouths of French creek in Pennsylvania, Wheeling creek, the Muskingum, the Great Kanawha and the Great Miami. Three of these plates have been found.

J. H. Galbraith of Columbus, Ohio, gives the following account of the finding of the plate at the mouth of the Muskingum:

"In the museum of the Antiquarian Society of Massachusetts there is a relic of great interest to Ohio people that ought properly to be in the State museum of the Historical Society on the state university campus. It is a portion of a leaden plate which Louis Celeron, French captain, planted at the mouth of the Muskingum river in token of his taking possession of the country tributary, in the name of the French king. By this action he hoped to reaffirm the possession of the country that it was claimed the discovery of the Ohio river by LaSalle long before, gave to this country.

"But two such plates were planted by Celeron in Ohio —the other one being at the mouth of the Great Miami. The latter may never be found—the washing of the two rivers having changed the scene very much, and the plate may be buried many feet deep. The plate buried at Marietta was found by boys while swimming in 1798, when the first settlement was only 10 years old. Lead was in great demand at that time for bullets, and the boys valued their find solely because of this value. Part of the plate they had already run into bullets before news of the find came accidentally to Paul Fearing, a lawyer and representative in congress.

"Not being able to read French he was only partly aware of the importance of the discovery the boys had made, but a French student translated the words on the plate to read "Louis the Fifteenth King. Ohio River." That established its identity fully and no more bullets were made out of it. Fearing saw that the plate got into the hands of Caleb Atwater, the first historian of Ohio, and Atwater gave it to Governor Dewitt Clinton, New York, who gave it to the Massachusetts Antiquarian Society.

"The plate buried on the other side of the Ohio at the mouth of the Kanawha, was found in the summer of 1846—also by boys while swimming in the river."

The inscription on the plate found at the mouth of the Great Kanawha, translated into English, is as follows:

"The year 1749 in the reign of Louis XV, king of France, we, Celeron, commandant of a detachment sent by Monsieur the Marquis de la Galissoniere, Commandant General of New France, for to re-establish tranquility in some savage villages of these tribes, have interred this plate at the entrance of the River Chinodahichetha August 18, near to the River Oyo, otherwise Beautiful River. as a monument of the renewal of possession which we have taken of the said River Oyo and of all those which fall into it, and of all the lands of both sides as far as to the sources of said rivers, as have been enjoyed, or should have been enjoyed, by preceding kings of France, and which have been declared maintained by arms and by treaties, especially by those of Risw.ck, Utrecht and Aix la Chapelle."

Celeron's mission was also to make friends with the Indian tribes and to prejudice them against the English. In this he was very successful, gaining the good will of the Delawares, the Shawnees and the Mingoes. He returned to Montreal by way of the Miami, the Maumee and Lake Erie.

In the Fall of 1750 the intrepid explorer, Christopher Gist, traveled up the Potomac and crossed over to the Kiskiminitas River, following it down to its junction with the Allegheny, which he also called the Ohio. He came to a small Indian town of the Delawares in what is now Pittsburgh, and there got provisions for his further journey. At Big Beaver he struck inland and reached the Muskingum, where George Croghan and Montour, scouts and special envoys, were busy endeavoring to induce the natives to favor the English. He went from there to the Scioto and then down that stream to the Ohio where he found the chief town of the Shawnees, which he called "Shannoah Town," situated on both sides of the Ohio. From there he roamed up to where Lima now stands and as far as the present Fort Wayne, Indiana, then returning to the Ohio at Shannoah Town. After resting he journeyed southeast nearly to the Falls at the present site of Louisville, and returned to Virginia by way of Pound Gap. He reported the best lands to be in Central Ohio and along the Muskingum, Scioto and Miami rivers, and also along the Licking river in Kentucky.

It is impossible to avoid noting the contrast between the brilliant martial display of the French under Celeron and the quiet yet bold movements of the solitary explorer sent out by the Ohio Company, both eminently characteristic of the nations represented. To the colonizing thrifty Englishmen it appeared that if one man could do the work, then one man was enough. He did it thoroughly, covering a vast territory alone and on foot, despite the fact that the French had been first on the ground and had endeavored to stir up a hostile feeling against the English.

At this period there were very few Indian towns situated on the shores of the Ohio, most of the villages being located on the tributary streams to the north. The hilly and mountainous country south of the Ohio was held as a common hunting ground by the Indians grouped around the Great Lakes and those of the Gulf, and was visited mostly in the Fall of the year for the purpose of securing buffalo meat and venison for the Winter. Buffaloes and deer are said to have traveled long distances to get to the many salt licks in West Virginia and Kentucky. Some of the salt springs were within the present limits of Pleasants county.

There is evidence that at one time a large settlement of natives existed at the mouth of Middle Island Creek, on both sides of the stream. Flint arrow heads and fragments of pottery are still to be found there, the latter showing such a degree of ornamentation that they might have been the work of a race anterior to the Indians. This view may be further maintained by the near existence of a large earth mound on the Reynolds farm, a mile north, and by the discovery of a large stone pipe, rudely carved in the image of a seated man, on Middle Island, only a few hundred yards from the site of the village. This relic was found about the year 1884 by George Riggs, a resident of the island, on his farm, and the carving seems to have been beyond the recognized ability or skill of the Indians. On the northside of the creek a fine pipe bowl of clay or soft stone was found, of ordinary size, plainly made, and possibly the work of Indians. There was also found a hard, flat piece of sandstone, evidently hollowed out into a mortar for the purpose of cracking corn or hominy, and near by were three or four round granite stones, small boulders, which might have been used as pestles. On the surrounding hill are many cairns, rude stone mounds thrown over the graves of warriors.

It is probable that the location was held in high repute because of the excellent fishing, and also because it is quite well hidden from voyagers upon the main stream of the Ohio. In times of very low water it was easily possible to ford the river at the head of Middle Island, so that it is reasonable to assume that this was one of the several crossings frequented by the northern tribes on their way to the hunting region of the mountains. From here the trail would naturally lead up Middle Island and McKim creeks, or on top of the ridge east of St. Marys.

In support of the theory that the trail led up the creek, early settlers tell of finding two never-failing springs, each hollowed out of the solid rock. One of these is on the hillside of the Locke farm, McKim creek, a few hundred yards east of the county's Four H Camp, and the other is on the James Wagner farm on Walnut Run, a tributary of McKim creek. This trail would be the most direct and secluded route to the dividing ridge between the waters of the Little Kanawha and those of Middle Island Creek.

The ridge east of St. Marys leads to the same point, so that it is possible by following it to travel from the Ohio river to the Alleghany mountains without crossing a stream of water. This trail would lead southeast through Pleasants county, then between Tyler and Ritchie counties, through the center of Doddridge and Lewis, and then into Randolph county, the general course being southeast.

While the Indians were in possession of all this country, unquestionably it was the scene of many fierce encounters among themselves, and it is certain that the land was not so cultivated as to produce the greatest good to the greatest number. A vast territory, capable of supporting comfortably many millions, was only occasionally traversed by a few thousand savages who cared only for their immediate needs and were apt to regard all intruders as enemies. From all accounts there was very little sociability among the several tribes. but on the contrary there was almost continual warfare.

It was this fertile land that excited the avarice of the French and the English. The former regarded it as a country abounding in furs, and proposed to use the Indian as a means of procuring them. The latter looked upon it as a place for permanent homes with rich agricultural prospects, and cared little or nothing for the Indian. The former claimed it by the right of discovery, the latter by right of purchase. There was a great deal of maneuvering by both parties, but as usual the issue was finally determined by force of arms. For nearly three years they eyed each other like well-matched dogs, each studying every twitching muscle of the other. The first move was made by the French.

They had already built a fort at Niagara, contrary to an agreement between them and the English, and in the Spring of 1753 they made preparations to extend their line of forts from Niagara down the Allegheny and Ohio rivers. The Virginians began to protest, and in November Governor Dinwiddie delegated George Washington, then a young man of only twenty-one, as a messenger to the French on the shores of Lake Erie, his guide and companion being that experienced backwoodsman, Christopher Gist.

The trip was made in the Winter, amid great hardships, but it was fruitless. It was a wonderful adventure for a youth, traveling over five hundred miles on foot, in the worst season of the year, through an unknown wilderness, knowing that every action was viewed with jealousy by vengeful savages.

Diplomacy was now at an end. Even before Washington returned to Virginia the English were preparing to erect a fort where Pittsburgh now stands. Captain William Trent was in charge, but before the work was finished, in April, 1854, the French descended in force and compelled him to surrender. The fort was then finished and called Fort DuQuesne in honor of the governor of New France.

Then followed what is known as the French and Indian War, Washington's success at the first battle of the war, Great Meadows, Braddock's defeat in 1755, the ultimate capture of Fort Duquesne in 1758 by General Forbes, aided by Colonels Bouquet and Washington, and all ending in the complete surrender to England of all the French possessions in North America except one little island near New Foundland.

The war of course interfered with the proposed settlements by the English down the Ohio Valley, but the movement westward across the mountains, which had begun a generation before. steadily increased. One set of pioneers came up the Potomac, and the other advanced down the valley of the New river to the Kanawha.

One of the first along the Potomac was Morgan ap Morgan, who set up a cabin in Berkeley county in 1726. This Morgan was a Welshman, as is indicated by the syllable "ap" which signifies that he was Morgan the son of Morgan. He was the ancestor of a very numerous family of that name which spread over the northern and western portions of the State, sturdy and patriotic citizens, many achieving fame and giving additional luster to the honor of our country. Eight years later Richard Morgan settled at New Mecklenberg, now Shepherdstown, and in the following year settlements were made on the South Branch of the Potomac. By 1753 some of the pioneers of the South Branch had crossed the dividing ridge and built cabins on Tygart's river.

About 1740 Stephen Sewell and Jacob Marlin made their way into what is now Pocahontas county and built lodges near the present site of Marlinton, and within fifteen years there was a considerable white population along the Greenbrier river, and extending down to the Kanawha. The outstanding family in that section was that of the Lewises, who became very prominent in the history of Virginia.

The first depredation said to have been committed by the Indians within the limits of West Virginia was in 1747, when they raided the cabin of Adam Harmon on the New River and stole his pack of furs. For a period of fifty years succeeding that event the border annals are replete with trouble between the two races.

It was a pitiless, ruthless warfare of hate and reprisal, conducted mainly on both sides by individuals or small parties of marauders. Indians stealthily crept upon the homes of squatters, killing the men and frequently the women and children, but the latter were sometimes carried into captivity, hundreds of miles into the wilderness, transferred from one tribe to another. Few made their escape, not many being endowed with the desperate courage of Mary Ingles, who finally reached her own people after passing through the most terrifying dangers. Many of the children, indeed, grew up like the savages and became so enamored with the wild life, that even when an opportunity to return to their kindred was offered, they declined to accept it.

Probably no other section of the United States passed through such horrors as the Ohio Valley, so frequent and so long continued. Certainly no other section produced so many noted "Indian fighters," chief among whom stands Lewis Wetzel, whose exploits in this immediate vicinity are familiar to everybody. Many of these scouts figured as heroes of the "Dime Novels" of sixty years ago. They were proficient in savage warfare, exceeding the Indians themselves in strength and cunning, and adopting many of the customs of their enemies, some going so far as to scalp their victims; but the usual procedure was to simply cut notches in the gunstock as a tally of those they had slain.

This border warfare endured until 1793, when the severe punishment administered to the Indians at Fallen Timber by General Wayne brought peace to the lands on both sides of the Ohio.

George Washington made a trip down the river in the fall of 1770, for the purpose of selecting land for himself and others, but there is no record that he chose any within the limits of what is now Pleasants county. His journal, part of which we quote, is rather interesting:

"Thursday, October 25th, 1770. About half way in the long reach we Incampd, opposite to the beginning of a large bottom on the East side of the River. At this place we through out some Lines at Night and found a Cat fish of the size of our largest River Cats hooked to it in the Morning, tho it was of the smallest kind here. We found no Rifts in this days passage, but pretty swift water in some places, and still in others. We found the bottoms increasd in size, both as to length and breadth, and the River more choked up with Fallen Trees, and the bottom of the River next the Shores rather more

Muddy but in general stony as it has been all the way down.

"Friday 26th. Left our Incampment at half an hour after 6 o'clock, and passed a small run on the West side about 4 Miles lower. At the lower end of the long reach, and for some distance up it, on the East side, is a large bottom, but low, and covered with beach next the River shore, which is no Indication of good Land. The long reach is a strait course of the river for abt. 18 or 20 Miles which appears the more extraordinary as the Ohio in general, is remarkably crooked. There are several Islands in this reach, some containing an 100 or more Acres of Land; but all I apprehend liable to be overflowed.

"At the end of this reach we found one Martin and Lindsay two Traders; and from them learnt, that the Person drownd was one Philips attempting in Comp. with Rogers, another Indn. Trader, to Swim the River with their Horses at an improper place; Rogers himself narrowly escaping. Five Miles lower down, comes in a large Creek from the Eastward, right against an Island of good land, at least a Mile or two in length. At the mouth of this creek, the name of wch. I could not learn except that it was calld by some Bulls Creek from one Bull that hunted on it is a bottom of good Land, tho rather too much mixd with Beach; opposite to this Island the Indians showd us a Buffalo Path, the Track of which we see.

"Five or Six Miles below the last mentioned Creek we came to the three Island before wch we observed a small run on each side coming in. Below these Islands is a large body of flat Land, with a water course running through it on the East Side, and the Hills back, neither so high, nor steep in appearance as they are up the Rver. On the other hand, the bottoms do not appear so rich, tho much longer and wider, the bottom last mentioned is upon a strait reach of the River, I suppose 6 or 8 Miles in length; at the lower end of which, on the East side, comes in a pretty large Run from the size of the Mouth. (Bull Creek). About this, above, below and back, there seems to be a very large Body of flat Land with some little risings in it.

"About 12 Miles below the three Islands we Incampd just above the Mouth of the Creek which appears pretty large at the Mouth and just above an Island. (Little Muskingum at Reno). All the Lands from a little below the Creek which I have distinguished by the name of Bull Creek, appears to be level, with some small Hillocks intermixd, as far as we coud see into the Country. We met with no Rifts today, but some pretty strong water, upon the whole tolerable gentle. The sides of the River was a good deal incommoded with old Trees, wch. impeded our passage a little."

In the meantime, no sooner was the war with France closed than the rush of immigration began down the valley, colonists literally fighting their way to the rich lands on which they hoped to build their fortunes as well as their homes. It was the actual beginning of that tremendous westward movement which has scarcely ceased even in our own time. When we note the vast expanses of lands still lying idle east of the Alleghanies, we are led to wonder at the feverishness of those pioneers who risked their lives in seizing upon a remote wilderness. At that time there were barely three million inhabitants in the Atlantic seaboard, with more good farm land than they could utilize. The movement cannot be reconciled to the teaching of calm philosophy. It was not a stampede for gold, and there was no necessity for more land. It can only be attributed to that westward yearning that seems to have actuated mankind even before the dawn of history, for never has there been a record of a general eastward movement.

The most favored route seems to have been up the Potomac to Cumberland, thence over the hills to Brownsville on the Monongahela, which became the great outfitting station and port. The canoe of the hunter and trapper was early replaced by the raft and the flatboat. But from the nature of their construction craft of these kinds were unable to return up stream, so the keelboat was designed—a vessel with a sharp prow, capable of being propelled with a sail or of being pushed up the river with the aid of long poles. The timber of the rafts and flatboats, when the destination had been reached, was used in constructing houses.

In his book, "The Ohio River," Professor Hulbert describes the flatboats on which the first permanent settlers descended the stream as mere rafts of lumber with a lean-to or tent pitched in the center. This sort of craft was called a "broad-horn." The next development was a real flatboat or shallow barge, with a cabin in the center, and succeeding that came the keelboat, having a regular cutting bow and keel, enabling it to be worked against a current. The keelboat was about fifty feet long and twelve feet wide, the whole roofed over, and had running boards on the sides on which the crew walked while propelling the craft with large poles.

As an illustration of the dangers faced by these early voyagers, we quote from Professor Hulbert's book the story of John May, in whose honor Maysville, Kentucky, was named. This tragedy occurred about the year 1784.

"Embarking on a flat at Kelly's Station on the Great Kanawha, in company with his clerk Johnson and a trader named Skiles, Point Pleasant on the Ohio was reached without incident. Here they were joined by a man named Flinn and two sisters by the name of Fleming. At daylight on the morning after leaving Point Pleasant, Flinn, who was on watch, awakened the whole crew with a cry of alarm. Far down the river the smoke of a large fire could be seen drifting above the trees and out over the water. Just as May had decided upon which shore the fire was and was heading for the opposite (Virginia) side two white men came down to the water's edge on the 'Indian' side and implored to be taken aboard; they told when and where they had been taken captive, how they effected their escape, and added that the Indians were hard on their trail. The veteran May remained unmoved at the story, and when he asked the reason of the fire and smoke and received a reply from the whites denying any knowledge of a fire, he scoffed at them. While the parley was taking place the boat was kept amid-stream in the current and the white decoys ran along the shore continuing their well feigned lamentations. These affected the Fleming women and also Flinn, who at last proposed to May to land and let the whites aboard. The request was refused, but after a time, through the entreaties of the woman and Flinn May agreed to run near enough the shore to allow Flinn to wade ashore and interview the two men. But this was not done until the boat had floated a mile beyond the decoys, who, probably, were stopped by the impassable nature of the river bank.

"However, the moment Flinn's foot touched shore, several Indians, well-nigh breathless from the exhausting run of miles in the forest, stepped out and seized him and opened fire on the boat. Johnson and Skiles sprang to their guns, but May, knowing that the current in the middle of the river was their one hope of escape, leaped to his oar. He called the others to leave their guns and help him, but the rain of bullets made it impossible to remain in range and the men sank behind shelter. The boat still lay in the backwater, and the Indians, wary of approaching kept up a continuous fire. One of the women received a bullet in the mouth and fell dead; Skiles was shot through both shoulders; when at last May arose and swung his night-cap over his head in sign of surrender, he received a bullet square in the center of his forehead and fell dead in his tracks. Soon the Indians came out to the boat and, boarding her, ostentatiously shook hands with the two unhurt voyagers, and coolly scalped the dead and plundered the cargo."

Concerning the early traffic on the river and the great rush made to Kentucky, the same writer says: "In the year ending in November, 1788, 967 boats, carrying 18,-379 souls, with 7,987 horses, 2172 cows, 1110 sheep, and 646 wagons, went down the Ohio past Fort Harmer."

As happens in all frontiers, there was an influx of the worst characters, and the terror inspired by the Indians was not yet over when came the new terror of lawless white men. Hard drinking and hard fighting became acknowledged characteristics of the Ohio river communities, frequently commented on by travelers. It is probable that some of the descriptions were overdrawn, but the rough habits of the old keelboat men clung long enough to the valley to be remembered by people still living, and there are places yet recalled by name as the scenes of bloody orgies.

The first comers took up what were known as "tomahawk claims," each comprising from one hundred to four hundred acres, roughly guessed at, and marked by hacking trees on the corners with hatchets or tomahawks, whence came the name. Usually these claims, when well established, were respected by the Virginia government and valid titles given. Other claims were by "patent," in which case a parcel of land was granted outright by the government for services rendered to the State or for purchase money paid.

Some of the "patents" comprised thousands of acres, often very loosely surveyed and overlapping other claims, causing a great deal of confusion and litigation even down to the last score of years. These larger purchases were of course for purely speculative purposes. Many an old parchment deed or patent is still in existence, signed by Patrick Henry as Governor of Virginia.

Except where large clearings had been made, it was generally considered that the country back from the river afforded a more wholesome atmosphere, and for that reason, and also to escape the depredations of the "river pirates," many of the later comers sought homes several miles inland. Uncleared land was very cheap, but town lots early assumed considerable value because of the protection afforded and of the opportunities for labor.

In 1796 a resident of Belleville in Wood county, who came from Connecticut, wrote to the folks back home, describing the Virginia side of the river from Wheeling to Belleville as a wilderness, with only a few inhabitants who had arrived in the last Spring and had no provisions but what they had brought with them. Belleville then had eighty inhabitants, town lots were selling at $36 and corn at two shillings the bushel. Weavers were paid one shilling a yard for weaving tow cloth.

The pioneers were obliged to do many things for themselves—from clearing and tilling the soil to building homes, from tending sheep and cultivating flax to converting the wool and the flax into cloth. But the garments they had brought from the East, when worn out, were often replaced with clothing made from the skins of deer, skirts for the women as well as shirts and trousers for the men.

Their actual wants were few, and for that reason more easily supplied. The home was a small log cabin of a single room and a loft, with a rough stone fireplace and a mud chimney re-inforced with sticks. In some the floor consisted of the bare earth, in others it was made of hewn puncheons. The furniture was home-made and of the crudest form, such as could be manufactured with an axe, a hatchet and an auger.

It must be remembered that the entire valley was covered with timber. There were no areas of treeless plains, such as were found in the northern parts of Ohio and in the West, so the rule was first to build a cabin, then to kill the trees surrounding it by cutting a circle through the bark. This "deadened" the trees so that they could be burnt while standing, saving the trouble of felling them. While this slow method of making a clearing was in progress, the men kept the family in food with their muskets and rifles, for game of all sorts was plentiful, and sufficient space was found among the deadened trees to raise a little corn and potatoes, together with tobacco—a very essential plant at that time.

And as their wants were few, so their recreations were simple; but their indulgences were almost always carried to excess—an inevitable result of having unlimited time at their disposal. Those who were religiously inclined were abnormally fervid and easily affected with mysticism, while the "scoffers" went to the other extreme, apparently to show by their viciousness as much contempt as possible.

As people innocently judged of their health by the quantity of meat they could consume, gorging at meals was a common failing. The roysterers were hard drinkers and hard fighters, their "manliness" being registered by the roughness of their sports. Physical prowess won the highest admiration among the men; even the favorite preacher being the one who was handiest with his fists upon just occasions.

CHAPTER III

OUR FIRST SETTLERS

It is interesting to note the changes that have been made in district and county lines since this country was discovered and claimed by the English. In the reign of Queen Elizabeth all that part of America belonging to England was known as Virginia, extending from the mouth of the St. Croix river, or the eastern boundary of Maine, to Cape Fear on the southern coast of North Carolina, and reaching across the continent to the Pacific Ocean. North of this lay the French possessions and south of it the Spanish.

King James, in 1606, divided the English territory into two parts, giving that to the north of the 41st degree of latitude to the Plymouth Company and that to the south of the 38th degree to the London Company; the land embraced between these two degrees was termed neutral territory, but either company might make a settlement within it provided there was a distance of 100 miles between it and any settlement already made by the other company. So the land of Pleasants county lay first within this neutral strip.

But in 1609 both companies were reorganized, the Plymouth Company being termed the Plymouth Council of New England and the London Company receiving the Virginia Charter, the fortieth degree being established as the dividing line, all north of that being known as New England and south as Virginia. This brought Pleasants into the Virginia colony.

In the eighteenth century Virginia set apart all that indefinite territory west of the Shenandoah mountains as West Augusta, including Kentucky, the Northwest Territory and that part of Pennsylvania in which Pittsburgh is situated. This was the land to which Washington proposed to withdraw if the British were successful in regaining the Atlantic seaboard.

The Northwest Territory was ceded to the Federal Government, Kentucky was permitted to erect itself in to a distinct State, and what remained of West Augusta was divided into Yohogania, Ohio and Monongalia counties, the first lying almost wholly in what is now Pennsylvania. Ohio extended from Cross Creek in Brooke county to the mouth of Middle Island Creek, thence the line followed the ridge between that creek and French creek and the waters of the Hughes river, and along the dividing ridge between the waters of the Monongahela and the Ohio to the head of Cross creek. Monongalia county embraced all the remainder of what is now West Virginia, so that Pleasants county was about equally divided between these two large counties.

In 1784 Harrison county was formed from Monongalia, extending from Middle Island creek to the Little Kanawha river, so the southwestern part of Pleasants was included in that county. When the county of Wood was formed in 1799 from Harrison the same part of Pleasants was transferred to the new county, while in 1814 the remainder of Pleasants became a part of Tyler county, and in 1843 a strip was taken from the southeastern border to help form Ritchie county.

These several subdivisions of the territory have sometimes caused difficulty in establishing titles to lands, for the records prior to the formation of Pleasants county in 1851 must be searched in the archives of Ohio. Monongalia, Harrison, Wood, Tyler and Ritchie counties.

So when Isaac and Jacob LaRue settled at the mouth of Middle Island creek in 1790 they became residents of Ohio county. Their nearest neighbors were at the settlement made by Isaac Williams and at the opposite village of Marietta on the Ohio shore. The country was still subject to depredations by small marauding bands of Indians, but in 1794 the establishment of small bodies of militia at several frontier points brought some degree of safety. At Neal's Station (now Parkersburg) was Ensign Bartholomew Junkins; at Fishing Creek (New Martinsville), where a settlement had been made in 1780 by Edward Doolin, who was killed by the Indians in 1784, Lieutenant Morgan was stationed, and at Middle Island was Ensign Jonathan Coburn. An expedition by Captain Morgan with thirty men up the Muskingum about two hundred miles, in the course of which they destroyed an Indian town, seems to have had a quieting effect.

The LaRues were not long the only white inhabitants of Pleasants county. In 1797 Basil Riggs crossed over the mountains and hills from Maryland and settled at Grandview, Ohio, soon afterwards returning across the river and establishing a home on the fine bottom land above Raven Rock narrows, where Edmond Riggs, Jr. was born in 1804. That part of Pleasants was then in Ohio county, and Basil Riggs was made a deputy sheriff of that county in 1799, serving until 1813.

The Tripletts were also among the first comers. Robert Triplett assisted in the formation of Wood county in 1799, and was made its first surveyor. It is remarkable that four generations of Tripletts have held the office of county surveyor—Robert Triplett being succeeded by his son in Wood county, his grandson, the late Francis M. Triplett, holding the position in Pleasants county and John Triplett, son of Francis, being the present incumbent.

In 1783 a Mr. Henderson of Dumfries, Virginia, obtained a patent for two thousand acres along the river at Cow creek, and in 1806 his two sons, J. G. and Alexander Henderson, brought a number of slaves and began a large clearing. A spring still remembered by the name of "Nigger Spring," at the foot of the river hill, is said to mark the place where the slaves had their cabins. This tract was orginally surveyed by Colonel William Crawford, who was murdered so cruelly by the Indians in 1782.

In 1808 Lewis Summers of Fairfax county, Virginia, made a tour of the Kanawha and Ohio valleys at the request of his father, Colonel George Summers, who desired to locate in the western territory. Traveling up the Ohio on horseback in July of that year, Lewis made the following entries in his journal:

"Dined at Williams' tavern. Crossed over and took a view of Marietta and proceeded to Henderson's quarter, 10 miles from Marietta. This farm contains 2,000 acres, about 200 in corn; expect to make 2,000 barrels. They work 30 hands. Stock of hogs, cattle and horses fine.

"Rode to Middle Island creek, 10 miles, to breakfast, a rough road and a hilly country. Six miles beyond this passed Chimney Bottom, in which I viewed an ancient encampent. The trenches are square and contain ten acres. Got to Mr. Chas. Wells to dinner. He is a very reputable old man and has often represented this (Ohio) county in former times. Left Wells' and got to Friend Payton's six miles."

Charles Wells, with whom he dined, lived at what is now Sistersville. He was father of 22 children, and it is recorded that two other families in the same neighborhood also boasted 22 children each. Friend Payton resided at what is now Paden City, other variations of the name being Peyton and Peden.

The Chimney Bottom referred to by Mr. Summers seems to have been the lower portion of the Long Reach bottom, but why called Chimney Bottom we have been unable to ascertain. Traces of earthworks are yet discernible, although they have been sadly worn down by the plow in the last hundred years. According to a description written recently by Mr. George P. Riggs of St. Marys they enclosed much more than ten acres. He has traced the remains of two earthen walls, an outer and an inner, running parallel and enclosing an estimated area of four hundred acres. They begin at Bens Run and extend up the river about one and seven-eighth miles, the total length of the outer wall being four and one-half miles, and the length of the inner wall perhaps a fourth of a mile less. He estimates the original height of the walls at about twelve feet.

Mr. Riggs also mentions a stone pavement on the farm of John Bolen in Pleasants county, located on the ridge of a hill overlooking the Ohio river, about three miles below Bens Run, and a corresponding pavement on a hill on the McKnight farm on the opposite side of the river. Both are described by him as being composed of stones set up on their edges. On the top of a hill between the two

two platforms, on the farm of Mr. Vogel in Pleasants county, he describes a mound formed of large stones, flat, and arranged so as to encircle a larger stone in the center, which he thinks might have been a sacrificial altar.

After 1800, all danger from Indians being then removed, the country began settling up more quickly. The Gorrells and a branch of the Smith family came to Middle Island creek about that year; the Harness family traveled overland from Hardy county and built their home above the mouth of Bull creek; in 1804 Nathan Rolston settled in the same vicinity. The development of that part of Pleasants which was then in Wood county was perhaps hastened by the completion of the "Old State Road," from Alexandria, Virginia, through Romney and Clarksburg to the Ohio river near Marietta. This was authorized by the House of Burgesses in 1789, before Parkersburg existed. Work of clearing and grading was commenced immediately, so that by the Fall of 1790 it was open for traffic. This road still is used in Pleasants county, following the top of the ridge between this county and Ritchie to the head of Cow Creek, then down that creek to just below the mouth of Sharp's run, where it takes up the hill, following the winding of the ridge over Ginger Hill, down Horseneck and Rawson's run to Bull creek, where there was a ford, then passing over the hill to about where Waverly now stands. It was a rough road, full of steep grades, its chief merit being that it kept the ridges wherever possible in the maintenance of its general direction.

About the year 1806 Thomas Reynolds came down the river and bought the lower part of Middle Island, his son, Daniel, at that time being about five years of age. Daniel married Sarah, daughter of Jacob LaRue. He took an active part in the formation of Pleasants county, and his descendants have been prominent in local affairs.

Near the same time the Taylor family made a home on the river bottom land at Grape Island, and the Ruttencutters settled on Middle Island creek about four miles above its mouth. Prior to 1810 the Williamsons were living in the upper end of the county, and Christopher

Wagner moved to the same locality from Pennsylvania in 1820.

A man named Sharp is said to have first settled on that fork of Cow creek which bears his name, and a few years prior to 1820 Christian Schultz came from New York and built a home in the wilderness at the mouth of Sharp's run. In 1830 came Thomas Browse from England and bought a large tract along the river at Grape Island.

About the year 1820 there was quite a stream of immigration into this section from Scotland and the north of Ireland. There were the Grahams, Ingrahams, Outwards, Douglases and McGregors. Most of them went back from the river to escape the malaria then prevalent in newly cleared bottom lands, settling in the western part, then Wood county. In the Tyler county section early settlers were the Baileys, Kesters, Barkwills and McFarlands; while farther back along the waters of McKim creek came about 1840 Ralph Wilson, William and James Hart and Job Locke, and farther up the creek were the Campbells, the Lamps, the Morgans and the Shingletons.

The most notable of these early settlers was Christian Schultz. He was born in the city of New York, probably a scion of the old Dutch stock that settled along the Hudson. His education, which was of the highest order, indicates that his family was well-to-do. He took up the practice of law, and while still a young man was elected to the office of judge. His success caused him to aspire to a membership in the Supreme Court, but it is reported that his ambition was thwarted by persons whom he had supposed were his staunch friends.

Embittered by this disappointment, he resolved to flee from what he considered a false civilization and take refuge among the denizens of the wilderness. Breaking loose from all his old associations, accompanied only by his devoted wife, he crossed the mountains and came down the Ohio to the village of Parkersburg, where he made a stop to explore the country.

The maze of hills and hollows suited his mood. It was a labyrinth in which he would certainly be hard to find.

He bought many thousands of acres about the head of Cow creek, a section which for years afterwards was known as "Schultz Range." On the north side of the creek, opposite the mouth of Sharp's run, he erected a home, for that day and place quite a pretentious dwelling. It was built of hewn logs, and besides two or three rooms on the ground floor it contained an upper story in which were sleeping apartments; in fact, it must have appeared palatial compared to the rude cabins of the country, most of which were limited to one room and an attic. This house was destroyed by fire many years ago.

Here he lived practically the life of a recluse, having no associates and no friends, his acquaintance limited to the few squatters in the neighborhood. It may have been because of his disgust for humanity that here he cultivated the friendship of reptiles. Scarcely could a biassed mind find a stronger method of showing its contempt.

One who was closely related to him informed me that near his residence he constructed a large cage in which he placed snakes. He gathered specimens of every kind then to be found in the forest, both harmless and venemous. Whether or not he himself entered this den and handled the serpents is not known, but undoubtedly it was so naturally arranged that the occupants felt perfectly at home, and he gave up his days to the study of their habits. He wrote several manuscript volumes about them, probably such exhaustive studies of serpents as no other man has made, as he had full time and opportunity for the purpose, and his inclination to do so was strong. These manuscripts were never published, but my recollection is that some of them were in possession of relatives near New York as late as twenty-five years ago.

He was only fifty-six years old when he died, in 1830, having passed fifteen years in solitude. His widow, who was one year younger, survived him almost exactly thirty-one years, dying in 1861. She was born one year after the first battle for the independence of the nation, and died in the first year of the war which threatened a dissolution of the nation.

The village of Schultz received its name from this remarkable man. In the edge of that village, where

Sharp's run joins Cow Creek, a pine tree stands on the lower part of the rocky point formed by the erosion of the two streams. Under that pine is the grave of the pioneer and that of his wife. It is a strange but romantic spot for a tomb, yet suited to the character of the man whose remains lie there.

Years ago a landslide almost demolished this last abiding place. The grave was once surrounded with a smooth wall of well-dressed freestone blocks, three courses high, surmounted with an iron picket fence. This strong wall has been thrown down and lies in chaotic confusion; the marble headstones have been pushed out of place and the large freestone slab covering the grave has been tilted out of position.

On one of the marble stones are engraved the backs of six volumes, inscribed "English, German, French, Latin, Greek, Hebrew," implying that Christian Schultz had mastered all of these languages. Below them is the inscription,

Hon. Christian Schultz, A. M., LL. D.
erected to his memory by
Mrs. Nancy Schultz, his wife
1858

On an adjoining marble stone, whose edges are decorated with a finely wrought sculpture of a grape vine, are these words:

Mrs. Nancy
widow of the
Hon. Christian Schultz
1861
Aged 85 Years
11 mos. 25 days.

The large freestone slab, which had been laid flat over the grave according to the custom of the period, bears the following lines, some of which are almost obliterated:

In Memory of
CHRISTIAN SCHULTZ
who was born in the City of New York
the 7th of November, 1774

and died at Schultz Range, Wood County, Virginia the 28th day of May, 1830.
This stone is placed on his grave by his widow Nancy Schultz

MRS. NANCY DE LA VAN
widow of
Hon. Christian Schultz
was born in
North Salem, Westchester County, New York
the 29th day of May, 1775
and died at
Bull Creek, Wood County, Virginia
24th of May, 1861
Aged 85 yrs. 11 mos., 25 days.

Christian Schultz was a "man of mystery" to the people of his vicinity, and still it is currently rumored there that he was an atheist or at least an infidel, who devoted his life to writing blasphemous works, all of which were destroyed in the flames which consumed his residence. Of this nothing authentic has come to my notice. It must be attributed to the residence among them of a man of such superior mental attainments, together with his probable taciturnity and his scientific studies into the nature and habits of reptiles. I venture a suggestion that in his political disappointment, fancying some analogy between himself and Herman Blennerhassett, he was morbidly led to bury himself in the same wilderness which had become famous through the celebrated trial of that individual and Aaron Burr.

It is refreshing to turn from a contemplation of this recluse, howsoever fascinating his history may be, to the study of another pioneer who came into this country with an entirely different purpose, a man of a hopeful, sanguine temperament, ready to make friends, helpful to the community and anxious for the general welfare.

Thomas Browse, a young Englishman of 27 years, came to this country in 1830 with his bride, of nearly the same age. They came from Paington, Devonshire, to set up a new home in this country west of the Alleghanies, in what was still a comparative wilderness, and must have seemed especially so to them, who had up to that time been surrounded by intimate friends and relatives, with all the comforts that had grown up in centuries of civilization. Our older citizens recall him as a plain, outspoken man, full of vitality, and actively interested in every movement for the public good.

From the letters of Mr. and Mrs. Browse and from his journal, which he kept from the year 1840 up to 1878, I shall quote matters which will be of considerable interest to readers in Pleasants county, at least. The fact that he made and retained copies of even letters to his relatives tells of the methodical and painstaking nature of the man.

In his first letter to his brother Nicholas, under date of June 26, 1830, he describes their passage on the sailing vessel, Caroline Augusta. It is not stated where they landed, but soon they were at Baltimore, boarding at a Mr. Brown's on Hanover street.

"I am still undecided where to settle, but believe it will be either Pennsylvania, Ohio or Indiana. The land around Baltimore is very indifferent, but the town will likely be very large, for a railroad is commenced between this and the Ohio river, and at Washington is cutting to the same place."

His next letter is from Wheeling, July 27, to which he had traveled in the mail coach, leaving Mrs. Browse at Baltimore. He complains of the heat, the thermometer indicating 91 degrees in the shade, and says humorously, "Since I have been in America the weather has been hotter than usual." So it seems that even one hundred years ago was used the phrase which is so common in Florida and California—"The weather for this season is so unusual!"

He states that when he arrived Mr. Cranford, the gentleman on whom he had called, scarcely knew of a farm for sale, but as soon as it was learned that he was a possible purchaser there were many on the market. He was soon joined by Mrs. Browse and they spent several months looking at estates near Wheeling.

"Persons can live here both cheap and comfortable," he writes. "Eliza and my living at a tavern would be only $105 each per year."

Two dollars a week at a hotel! That gives one a very fair idea of the cost of living in those days, and I am tempted to interpolate that in 1800 Rev. Joseph Doddridge, a noted preacher, contracted to preach the Gospel, to baptize and catechise children, to preach funeral sermons, and read funeral services, and to administer the Holy Sacrament at least twice every year to each of four congregations in Ohio and Brooke counties, for all these services his remuneration to be $246.25 "in cash or merchantable."

Desiring to look farther before buying, early in the Fall of 1830 Mr. Browse journeyed in a skiff to Cincinnati in company with a Mr. John Harris. "From Wheeling to Cincinnati is 363½ miles, which we passed over in ten days, considered exceedingly well. A steamboat left with us, and from delay of wooding and grounding was only two days ahead of us."

From Cincinnati he went by land to Lexington, Kentucky, and describes that country as the finest he ever saw. He was tempted to buy on Mad river, but was deterred by the insecurity of title. He returned to Wheeling by way of Dayton, Springfield, Columbus and Zanesville, 264 miles, of which he trudged 200 miles on foot. "From Zanesville to Wheeling all I saw to admire was the National road macadamized."

On March 30, 1831, he writes that he has at last found the place that suits him.

"I have at last purchased an estate of 400 acres on the river bank for which I am to give $5,216. I shall get possession of the place in the Fall when the tenant leaves it. I have also purchased 37 acres adjoining for $300 with possession directly. It is situated in Tyler county, Virginia, 20 miles above Marietta and about 60 below Wheeling, 150 acres cleared and four in orchard."

He bought from a Mr. John McDonaldson, who lived in the interior of the State. Then he describes the farm:

"On it are 250 acres of river bottom of first rate quality, with not one acre of gravel bottom. It is very level and unbroken by runs. Two come from the hills and pass to the river, one above and one through the 37 acres. I have not so high an opinion of river bottom land, as no crops come to great perfection and grass dies out in hot weather. My hill land is good and stocked with excellent timber. Persons tell me it is the first estate in Tyler county to its size, and I do verily believe it. The soil is stiffer than on the river bottoms and raises first rate wheat. I have fine freestone for building, and a most beautiful spring that never fails up a hill and could be taken anywhere. I have a run which would do for a sawmill some months in the winter, but a little up Middle Island creek I can purchase boards at from one-half to one cent a foot, and float them to my river bank, a distance of four miles. The farm above me has a grist mill."

That does not read like a man who has fled into the wilderness to nurse revenge or humiliation. It expresses hope and rich appreciation of the blessings of life; pride in achievement and belief in the strength of his resources.

The sawmill on Middle Island creek was the one built by Jacob LaRue at the mouth of Broad run, near the present home of L. W. LaRue. An upright saw was used, and its capacity was 1500 to 2000 feet per day. That was built about the year 1810, and about the same time that Basil Riggs set up a grist mill on Java run where Raven Rock stands now. It is said that one of the mill stones is still lying in that neighborhood.

Mr. Browse built a small cottage on the 37 acre tract, into which he and his wife moved in July, 1831. That was part of the house now occupied by Mr. Edmund Holdren. That same Fall another Englishman, John Edwards, with his wife, five children and a brother, arrived and moved upon the Browse land. Descendants of this family now reside on the Ohio shore opposite Raven Rock.

The great flood of 1832 is vividly described by Mr. Browse:

"On the 11th of February the river presented such a scene that I can give you but a poor idea of it. Every kind of property that could be floated covered the whole breadth of the river, which rose six feet higher than was ever before known. I feel convinced that 1,000 horses must have floated past, with innumerable stacks of wheat, hay, oats, rye, etc., with shocks of corn, warehouses, mills, corn cribs, planks, barrels of flour and whiskey, apples and so on. My neighbor, Mr. Riggs, lost 15 head of cattle and 2000 bushels of Indian corn. People had contrived just to endure the highest freshet, but six feet beyond played the devil and all. It must have ruined hundreds. Lower Wheeling, a very little place, lost forty houses, upper Wheeling several. * * The only recompense I have is about one hundred acres of the most choice kind of mud, and between ourselves I do believe that the crops in future will amply repay the value of all the fencing lost."

He boasts of having seven hogs in salt and 16 venison hams in smoke. The hams could be bought in Winter from the hunters for 32 cents a pair. That they lived well is shown by a letter written by Mrs. Browse: "Our breakfast consists of fried meat or hot chicken and fried ham, venison, game or fish, with cream, preserves, honey and molasses. Dinner as in England, and teas, or tea and supper together, similar to a breakfast."

She tells about the use of rocking chairs, something unknown then in England, and says "It would seem strange to you at first to see three or four people rocking themselves." She praises the fruits, and especially the fine vegetables. Of maple sugar she says, "We could make sufficient sugar from the trees that grow on our farm to supply five or six families, for one of our tenants last Spring made 300 pounds."

Since then rocking chairs have become common in England, also other articles which were first made and used in this country, among them iron stoves and rubber goods. Mr. Browse hopes that his brother Nicholas "got the gum elastic shoes and the buffalo robe" to take with him to England.

The journal begins with June 1, 1840. It is not in the least descriptive, being kept only for the purpose of refreshing his memory, but it serves to give us some idea of values and the names of residents. In looking over it, one is forcibly impressed not only with the alterations made in the manner of living by such physical improvements as railroads, telegraphs, telephones, steam and gasoline engines, to say nothing of the many housekeeping improvements, but also with the changes wrought in the very lives, customs and thoughts of the people.

Whereas now we depend on the public authorities for all public improvements, and individuals depend only upon themselves in making private improvements, in those days the people of a community worked together in all things, public as well as private. Neighbors joined merrily in husking corn, without a thought of compensation; cheerfully lent a hand in butchering time, and when a beef was killed large portions were sent gratuitously to the neighbors. Quilting bees were occasions of busy activities and feasting. When the community needed a church or a school house, all the able-bodied men gave a helping hand or contributed stone, wood or money.

The common fuel was wood, in most cases burned in an open hearth; but sheet iron stoves were gradually coming into use and some of the more modern fire-places were improved with grates. Soft or bituminous coal could be burned in these, but while there were outcroppings of coal on the hillsides, the seams were thin and remained unworked for many years. This sort of fuel, however, was often amply though accidentally provided by the coal fleets that swept down the river from Pittsburgh during high water. The numerous islands in the river made navigation very difficult, especially in a freshet, when the current was unusually swift, and towboats pushing a large fleet of laden barges found it exceedingly difficult to keep in the channel when approaching the wide-spreading head of an island. Thus it sometimes happened that one or perhaps two barges were run so high up on the sand bars that they were hopelessly stranded and must be abandoned.

In such cases the steamboat companies were very glad to dispose of the coal to responsible parties at a merely nominal price, anxious to save what they could of their barges. The journal of Thomas Browse states that the price generally obtained was five cents a bushel. Sometimes enough could be unloaded into small flatboats so that the barge would float and then be hauled to the shore, where the coal could be shoveled into wagons.

Long before the great wheat lands of the Northwest were developed, wheat was one of the principal crops on the wide river bottoms, and we find Mr. Browse mentioning on many occasions with pride his "great wheat field." In 1840 and 1841 the price of wheat was from 75 cents to 87 cents a bushel, which, measured by the prices then paid for other commodities and for labor, was equivalent to about three dollars according to the standard of today.

Harvesting was done with the scythe and cradle, therefore requiring a considerable number of hands. Among those employed during the July harvest of 1840 he records Kelch, Ellifritz, Squire D. Riggs, Barkwill, John Taylor, Jackson, John Bailey, Coen, Owen Riggs, Josiah Riggs, Edmund Riggs and James Williams.

At this time occurs the first direct reference to employing a teacher. Immediately after the harvesting was finished, Kelch was sent to Wood county with two horses to bring up a Miss Stanley, who was to teach in the "Good Intent" school house. This, one of the first school houses in the county, was situated on Spring Run, a short distance above the great spring and on the northern bank of the stream. Miss Stanley secured board at the home of Mr. Riggs.

Besides serving as a place for instruction, the school house was also used for religious worship and for dispensing justice. Thomas Browse and Edmund Riggs were magistrates of Tyler county, the former being also a surveyor, and together they were accustomed to meet at the Good Intent school house to hear petty cases.

The year 1840 was a memorable political year throughout the United States, Martin Van Buren had been renominated for the Presidency by the straight-out Democrats and was opposed by General William Henry Harrison, the Democratic Whig candidate. Never was there a more unpopular administration than that of Van Buren. The people of the North had been particularly dissatisfied with the Seminole war and everywhere the country was suffering because of the great financial panic of 1837. The feeling of the populace was demonstrated in the wildest and most boisterous manner. It was the famous "Log Cabin" campaign, when log cabins on wheels were hauled over the country, freely dispensing cider, so that every touring speaker was certain to have an audience.

The excitement was shared in this section. On August 5 the journal says: "Nicholas and I, with Mr. Bailey, Daniel and James, Nicholas Wells. Edmund Riggs, Basil Riggs, Isaac, Edmund, Squire D. Riggs and Greenberry, Isaac LaRue and others went to a political meeting at Cow Creek. There was a band of music from Marietta, with refreshments for all. Joseph Barker, George Woodbridge and John T. Jackson addressed the meeting, advocating the Whig cause. The address of Jackson was truly admirable and pleased all the Whigs, at least. The whole gave us great satisfaction."

William Bills came to this section in the Spring of 1841 and purchased the northern part of what was then known as Pickens Bottom, Mr. Browse doing the surveying. On this farm has been laid out the Billsville Addition to St. Marys.

His original name was William Williams, and as such he had been enrolled as a soldier in the war of 1812, first as a private in the company of Captain William Irwin's "Wheeling Light Infantry," and later as ensign in Captain Moses Congleton's Company from Brooke county. It is reported that the change of name was made because several others named Williams were in the same company.

The low price of labor as measured by the standard of money then is shown in the contract Mr. Browse made with Alexander Core, who was to work a year for $100. This probably included lodging and meals. In March he makes an entry concerning his contract with Kelch:

"Saw Kelch and it was agreed that he is to live in Mr. Riggs's house, have an acre for a truck patch and to sow a bushel of Flax seed. He is to live in the back part of the house if required. I am to pay him for any meals he eats at home instead of at my house at the rate of $1 per week, that is, $1 for 18 meals. The other matters stand as last year."

It is interesting to note the prices of some commodities. Coffee was then selling at $13\frac{1}{4}$ cents a pound; whiskey at 48 cents a gallon; brown sugar seven cents a pound; pine boards eight dollars a thousand feet; salt $\frac{3}{4}$ of a cent a pound; nails 7½ cents a pound; potatoes 25 cents a bushel, and "Old Gooch," it was written, was around bargaining for hoop-poles at 12½ cents per hundred, to be paid for in the Fall.

Farmers and their families were glad then to turn their hands to anything for a little money, and there was a large trade in hoop-poles as late as 1880. At almost every landing along the river great piles of the poles were lying on the shore waiting for the coming of a steamboat.

The difficulty of taking a grist to mill then is made apparent by this entry in 1841: "May 30. I prepared to go to mill with 26 bushels of wheat in a large flatboat in company with James Bailey and Charles, Roswell Amlin, John Taylor and Kemp. Left about sundown and floated as far as Little Muskingum river up to Corner's mill." The next day he could not get his turn to grind, so he went to Marietta and spent the night there with John Bieldz. "June 2 returned to the mill and commenced grinding. Could get no supper." June 3 the grinding was finished and at two o'clock in the afternoon they started back up the river, getting five miles on their way by dark, when they tied up and slept in the boat. June 4 they got home with the grist about four o'clock.

He tells of riding to the creek on January 8, 1842 to attend a meeting of the citizens of Wood and Tyler counties at the Union school house, held with a view of forming a new county from parts of Tyler and Wood. This is the first mention of any desire to establish a new county. We have not been able to locate the Union school house, but judging from the name it was probably the building on what has since been known as Gallaher's run, the land, then a part of the Pickens farm, being purchased by Silas Gallaher about ten years later. This building was located above the first fork of the run, where the ground slightly rises at the foot of the hill. A few scattered stones still mark the place where the chimney stood. At one time a fine grove of trees adorned the little hollow, and under their shade was the old burying ground, wherein still lie the remains of William Bills and others who died in that period. Like all other school houses this was also used for worship and as a community gathering place. It was probably called the "Union School House" because it was situated near the borders of Wood and Tyler counties. No action seems to have been taken towards forming a new county.

A quaint custom of that time was the "shooting up" on New Year's eve. It simply consisted of several men of the vicinity gathering with their guns and discharging them in front of a neighbor's house, the sound of the firearms being accompanied with wild yells and halloos, the whole being, in fact, a rude sort of charivari. The rioters were always asked into the house, where they were hospitably entertained and the evening spent in playing cards.

There was a very large trade in cattle, hogs and sheep, the animals being driven through in droves of hundreds to the Pittsburgh and Baltimore markets, coming even from far off Indiana. On account of the large enclosed pasture on the Browse farm the cattle men made an effort to put up there for the night, and the fee charged was certainly very small. One item records that a drove of 130 cattle, with five men and two horses, were charged only $4 for the night, and another case is mentioned of 234 cattle and 400 sheep, for which the charge was $5.50. "Too cheap," he adds. And they had to be watched, for apparently there were rustlers in those days as well as later on the western plains. One drover at least was caught making off with two of the Browse heifers.

In June, 1842, Mr. Browse records that he and Mrs. Browse rode to McKinley's store at the foot of Middle Island. It has been reported that Alexander H. Creel had decided at first to establish a town at the foot of the island, but changed his mind and located at Vaucluse. In all probability Mr. McKinley had come with the intention of getting a good location and had decided to remain, notwithstanding that Vaucluse was by this time become a considerable shipping point, and it is very likely that he erected a building which antedates any of the so-called earliest houses, which were built about the year 1850.

Mr. Creel came in 1834 from Eastern Virginia with the intention. according to the older inhabitants, of founding a town on Pickens Bottom which should rival the then rapidly growing city of Parkersburg. It is regretted that no accurate description can be given of him. He was of slight build, with a rather nervous manner. There can be no doubt that he was a "man with a vision," full of enterprise and with ability to carry out most of his undertakings. He was scholarly, as is shown by the fragmentary documents he drew up, and his love of literature is evidenced by his splendid set of Shakespeare's completely annotated works, solidly bound in leather, a few of which have come into possession of the writer, and which bear the autograph of their original owner.

The land which he or his father bought is a beautiful and broad stretch of bottom, with two distinct terraces, the upper being many feet above the highest flood mark. It is a semi-circular nook, defended practically on all sides by the hills, so that it is very slightly subjected to high winds. Just why he should have decided to abandon this site for that of the narrow gorge at the mouth of Greens Run is a mystery; but in 1837 he sold the tract to H. L. Pickens and laid the foundations of the place he called Vaucluse, after the place in the southeast of France made famous by the residence of the poet Petrarch.

He procured the building of a ten mile stretch of road to tap the State road at the head of Whiskey run, and connecting with the road down that stream to the Northwestern Pike at the village now called Pike. The construction of this road shortened the distance from Clarksburg to the river by about fifteen miles.

Immediately Vaucluse became a prominent port. Merchants from Parkersburg hurried up and built storehouses, seriously interfering with the trade of that city. Flatboats and steamers stopped there to take on merchandise for the South and West. Houses were built on both sides of the narrow gorge along the run and buildings were strung along the rough, rocky ledges of the river shore wherever they could be perched. Steamboats burned wood then, and William Carroll, who came here from Maryland, made a lucrative business supplying them from his woodpile.

The Winter of 1842-3 was very long and severe. Mr. Browse tells of crossing the river on the ice on December

2, an exceedingly unusual occurrence for the river to close so early. And on March 25 he says the temperature was below zero and the river almost closed with ice.

Not many slaves were held in this section, for which there were possibly two good reasons. First, the price of labor was so cheap that very little could be gained from the toil of slaves, after deducting the purchase price, the cost of maintenance and taking care of them in illness. Then Ohio, a free State, lay just across the river and was easily attainable, while there were many persons over there who gave all aid they could to escaping slaves, helping them on the way to the British posession of Canada, where they would be safe from pursuit.

In 1843 a general movement for liberty seems to have possessed the blacks. Early in the year two or three ran away from the Browse farm; in August ten escaped from the Harness farm and one from the Corbitt place, while five were reported to have fled from Parkersburg. These instances are probably only a few of many, and seem to bear out the idea that some secret influence was at work among them.

There was a school house at Clay Point in 1843, not far from the Ruttencutter home on Middle Island Creek, at which religious services were held. So far as can be ascertained there was not then an established church within the present limits of the county, yet the ground was fairly well covered by itinerants of various denominations. Some of the preachers of the period were Rev. Wood, Winstanley, Warren, Morrison, Gallahue and Smith.

As early as 1844 it was rumored that the Baltimore & Ohio railroad would be extended to the Ohio River, and it was calculated that it would take a directly westward course, which would naturally bring it down Middle Island creek. In September several meetings were held with the object of influencing the company to bring the road through Clarksburg to Middle Island, where the river would be bridged. It is said that engineers made a survey and reported favorably upon this route, but the citizens of Parkersburg offered greater inducements.

In January, 1846, Joseph Taylor was sworn in as postmaster at Grape Island under bond of $300, with Thomas Browse and William Hammond as securities. The business of the mails was not then carried on with the same system as at present. Letters were paid for on delivery the amount of postage depending on the distance carried, and stamps were unknown. Postage on newspapers was not prepaid, but the accounts were usually let run for several weeks or even months, when the subscriber was called upon to settle. The postage for periodicals was based upon the number of inches measured by the columns or pages.

Thanksgiving Day, while not officially proclaimed as a National feast day until 1863, was observed here at an early date, the custom probably emanating from New York. The day, when the weather permitted, was devoted to the old backwoods sport of shooting at a mark, the prizes being turkeys and other fowl. This pastime was kept up in St. Marys until near the close of the last century, and the writer has seen nearly the whole masculine population of the town gathered on the shooting ground, the low bottom just below Creel street, where some remarkably fine rifle practice was exhibited.

In fact, every occasion was seized upon for getting together and having a good time. For the men there were log rollings, house raisings, harvesting and threshing; for the women there were quilting bees, and there were corn huskings for both. Where the men gathered there was whiskey, which was then both pure and cheap, but always intoxicating. It could be bought for less than fifty cents a gallon, and was so freely drunk that most of the men were intoxicated by evening and the day frequently wound up with a fight.

The habit of judging men by their physical prowess obtained in the Ohio Valley from the days of the old Indian fighters down almost to the present. Within our recollection the common phrase of "He is a mighty good man" referred not to the qualities of his heart but to his ability to use his fists. Old men still relate stories of terrific encounters between celebrities, bare-fisted, rough-and-ready affairs, almost always merely to discover which was "the best man." If there could be any redeeming feature about them it was the fact that they were not fought for money, but for honor and glory as understood by the combatants and their associates. Sometimes, like the knights-errant of old, these worthies traveled far to win renown or to meet a challenge. One illustration as related to us will suffice:

A man named Decker lived in a houseboat, leisurely journeying up and down the river, dispensing whiskey and affording accommodations for gambling card-players. He prided himself on his ability to knock out any other man along the river, and directed his remarks especially to a certain resident of St. Marys. It was not long until the latter heard of this challenge, and learning that Decker's boat was then lying in Fishing creek at New Martinsville, he made his way to that place. Neither of the men knew the other except from description. Both were large and powerful. The St. Marys man found the houseboat, in which a game of cards was in progress. He was met by Decker, who eyed him and asked his business. Scarcely was it told when the two began the combat. Witnesses say that they fought fairly, as fighting with fists was understood then, not using any weapons, but that it was the wildest rough and tumble fighting ever seen. How long it lasted no one could tell, but it seemed to have extended all over the boat, and in the end Decker acknowledged that his opponent was "the best man." There was no money at stake, no hatred, no wrong to avenge. It was simply for reputation and honor.

Refined sugar was a luxury exceedingly rare, and until towards the middle of the century few persons in the valley used it or had even tasted it. Most of the sweetening was done with honey, sorghum and maple sugar, the last being very plentiful, large groves of sugar maples being found in several parts of the county, whence come the names of Sugar creek, Sugar Camp run, Henry Camp run and others. February was the month for tapping the trees, and usually the entire neighborhood turned out for a frolic in the sugar camp, gathering the sap and boiling it down.

Clothing was made of wool and linen, both home-grown products, and carded, spun and woven at home. Still may be found, treasured in old chests and drawers, table cloths and bed sheets made by the great-grandmothers of the present generation as their wedding contribution to the home; and men now living can recall the rough and curiously streaked suits of homespun jeans they wore in their youth.

For finer materials trips had to be made to Wheeling, or there was frequent opportunity to procure them from some store-boat that floated down the river, laden with merchandise of all sorts. These boats tied up along the shore until all the wants of the neighborhood were supplied, exchanging wares for such produce as could be stored on board until they returned to Wheeling. These traveling merchants usually had their families with them on their long journeys. Two frequently mentioned by Mr. Browse were George Bier and Thomas Hornbrook, the latter making yearly trips.

Peddlers, of course, tramped over the country with their packs, and there were itinerant cobblers, tinkers and tailors, all capable men and often remaining several days at a house to finish their work. The cobblers did not confine themselves merely to mending shoes, they also made them.

Here are a few prices quoted at the stores in Newport in 1848: Sugar $5\frac{1}{2}$ cents a pound; coffee $8\frac{1}{2}$ cents; rice 6 cents. As for live stock, heifers were quoted at $6, milch cows at $9 to $13, steers at $9, young pigs at fifty cents and as low as $37\frac{1}{2}$ cents each, hogs weighing 150 pounds at $3.10. old sheep at $1 and lambs at fifty cents. There were brickyards at Matamoras, where hard bricks could be bought at $5 a thousand. Wheat brought 65 cents a bushel and corn 10 cents to 31 cents; potatoes were sold for 25 cents.

Money was scarce, and as there were no banks nearer than Wheeling or Marietta, small sums were frequently borrowed from neighbors to tide over an emergency. In this neighborhood Mr. Browse was regarded as a moneyed man, and persons from quite a distance traveled here to make a loan; but often his journal shows that he also was a borrower.

Land continued to be very cheap up to the middle of the century. On McKim creek six hundred acres of unimproved land were bought for 56 cents an acre, and this low price brought about the rapid settlement of the section between the years 1840 and 1860, when many of those we call our old families moved in, mostly from the eastern part of the State or from Pennsylvania.

And as land was cheap, so was timber. In fact, it was more often considered an incommodity rather than a commodity, because clearings had to be made in order to raise crops. The custom was to ring or girdle the large trees with an axe near the base, thus killing the tree in one season, then, when thoroughly dead and dried, it would be burned, if possible; but often only the limbs and outer portions of the trunk would be consumed, the fire-hardened stump standing for many years in the field as a monument of apparently reckless waste.

Also great quantities of timber which now would be very valuable were then devoted to the building of fences and houses. Walnut was especially desirable for fence rails because of the ease with which it could be split. The same valuable wood was used in furnishing the heavy beams for houses, as has been repeatedly shown when tearing down some of the older homes in St. Marys. The best wood for fence posts was locust, which, when mortised for the insertion of the rails, brought $6\frac{1}{4}$ cents each, while the split rails sold for 75 cents the hundred.

This locality seems to have been particularly favorable to the growth of such hardwoods as oak, hickory and maple, also yellow poplar or tulip trees. White oaks with a diameter of five feet were not uncommon, and yellow poplars attained a diameter of seven feet from sap to sap.

52

THOMAS BROWSE.

CHAPTER IV

MAKING A NEW COUNTY

Perhaps it will never be known who originated the idea of forming a new county out of Wood, Tyler and Ritchie. It might have sprung from some apparently idle talk, some chance remark made while a group was sitting around the fire in one of the Vaucluse stores, but it is reasonably certain that some of the most active promoters were Alexander H. Creel, Thomas Browse, Edmund Riggs and Daniel Reynolds.

The first mention we have of any desire to form a new county was when Thomas Browse rode to the Union school house in January, 1842, to talk the matter over with his neighbors. Then for several years the affair seems to have rested in abeyance, until in September, 1846 Mr. Browse, who was then surveyor of Tyler county, records that he had begun making a map for the new county, On the fifth of the same month he says he finished a new map and then rode with Edmund Riggs to the Union school house "to the meeting of Wood, Tyler and Ritchie citizens, who appointed me to fix boundary lines and to meet again next Friday." And on Friday he says he rode to Vaucluse about the county lines, but gives no further information.

In January, 1847, he mentions being in Middlebourne, the county seat of Tyler county, and seeing there posted a notice of the proposed new county. On March 13 he went to the Pickens school house, which was probably the Union school house mentioned before, to attend a meeting about the new county, at which the following subscriptions were laid for the public buildings:

William Bills	$400.00
Samuel Pickens	400.00
Alexander Creel, One Acre for Court House and	700.00
Edmund Riggs	300.00
D. Reynolds	300.00
Isaac Riggs	200.00
Harris	50.00
B. Brandis	25.00
Isaac LaRue	100.00
Wm. Medley	50.00
Brown	25.00
Thomas Browse	100.00
Jos. Taylor	50.00
Wm. Hammond	50.00
James Patterson	100.00
	$2850.00

The object was to obtain $3,500, of which $3,000 was to be raised on the island and below the creek, including Isaac LaRue, and $500 above the creek and up McKim. Edmund Riggs, D. Reynolds, Harris, Brown and James Patterson were not present at the meeting.

Under date of April 17 Mr. Browse writes: "Went to the school house at Pickens about the bonds for the new county, and found none there but Bills, Isaac LaRue, Perry LaRue and Samuel Pickens. This clearly shows how much confidence can be put in promises. All will subscribe but no one will bind themselves."

However, the matter seems to have moved forward, for on April 27, 1848, an election was held in which it figured. At the Grape Island precinct the new county proposition received 30 votes with only one against it, the objecting voter being Josiah Riggs. At that time the elections were conducted vive voce, every voter audibly announcing his vote to the commissioners, so that all bystanders could hear. At Allen's precinct, which included the Sugar Creek neighborhood, there were five for the new county and 16 against it. Mr. Browse's journal gives no further news of the election, but it is presumed to have carried, for an act establishing the new county was passed by the Virginia Assembly in the session of

1850-1851. It was named Pleasants in honor of James Pleasants, who was Governor of Virginia from 1822 to 1825, and died in 1836.

From Wood county was taken a section from Bull creek along the river to Middle Island creek and extending back about five miles; from Ritchie county came a narrow strip west of the ridge dividing the waters of Goose and Bond's creeks from the sources of Bull creek, Cow creek and French creek; and from Tyler county came the remainder. The area is given at 132 square miles.

It was a mistake to make the boundary so contracted. More of Wood and Ritchie should have been taken, so as to equalize the area and population of the four counties. The division left Wood with 364 square miles, Ritchie 453 and Tyler 260. One hundred more square miles could easily have been spared by Wood and Ritchie.

The population of the new county could not have been more than 1500, and the total valuation of property was not sufficient to decently operate a county government even in that time of small salaries. It was a purely agricultural and timbering country, with only here and there a grist or saw mill operated by water power, excepting a steam saw mill on Cow creek, which is said to have been operated in 1838.

In the first book of the county records, kept in the remarkably neat handwriting of Rodney Hickman, are related the early events of the organization, which was effected in a house owned by A. H. Creel. These records were written with old fashioned goose quills, pointed by Mr. Hickman, who obtained the quills from poultry on the farm of Thomas Browse.

The first meeting of the justices of the new county was held May 15, 1851. They had been appointed by Governor John B. Floyd of Virginia. Present were Moses Williamson, John K. Prince, Abner Martin, Thomas Browse, Samuel Hammett, Abraham S. Gorrell, Isaac Williamson, Edmund Riggs, Alexander H. Creel and John Stewart. They took the oath of office and organized themselves into a court.

Following this initial step came the election of a clerk. There were several candidates—Rodney Hickman, Uriah

V. Gill, Phineas P. Feeney and Jesse C. Beeson. The voting, as at all elections then, was viva voce. Martin, Browse, Gorrell, Riggs, Isaac Williamson and Moses Williamson, all residing in what had been the Tyler county section, voted for Rodney Hickman, who came from Middlebourne. Prince and Hammett, who lived in the Wood county section, voted for Feeney of Cow creek; Creel voted for Gill of St. Marys and Stewart voted for Beeson. Hickman was declared elected for the term of seven years, and his records show that he made a very good clerk.

Greenberry Riggs was appointed crier for the court; Thomas Browse, late surveyor of Tyler county, was recommended for the same position in the new county, and John K. Prince was unanimously chosen commissioner of revneue.

The county was laid off into two constable districts, the dividing line running with Washington street and the Middle Island Creek Turnpike, now known as the Ellenboro Pike, to the Ritchie county line, the northern district being No. 1 and the other No. 2.

Moses Williamson, John K. Prince and Abner Martin were recommended severally to the governor for sheriff, with preference in the order named. The following attorneys were admitted to practice before the bar of the court: William I. Boreman, John W. Horner, Joseph Spencer, John J. Jackson, Jr., Arthur I. Boreman, William L. Jackson, Benjamin W. Jackson, Leonard S. Hall, Joseph C. Moore and Jacob B. Blair.

Several of these young lawyers later took dintinguished parts in the history of the State. John J. Jackson was appointed a Federal judge by President Grant and became known as "the Iron Judge." Arthur I. Boreman was the first governor of the State of West Virginia. James M. Jackson served many years as a circuit judge. William L. Jackson became a general of the Confederate army and Leonard S. Hall was a member of the Virginia Assembly of 1860 in which he voted for secession.

William L. Jackson was the unanimous choice for commonwealth attorney, and John W. Widderfield was appointed deputy clerk. A. H. Creel, John Stewart and John Logan were appointed a committee to secure a suitable place for holding court. Edward W. Johnson and Ambrose Smith were appointed constables for district No. 2 and Joseph Gorrell, Thomas Rymer and Jesse C. Beeson for No. 1.

The following day the court marked out four districts for overseers of the poor; later the same districts were created school districts. Henry Flesher was overseer and school commissioner of the First district, William Hanes of the Second, Phineas P. Feeney of the Third and Robert T. Parker of the Fourth. Although the bounds of the districts are not given, one may deduce from the residences of the overseers that the First district probably embraced what is now Lafayette district with a portion of McKim, the Second was Union district with a part of Washington, the Third Jefferson with a part of McKim, and the Fourth Grant and a part of Washington.

Greenberry B. Riggs declining the position of court crier, Henry C. Creel was appointed in his stead, and was also made collector, besides becoming deputy to John Widderfield. who was commissioned coroner.

William Dils was licensed to sell spirituous drinks, "so as such liquors be not drank in said store house."

The question of public buildings arising, the justices appointed a committee composed of A. H. Creel, John Widderfield, Edmund Riggs, Thomas Browse, John K. Prince and Abner Martin, to draft suitable plans, and also named A. H. Creel, Thomas Browse, John Stewart, Joseph Taylor and John Widderfield a committee to select a site for the buildings. The sparseness of the population, in which few able men were found, is indicated by the several duties given to certain individuals.

William Rymer was granted license to keep "a house of private entertainment" in St. Marys; Ervin D. Myers was licensed to keep an ordinary at Vaucluse, "the court being of opinion that he is a man of good character and not addicted to drunkenness or gambling." Ambrose Smith was licensed to keep a house of private entertainment at St. Marys, and Logan Brothers and Hopkins & Dils wers given permission to sell liquors in St. Marys, the court deeming that their "places are fit and convenient to the neighborhood thereof for the retailing of such liquors."

In 1848 pledges had been given for raising $4,500 for the purpose of erecting the public buildings, A. H. Creel heading the list with $700 and the promise of a public square for the court house and jail. Other subscribers were Joseph Taylor, James Patterson, U. V. Gill, Thomas Browse and Daniel Reynolds. The amount needed was raised with considerable difficulty, and at last a contract was awarded to George Sharp and John Stewart to build a combined court house and jail for the sum of $5,300 and to complete the same on or before December 15, 1852.

For a time it seems that Mr. Creel rued his bargain, as to giving the public square, but at last, on July 11, 1851, Thomas Browse drove the first stake in surveying it, and immediately the contractors went to work. The court house lot was made 160 feet square, with a driveway surrounding it, the plat showing an avenue leading directly from the square to Washington street, but that part of the plan was apparently abandoned. Perhaps it was an attempt to make a thoroughfare to connect with the Ellenboro Pike, which was done years afterward when Barkwill street was opened up.

The brick for the building was burned on the Gallaher farm along the lane, where yet remains a slight depression formed by taking out the clay. The work went on slowly, and it was not until June 11, 1854, that court was held in it for the first time. During this waiting period the house of Isaac Reynolds was used as a court house. This building is yet standing, on the southeast corner of Second and Lafayette streets. Its owner was a son of Daniel Reynolds and was father of Daniel Webster Reynolds, who became sheriff of the county.

Governor Floyd appointed Moses Williamson the first sheriff, accepting the recommendation which had been made by the justices, and at the same time commissioned James Ruckman as a justice. Christian Engle was made deputy sheriff.

At that time all the magistrates of the county joined in holding court, being empowered to try civil cases in which the amount involved did not exceed a certain sum. After the formation of the State of West Virginia, a distinction was made between justices of the peace and members of the county court, but the latter continued as a juridical body with privilege of deciding cases in which the amount involved did not exceed $300, until the constitution was amended in 1880, when it became a purely administrative organization, composed of three members only.

The first grand jury, called in July, 1851, was composed of Daniel Reynolds, foreman, John Harness, Moses Ruckman, Robert Triplett, Francis Triplett, George May, Benjamin Prince, Giles Hammett, Edmund Riggs, James Dils, Robert Parker, John Taylor, Joseph Bills, William K. Hanes, Granville Stout, Hiram Curtis, Isaac Cecil, Benjamin Hallett, Isaac Riggs, Greenberry B. Riggs, Thomas Bramel and John Williamson.

It seems that there was a great demand for "ordinaries" and a license for that purpose was granted to Samuel M. Hibbs.

The first person admitted to citizenship in the new county was Samuel Barkwill, late of Boyle Parish, Cornwall, England.

In September, 1851, the new county lines were surveyed by Thomas Browse, surveyor of Pleasants county, A. W. Duty, surveyor of Tyler, Abner Martin, John Bullman, William Cornell and Elza Smith. For his services in doing this work Mr. Browse received $35.

In December, 1851, W. L. Jackson resigned as commonwealth attorney and Joseph Spencer was appointed to the office.

What we now know as a circuit court was originally called the superior court of law and chancery, the judge having a life tenure, but the constitution was amended in 1850-1, changing the title to circuit court and making the term of the judge eight years. The last judge of this circuit under the old constitution was David McComas, who held the office from 1844 to 1851, and was therefore the first judge to hold "superior" court in Pleasants county.

Joseph Taylor, one of the pioneers who had settled in the river valley at Grape Island, died January 14, 1852, aged 53 years. He had borne a prominent part in establishing the new county and held the office of road overseer at the time of his death.

About the middle of April there were several days of hard rain, causing the river to rise very rapidly. On the 19th it rose at the rate of nine inches an hour and on the 20th a great deal of drift floated down. The crest of the flood was reached April 21, 28 inches lower than the flood of 1832, but the rapid rise and strong current had done great damage. It was said that it carried away six acres from Middle Island.

May 26 an election was held, in which T. Locke, F. Williamson, Samuel Seckman and Abner Martin were elected magistrates, defeating Thomas Browse, Thomas Gorrell and William Virden. William Dils was elected sheriff, Rodney Hickman clerk, P. P. Feeney surveyor and H. Lee Pickens commissioner of revenue.

In some way the citizens of St. Marys had gotten possession of a cannon, which figured in many of their celebrations. On the afternoon of Christmas Day, 1852, a party took it on the steamer Venture up to Grape Island to fire a salute to Mr. Browse, but on trying to get it on shore it fell into the river. In the party were Messrs. S. Logan, Smith, Myers, Kelsall, Strous, Little and John Strafford. The cannon lay in the river until New Years Day, when it was gotten out and taken back to the town. That evening while firing paper cartridges it was discharged prematurely, killing David Seevers. His remains were buried on the Kelley farm on Middle Island creek, marked by a stone which briefly tells of the disaster.

It is a pity that we have not more particulars of a horse race which took place on the Browse farm December 15, 1855. It is mentioned here because it shows the diversity of amusements indulged in by that generation, and also because it occurred in a season that is usually inclement. A crowd went up from St. Marys, and three races were held in an open field, a straight course from a small stream to a board fence. The chief race was between a horse owned by a Mr. Cain—perhaps Zachary Cain—and one brought here by a Mr. Malone from Doddridge county, the wager being about $200 a side. The Malone horse won.

The latter part of that Winter was very severe. On January 9 the Browse record says it was twelve below zero. The snow was deep, logs were dragged over the roads to break a way for teams, and the snow on the hills made it impossible for people to get out. In the latter part of February Mr. Browse rode a horse on the creek ice, which was two feet thick, from the ferry to Sylvan mills, and on March 10 the mercury was ten below zero. The river of course was frozen over, and the ice did not break up until March 21. The following day about seventeen steamboats went up the river.

In 1856 there was a political upheaval in the United States. The old Whig party melted away; in the North the new Republican party was organized with John C. Fremont at its head as the candidate for President, and everywhere there was a strong sentiment for Know Nothingism. In Pleasants county there were only two parties—the old line Democrats and the Know Nothings, the former being successful throughout, although the voting in most instances was very close. Many of those who were Know Nothings afterward returned to their former Democratic allegiance.

Jacob B. Jackson, Know Nothing, afterwards Democratic governor of West Virginia, was defeated by W. L. Jackson, Democrat, for commonwealth attorney; H. L. Pickens, Democrat, defeated John Kester, Know Nothing, for sheriff; John Watson, Democrat, defeated Mahlon Hanes, Know Nothing, for commissioner of revenue, and Samuel B. Seckman, James Williamson, Thomas Browse and James L. Hanlin, Democrats, defeated Asa P. Allen, Greenberry B. Riggs, Clark Smith and John Fetty, Know Nothings, for magistrates.

The old Virginia law requiring regular muster and drill on the part of all able-bodied male citizens of military age was rather loosely carried out for several years in this county. These musters were held twice a year, sometimes at St. Marys and again at Sylvan Mills. The law was founded on the old English principle that every freeman should be trained to defend the country; but for lack of efficient drill sergeants the training was rather crude. On October 27, 1859, Robert Henry Browse was elected the first major of militia of Pleasants county.

CHAPTER V

THE BEGINNING OF ST. MARYS

In the Revolutionary War every colony was expected to remunerate its own soldiers, and Virginia adopted the plan of paying them off so far as possible with grants of land in her western territory, of which she claimed an almost unlimited area. These grants were called warrants, and were issued to the soldiers on request, so it happened that while Patrick Henry was governor of Virginia many warrants were given under his hand. A few of these tracts were actually settled upon by the grantees, but most of them were disposed of for small sums to speculators, and the land now occupied by St. Marys was transferred by the original grantee to another party without having been occupied by him.

The first owner of the tract was a certain Henry Thomas, who transferred his title to a William McClerry, and he in turn to Stephen West, and afterwards by West's heirs to the father of Alexander H. Creel, the founder of St. Marys. The original warrant to West is on file in the court house at Clarksburg, but has recently been copied into the records of Pleasants county. We here give an exact transcript of it:

"Patrick Henry, Esquire, Governor of the Commonwealth of Virginia,

"To all to whom these Presents shall come, Greeting:

"Know ye that by Virtue and in Consideration of part of a Preemption Treasury Warrant No. 1501, issued the 28th day of August, 1781, there is granted by the said Commonwealth unto Stephen West, Assignee of William McClerry, who was Assignee of Henry Thomas, a certain Tract or Parcel of Land containing 700 acres by Survey, bearing date the 13th Day of May, 1785, lying and being in the County of Harrison on the lower side of Middle Island Creek, and bounded as followeth, to wit:

"Beginning at a Sugar Tree and Buckeye Tree on the Bank of a Gut made by the Ohio River and said Creek, and running thence down said Gut with the Meander thereof 374 poles to a Sugar Tree and Buckeye Tree on Bank of said River, thence S. 65 degrees E. 312 poles to a White Oak, N. 21½ degrees E. 373 Poles to a White Oak, N. 61½ degrees 212 poles to a Poplar, N. 76 degrees, W. 80 Poles to the Beginning, with its Appurtenances.

"TO HAVE AND TO HOLD the said Tract or Parcel of Land, with its Appurtenances, to the said Stephen West and his Heirs forever.

"In Witness Whereof, the said Patrick Henry, Esquire, Governor of the Commonwealth of Virginia, hath hereunto set his Hand, and caused the Lesser Seal of the said Commonwealth to be affixed, at Richmond, on the 2nd Day of October, in the Year of Our Lord one thousand seven hundred and eighty-six, of the Commonwealth the Eleventh.

(SEAL) "P. Henry".

This tract embraced all the land from the mouth of the creek to the alley south of Creel street, extending back to about the low gap where A. J. Underwood resides, and from there to the LaRue farm and back to the starting point, including what later became the farms of Samuel Barkwill, Silas Gallaher, Solomon Bills, Charles Bills and Joseph Hubbs, in addition to the original territory of St. Marys.

On the 26th of May, 1849, Thomas Browse says he rode to Creel's and laid off the lower half of St. Marys. A few days later, June 8, he rode down to Edmund Riggs's Jr., for the purpose of laying off lots for a town. "Old Mr. Riggs and his brother Edmund, and Abner Martin was there sick. Edmund Riggs was undecided, so all labor was lost."

It will be recalled that Alexander H. Creel came from Eastern Virginia in 1834 and was said to have bought the land known later as Pickens Bottom. The following curious legend has prevailed concerning this, but so far as we have been able to learn it has no authenticity; however, it is as interesting and perhaps as authentic as many of the stories related of cities greater than St. Marys.

It is said that Mr. Creel, who was engaged in business along the Ohio, was traveling by steamer to Wheeling. In his sleep one night a vision of the Virgin Mary appeared to him and directed him to look upon the Virginia side of the river.

"There," said she, "you will behold the site of what some day will be a happy and prosperous city."

Awaking, he opened the outer door of his state-room. Illuminated by a brilliant moon he saw clearly the lower end of Middle Island and beyond it a spacious cove surrounded by a rampart of densely wooded hills. Marking the place well in his mind, he proceeded on his journey.

The memory of his vision never left him. He returned and bought the land. For some reason unknown, he was temporarily diverted from the purpose of founding a city there, for he sold the tract to Hugh L. Pickens, and located a mile below at the mouth of Greens Run; but in 1849 he came back, repurchased that portion of the land on which St. Marys was first marked out, and devoted his energies to the fulfillment of his dream, naming the place in honor of the Mother of Our Lord.

The legend is faulty in the fact that the land was not originally bought by Alexander H. Creel, but by his father.

Is the absence of any definite light on the question, it is reasonable to suppose that the certainty of forming a new county brought Mr. Creel back to this location. There would have to be a county seat, with a court house and a suitable area for a town, and all that was out of the question at Vaucluse, albeit the latter place afforded a better landing for steamboats. But the possibility of the railroad was also to be considered, and there was a strong probability of the Baltimore and Ohio coming down Middle Island creek and crossing the river on a bridge, so as to shorten the distance to Marietta and connect there with he proposed railroad to Cincinnati.

So in 1849 he employed Thomas Browse to mark out the town. There were then only three or four houses in the neighborhood. One was owned and occupied by Edmund Riggs, Jr., just below the town; another was on the brow of the upper terrace, Second street, on the site now occupied by the offices of Dinsmoor & Company; a log house near the present court house and another log house near Third and Lafayette streets. It is very likely that McKinney had a store near the landing.

The town was laid out regularly in the shape of a parallelogram, the southwestern boundary being an alley, then Creel street, Lafayette, George, Washington and Clay streets, the last forming the northeastern limit. Beginning then with First street along the river, next is Alley A, then Second street, then Alley B and lastly Third street. The town lots were of generous size, 80 by 160 feet; the streets 60 feet wide and the alleys 20 feet. George street was extended up the upper terrace to an acre donated by Mr. Creel on which the court house should stand.

Such was the general plan, but for many years it remained only partially carried out, the reason being that it overlapped property which did not belong to Mr. Creel. The Gallaher farm extended diagonally across Clay street from Second to the river bank, and two other small parcels of land embraced the proposed lots from Second street along Washington to the river, and it was not until many years later that these streets were fully opened. That is to say, for a long time First street extended only from Creel to Washington, and Second street above Washington was narrowed to but little more than the width of the county road into which it merged.

The first county road came down the banks of the Thoroughfare from the ferry over Middle Island creek. traces of it being noticeable fifty years ago, lined on one side with fragments of a post-and rail fence. The road has been washed away or overgrown with trees and the remains of the fence carried off by high water. This road continued along the river bank through the narrows below town to Vaucluse, but every vestige of it has disappeared.

The activities of the village for many years centered on Creel street, at the western end of which was the steamboat landing. The first building erected, according to old inhabitants who have been consulted, was the large frame house on the corner of First and Creel streets now owned by H. A. Carpenter. It was built by Logan Brothers and occupied by them as a mercantile store. This was about 1850, possibly 1849. At the same time was commenced the large brick building on the opposite side of Creel street, occupied by A. H. Creel as a store and hotel—or tavern, as inns were then designated, now for many years known as the Cain House.

Other houses built about that time were the Exchange Hotel, on the north side of Creel street; the Commercial Hotel across the alley from it and nearly adjoining the Logan store; the Isaac Reynolds home on the corner of Second and Lafayette streets, and the first M. E. Church South, on the site of the present structure. All of these, except the church, are still standing. Other buildings now existing, nearly competing in antiquity with those mentioned are the Aaron Doutt house and the houses occupied by J. C. Noland, William Hughes, J. M. Imlay, Mrs. R. A. Gallaher, W. L. Neely and the George Kelsall store and residence.

Alexander Creel was a believer in roads. He had caused the road to be constructed from Vaucluse to intersect the old State Road and the Northwestern Pike, and now he saw the necessity of having a good road to the East from St. Marys. There was an old road, the remains of which may yet be traced, from the Ellenboro Pike at the top of the hill through the Gallaher estate, but it was very rough and had almost insurmountable grades. It climbed the hill from the Pike near the residence of Andrew Boley, followed the ridge through the Barkwill farm to the house built several years ago by Thornton Hooper, then northward, passing the spring on the Gallaher hill, along the ridge and slanting down through the strip of woods to the present farm road on the Gallaher land, following that down Gallaher Lane until it intersected what is now Second street at the Sycamore street corner.

REYNOLDS HOUSE, OUR FIRST COURT HOUSE

The new road effected by Mr. Creel is the one now used, coming down the north side of Barkwill's hollow. Recent road engineers have pronounced it a work of great skill, providing an easy and steady grade for the distance of a mile and one-eighth. It was no uncommon thing, said one who came here about 1851, to see from thirty to forty teams coming into town over the Ellenboro Pike, bringing merchandise of all kinds from Clarksburg and points farther east. Great wagons, drawn by four or six horses, came dashing down the hill at breakneck speed, making the sharp turn on the face of the hill without drawing rein.

And one can easily picture to himself the scene on Creel street, where were located the stores and warehouses, the postoffice, the taverns and the boat landing. What a bustle each wagon must have occasioned, with the unloading and sorting out of the freight, some consigned to the local merchants but most of it to be laden on a steamboat for transportation down the river. The teams had to be taken care of, the thirsty and hungry drivers had to be refreshed, and the inns or taverns were probably noisy until late at night with drinking and singing, for from all accounts those husky teamsters had a way of their own and maintained it.

It is to be remembered that in those days strong liquor was freely used, and was sold by the drink or the quart in the regular stores just as any other commodity.

The establishment of the county of Pleasants and making St. Marys the county seat had the effect of practically depopulating Vaucluse, all persons of that community engaged in business removing immediately to the new town. The buildings, flimsy structures at the best, were left to decay, and most of them were swept off by floods, so that in a few years all the houses along the river had disappeared and there were left only three or four little habitations situated in the gorge of the run well above high water. Nothing remained but the high-sounding name, which still serves on the railroad time cards as marking a stopping station for passengers to and from Newport, directly across the river.

The first mercantile firms of which we have any record in St. Marys were McClure & Watson, Logan Brothers and Hopkins & Dils. A tailor shop was kept by a Mr. Core, a resident physician was Dr. Bottom, and Isaac Roby operated the ferry over the creek near its mouth, selling annual passes at four dollars a year. As early as 1853 there was a tannery, operated by a Mr. Myers, but owned by Logan Brothers. Mr. Myers was succeeded by Richard Towzey, who bought the business in 1860 and kept it going until 1866, when it was purchased by the King Brothers, who later removed to Washington, D. C.

Mr. Towzey was perhaps the most erudite man in the county. He was born in England in 1806 and came to America in 1833, preaching the Gospel for twenty-five years as minister of the Methodist Episcopal Church. In 1855 he came to St. Marys, where he remained until his death on August 21, 1889, in the 84th year of his age. For a few years he labored in the tannery and then taught school, while serving at times as mayor or recorder of the town. He was a man of very pleasing manner, and delighted in conversation of either a literary or a theological turn.

In 1855 Mr. Myers is mentioned as postmaster of the town, while James Bailey had become postmaster at Grape Island.

For some years the chief business of the town was handling the freight brought in by teamsters from the east, but this was seriously threatened by the completion of the Baltimore & Ohio railroad to Wheeling in the latter part of December, 1852. To forestall the intention of building a branch line of this road to St. Marys or Parkersburg, a movement was set on foot in Marietta to construct a line on the other side of the river. Capital was subscribed, the right of way secured and work was actively commenced in the year 1853. A large part of the proposed road was graded and stone bridges and culverts built, when the plan collapsed. At this day the traveler may see the great fills and cuts and the stone work of that abandoned project.

Disregarding this enterprise, the Baltimore & Ohio company began surveying for their branch line, and completed it to Parkersburg on May 1, 1857. This put an end to the ambition of St. Marys as a great shipping port. Creel's vision of a large and prosperous city faded, and for years the county seat remained only a dirty and squalid village of less than two hundred people, with no special industry until sometime after the close of the Civil War, when suddenly it became of some importance in the manufacture of oil barrels.

In the first twenty years of its existence the town had only grown up to George street along Second and to Washington street along First. Every business house was on Creel street, and the few dwellings above that street were very noticeably scattered, each standing on its large lot of eighty foot frontage., The farm house of Samuel Barkwill, on the corner now occupied by the First National Bank, was the only building within the town limits above Washington street, and back of it an apple orchard extended to the bank of the Thoroughfare. The square on which the Odd Fellows Hall stands was all vacant and was used as a ball ground.

In 1872 the town was incorporated by an act of the Legislature, but the privileges not being satisfactory, on petition of the mayor, Richard Towzey, and others, the charter was repealed in 1876. Four year later, in 1880, it was again incorporated, this time by the Circuit Court. Robert Patterson was elected mayor and Daniel W. Reynolds recorder.

CHAPTER VI

DURING THE CIVIL WAR

It is regrettable that accurate data of events occurring in Pleasants county during the Civil War are not found in the county records, such as the official acts, the enlistments, the companies formed, with their officers, and the ballots taken.

Slavery had never gained a strong foot-hold here, yet when dissension arose between the South and the North over that question, covered as it was by the apparently paramount matter of the right of secession, there were many adherents of the South in this county. After the fading away of the Whig and Know Nothing parties the sentiment here was overwhelmingly Democratic. This was shown by the balloting for President in 1860, Breckenridge receiving 165 votes, Bell 142 and Douglas 121, while only one vote was cast for Abraham Lincoln, the Republican candidate. It is said that James Reynolds of French creek was the sole supporter of Lincoln.

The secession of South Carolina in December, following the announcement of Lincoln's election, was an example for other slave holding States. Virginia was slower than most others, but Governor Letcher called an extraordinary session of the Assembly in January, 1861, for the express purpose of deciding for or against secession. The Assembly, apparently unwilling to assume full responsibility for such a drastic move, issued a call for a convention to be held in February.

Ritchie and Pleasants counties were united into a delegate district, and in the election held February 4 Cyrus Hall of Ritchie was chosen a member of the State convention. On April 17 an ordinance providing for secession was passed by the convention, Cyrus Hall voting for it. The ordinance provided that the matter should be left to a vote of the people, at an election to be held May 23. Of the forty-seven members of the convention representing the counties now composing West Virginia thirty-two voted against the secession ordinance, but two of them afterwards changed their votes. In the election of May 23 Pleasants county gave 158 votes for the secession ordinance and 363 against it.

In the meantime the sentiment against a division of the Union had become so far crystalized that a convention was called to be held at Wheeling, May 13, known afterward as the First Wheeling Convention. Delegates to this convention were chosen mostly at mass meetings of the citizens, and Pleasants was represented by Friend Cochran, Robert T. Parker, R. A. Cramer and James W. Williamson.

The first convention merely paved the way for a second convention, to which the members were elected by popular vote instead of being chosen at mass meetings. The Pleasants and Ritchie district sent James W. Williamson as member of the House of Delegates, and C. W. Smith and William Douglas as delegates to the convention. This body met in Wheeling June 11, 1861, and provided for the formation of the new State of Kanawha, the name being changed afterward to West Virginia.

The Third Wheeling Convention met in that city November 26, 1861, for the purpose of preparing a constitution for the new State. Pleasants county sent Joseph Hubbs as its representative. The following February the convention finished its work, the constitution was submitted to the voters, who ratified it by an almost unanimous vote April 11, 1862. In Pleasants the vote was 322 for ratification of the constitution and only two ballots against it.

This vote is rather surprising in view of the fact that at the other election more than one-third of the voters had expressed themselves as in favor of secession; but perhaps it may be partially accounted for by the rapid progress of the war, the practice of intimidation usual in such cases, and the virtual disfranchisement of voters.

The Unionists were in a large majority; every person suspected of sympathizing with the Confederacy was under strict surveillance, and prevented, if possible from voting. An example is taken from the Browse Journal:

Three days before the election on the constitution, James Ruckman, John Hammett, Thomas Browse and his son, Robert H. Browse, were required to report to Captain Myers at St. Marys and were confined in the guard house. Joseph Powell was brought in also on the day of the election. On April 12 they were put on board the Eagle, under guard of Lieutenant Ross, and taken to Wheeling. A stop was made at Grape Island to gather up all the fire arms to be found there—two double-barreled shot guns, a rifle, two flint-lock pistols and two revolvers.

At Wheeling they were placed in the Atheneum as prisoners with about one hundred others. James Barker, Thomas Seckman and David Houser, all of Pleasants, were added to the party. On the 19th the men from this county were taken before Judge John J. Jackson of the Federal Court, and were released after taking the oath to support the constitution and having given securities. They returned home on the steamer Liberty. Being taken up by the Eagle and brought back by the Liberty sounds like poetic justice.

Whatever men might think, they had to be very careful as to what they said. Such a thing as freedom of expression in time of war is unknown. Nicholas Wells, who resided above Bens Run, happened to remark that it "was an Abolition war from the beginning," and that was cause sufficient to arrest him and take him to Parkersburg, where he was compelled to take the oath and to give a security of one thousand dollars.

This section was not troubled with actual hostilities, although on one occasion there was a raid made by Confederates. On October 26, 1863, a small body of Confederate soldiers suddenly descended upon St. Marys, where they are reported to have destroyed ninety muskets, captured twenty-five citizens, whom they released, and then departed down the river road with horses taken from Pethtel, Hubbs, Gallaher, Patterson, Creel and Boylen.

Always the people were in dread of these raids, and it is said that several citizens buried their silverware and cash on the island. At the slightest rumor, too, some would cross the river into Ohio and remain there until all danger was reported over. When Morgan made his celebrated cavalry dash through southern Ohio it was supposed that he might attempt to cross back to the southern side of the river at Grape Island, where the river was fordable in low water, so a company of fifty soldiers under Lieutenant Howe came on July 23, 1863, and occupied the river bank near the Browse home. The men remained there four days, until news came of Morgan's capture not far from Steubenville.

In September, 1862, Mr. Browse records going on the steamer Science to Wheeling and meeting a Miss Wilson on the boat. She had been teaching school at Sistersville, but was dismissed because of her suspected sympathies, receiving the following note:

"Sistersville, Va., August 29, 1862
"Miss Wilson:
"At the instance of the citizens of this place I have considered the circumstance of your station here and have concluded that it would be best for you to give up the idea of teaching here. You will leave this county by the first boat.
"Respectfully,
"Edgar Boyers, Provost Marshal."

As the war proceeded, there were continual demands for enlistments, and in order to help the Federal government as much as possible the counties of the new State of West Virginia laid levies for funds with which to pay bounties to the enlisted men. For this purpose Pleasants county raised the sum of $37,900—a very large amount, considering the then limited resources of the county and the sparse population.

Later, the drafting plan was put into effect, and in September, 1864, the following were drafted into the Union army from Pleasants county:

Twenty-second Subdistrict—Brady Lemaster, George D.
Stout, William Locke, Charles E. Locke, William M. See
vers, Rodney Reynolds, Sylvester Wilson, John S. Morgan,
Frederick Shafer, John Virden, Jeremiah McCune, John
Kelley, William C. Ruttencutter, Thomas J. Birkhimer,
Joseph Rice, Job Smith, Jacob Idonise, George Kechaline,
Crayton Flesher, Isaac B. Cox, Joseph Bookman, Elias J.
Satterfield, Joshua Lamp, Joshua R. Ruttencutter,
Abraham Ruttencutter, Calvin Campbell, Robert Stanley,
Albert A. Stephens, Thomas H. Hart, Paul King, Andrew
M. Seckman, John W. Gatrell, Joseph Mason, John Arn,
Isaac Holland, Benjamim F. Seckman, Joseph Reynolds,
Jacob Speece, Jacob Dearth, John F. Hart, Reuben
Wright, Geo. W. Reynolds, Jr., John W. Riggs and David
Cunningham.

Twenty-third Subdistrict—William Wilson, Harvey
Hendershot, James E. Robinson, Samuel C. Hammett,
John Bryson, Marion Cochran, William Malone, William
F. Robinson, James Carney, Abel Bonar, Lewis Gibboney,
William Outward, Joseph H. Kester, John G. Wigner,
George F. Wiseman, Israel B. Smith, William Kester,
James E. Reynolds, Austin G. Wells, Joseph Brown, Francis M. Irwin, Newman Wilson, George S. Hammett,
Charles Robinson, David Rawson, Daniel Corbin, Charles
I. Wood, David Gregg, Jacob Lemley, Abram Joy, John
W. Norris and Emanuel Smith.

These men reported at the Atheneum Theater in
Wheeling.

Mr. Browse tells of being at Wheeling in the latter part
of that month and seeing a large number of drafted men
from other places, some being able to escape the service
by hiring substitutes, paying in some instances as high as
one thousand dollars. There were scamps who made a
practice of accepting bounties and then evading the service who after the war were stigmatized with the term of
"bounty jumpers."

CHAPTER VII

EARLY INDUSTRIES

The first census of Pleasants county was taken in 1860, after it had been in existence about ten years. The enumeration then gave a population of 2,945, about twenty-two persons to the square mile. Whether or not the war had a hindering effect upon its growth we cannot say, but the census of 1870 gave the population as 3,012, an increase of only 67. These people were scattered among the hills and hollows, excepting nearly three hundred who resided at the county seat. The only other place approaching a village was Hebron, in the extreme eastern end of the county, and there were found only a country store, a church, school house, blacksmith shop and a few houses nestled in the neighboring hollows. The place was humorously called "Giter."

Wild land or uncleared woods covered most of the county. It is true that much of the finest lumber had been taken out, but it had been done recklessly and the land allowed to grow up in brush.

Timbering was the first general industry. Old residents have taken great pleasure in telling of the fine stands of timber which once flourished on the hills. Practically every stream has had a sawmill located along its course, and piles of rotting sawdust and slabs remain as evidences. These mill sets were usually placed where the logs could be chuted down the steep hillsides with the least labor.

In journeying on foot over the county one is impressed also with the ruins of squatters' cabins, seen in almost every hollow and on many a sheltered hillside. Frequently these were built and tenanted for a time by the hands working at the saw mills, but some of them are known to have been occupied by a somewhat roving class, of which there never were many in this county, known as "seng diggers." These were families of thriftless habits, granted the privilege of settling down for a time either from pure charity or for some small service. Most of them were well acquainted with ginseng, yellow root and other native medicinal plants, which they traded to the stores for such merchandise as they needed.

Because of the necessity of clearing off their land, farmers themselves devoted a large part of their time and energy to timbering, and also to bring in a little ready money they put in their spare time getting out hoop-poles and tanbark. They found a ready sale for the bark at the tannery in St. Marys and also at the office of Aaron Doutt, who bought large quantities to be shipped in barges to Pittsburgh and Cincinnati. Mr. Doutt was of Pennsylvania Dutch extraction, and resided in the cottage now occupied by Mr. Alonzo Lawson on Second street. He was regarded as a very honest but quaint gentleman, and nothing delighted him more than to tell about his many trips down the river and his experiences in New Orleans.

The business of lumbering was carried on extensively the whole length of Middle Island creek, being at its height along in the 80's. The Spring freshets brought down the rafts with their crews of hardy navigators, apparently reckless of dangers. In an air line it is not more than twenty miles from the mouth of McElroy creek in Tyler county to the mouth of Middle Island creek, but by the eccentric course of the stream it is from sixty to seventy-five miles, some say one hundred, and with a current flowing at the rate of seven miles an hour, or even faster, the rafts would make that distance in the course of a long day.

The sudden, acute angles of the stream continually menaced the lives of the raftsmen, but those hardy navigators negotiated them with a carelessness that ignored a wetting or the breaking up of their rafts. But the latter danger was something that very seldom happened, for the timbers were so well pegged together with wooden pins that it would have required an Atlantic billow to tear them to pieces; yet they were pliant to a high degree.

Running a raft was a grand unceasing struggle throughout the whole of that hundred mile course. Constant care was necessary to keep it from running aground or getting hung up on the many rocks which lay in the channel, or to guide it over the numerous dams which then existed along the creek. It was far more exciting than the sensation of "shooting the chutes" at one of our modern amusement parks. To the onlooker who watched a raft making such a sharp turn as at Next, or Shiloh, or Ruttencutter's Bend, it seemed about as perilous an occupation as one would care to risk.

The yellow, swirling waters of the creek carried them onward sometimes at racehorse speed. When making a sharp bend it was often necessary for some of the men to leap ashore and with poles keep the raft from striking on the rocks; then, that duty over, it was left to them to get aboard again in the best way possible. At times, in passing over a dam, the raft would shoot down under the water. tossing the men about, much as a great wave in a storm at sea deluges the deck of a ship.

Usually they moored for the night in the backwater at the mouth of the creek, the men going to town for the night, frequently soaking wet and always hungry. Good, substantial meals they demanded, plenty of meat, with bread cut an inch thick, and the evenings were spent in recreations and recounting the experiences of the day.

The lumber market was at Marietta, and sometimes the men would continue the voyage to that city in the morning; but many of these hardy, daring voyagers were afraid of the Ohio. In the narrow confines of the creek the shores seemed always convenient, and leaping off and on their rafts was mere amusement; but the broad, vast surface and unknown depth of the great river filled them with dread.

We have mentioned the LaRue saw mill on Broad run, near its mouth, as the first of its kind in the county, operated by water power and using a vertical saw. This was run by Perry LaRue well into the middle of the last century. A mill on Cow creek in the 30's is said to have been the first one in the county operated by steam.

The largest lumber business carried on was that begun by Simpson Jones and Ralph Haines, under the firm style of Jones & Haines, in 1876 on McKim creek. They went into the business extensively, the village which built up around the mill being called Jonestown. They built a large saw mill and grist-mill, operated with water power, making a dam in the creek and building a splendid mill-race with huge cut stones. There was a general store, a blacksmith shop, a cooper shop; while down at the mouth of McKim creek they had a boat yard, where large barges were built. At one time they had a hundred teams at work. Several houses were erected for the men and their families, a school house and a church were built near by. For a few years Jonestown and its business were the talk of the county, and then came financial embarrassment. Gradually the place was deserted, the buildings removed or destroyed, and now only a farm house and the school building remain. The site of this deserted village is on the south side of the creek, a little above Zoar Chapel and the county Four-H Camp. A part of the solidly built mill-race is yet in place, but many of the stones have been removed.

Soon after that the Cochran Brothers entered the timbering business in Jefferson district, and on the ridge between the waters of French and Cow creeks constructed a tram road for carrying lumber. The title of this road was "The Eureka, Cochranville and Cornwallis Tram Railroad," and the ambition of its promoters was to connect Cornwallis in Ritchie county with Eureka on the Ohio river, but the road was never completed. Its course may still be traced from the top of Henry Camp hill along the ridge eastward to the head of Schultz Fork.

Owing to litigation over boundary lines the development of the eastern part of Jefferson district was retarded, and most of the land had grown up "wild." It was before the days of cheap wire fencing, and many large tracts, owned by non-residents, were not enclosed. To some this was a great temptation to trespass on the lands of another and cut timber. During the many prosecutions for this offence the term "vanderberging" became applied to it, in a jocular way.

Along with timbering, another matter that helped the farmer to a little ready money as he cleared his land was getting out staves for oil barrels, and for nearly a score of years coopering was the chief business of St. Marys.

Long before Drake drilled his well in 1859 petroleum, or Seneca Oil, as it was then called, was a marketed product of West Virginia. It was first gathered from pits dug in the sands in Wirt county at the mouth of Hughes River, soaked up in blankets, then strained and bottled. From fifty to one hundred barrels a year were gathered by this tedious process and sold to wholesale druggists. It was highly esteemed as a remedy for all sorts of ills, especially of the throat and lungs, and its medicinal uses are valued to this day, whether in the crude state or chemically prepared.

Bosworth, Wells & Co. of Marietta were the largest purchasers, shipping it to eastern markets where it was sold under the name of Seneca Oil. In 1855 they paid thirty-three cents a gallon for it, and by 1857 the price had risen to forty cents.

For sometime it was also called "fossil oil," from a belief that it originated in vast remains of shellfish whose oil had been extracted by the interior heat of the earth, but the production of enormous quantities caused that belief to be laid aside, and in lieu of a better term it has been given the general name of "rock oil," or petroleum. Scientists are still at a loss to account for its origin.

In the same year in which Drake drilled his Pennsylvania well, the Rathbone brothers drilled a well near Burning Springs in Wirt county and found oil at a depth of 200 feet, pumping several barrels daily. A quarter of a mile away another well was bored and at 303 feet a larger quantity of oil was found, pumping one hundred barrels a day. Soon after another well was put down in that neighborhood, which produced 1200 barrels a day. Then the excitement was intense. That was in 1860, and the work of production went on notwithstanding the war until, in 1863, General Jones of the Confederate army raided this section and set fire to the oil barges.

Burning Springs is on the great anticlinal which runs through Volcano in Wood county and Horseneck in

Pleasants. Far back in the ages when the earth was young there had been a tremendous upheaval of the earth's crust, perhaps the result of a lateral pressure. The formerly level-lying series of rocks to an unknown depth were lifted up into an irregular ridge. In the millions of years that passed after that, the summit of this ridge was worn down by erosion until the primal sandstone lay exposed. This grayish white rock, studded full of worn, round quartz pebbles, is now known as the Horseneck sand, and is a member of the Cow Run series. Large masses of it may be seen along the river road on the Hammett farm. Break off a fragment, let it lie in water for sometime and a thin scum of oil will form on the surface. This pebbly sand crops out all along the summit of the anticlinal from Burning Springs to Eureka.

The same conditions seem to have been observed on Horseneck Run as at Burning Springs, but there were no enterprising Rathbones to experiment with the desirable fluid. Mr. E. B. Steere, who came to this county about the year 1865, has kindly furnished us with some memoranda of the first oil excitement in the Horseneck field. He relates that along in the early '50's oil was discovered floating on little pools of water on Horseneck Run and its little branches, and for a time it created considerable wonder. Finally it was ascertained that the oil escaped through and from the exposed rocks, and this idea led to the belief that there must be a quantity of oil somewhere below. Several companies secured small leases on the Jacob Hendershot farm of 80 acres and other adjoining farms, and proceeded in a crude way to drill wells, which produced from ten to thirty barrels a day.

This started a wonderful rush of oil seekers to that section. Hendershot received enough in bonuses and rental to enable him to buy a fine farm on the Ohio shore. The excitement spread. Capitalists came in and bought much of the land for miles around. Many wells were "springpoled" down, some showing a little oil, others not any.

The first lease on record was dated about one month after the raid of General Jones on Burning Springs—June 16, 1863. Jacob B. Blair, A. S. Core, John Gilfillan and Thomas S. Conley of Parkersburg obtained a lease from Jacob Hendershot for the term of eighteen years, "for the purpose of boring for, pumping and mining for what is known as Petroleum or Carbon oil, the following piece or parcel of land lying on Horseneck Run, a branch of Bull Creek, in Pleasants county, W. Va." The boundaries are given in the lease but not the number of acres, and the document proceeds: "in consideration of the premises, the said Blair, Core, Gilfillan and Conley agree to deliver to the said Hendershot, his heirs and assigns, one-eighth on the vat or tank of all the oil they may pump from the well or wells bored on said land, and pay the said Hendershot the sum of $250 as a bonus, the receipt whereof is hereby acknowledged."

The third well drilled by this company at a shallow depth struck an immense flow of oil, estimated variously at from 1200 to 1500 barrels per day. They had no means ready to save such a vast quantity of the fluid, but at once they proceeded to dig pits over an acre of ground. Many of those pits can yet be seen. It is said that some of the ground timbers of the original derrick also remain on the edge of the creek. The stream has changed its course a little and now runs over the well, which was located nearly half a mile below where the road from Calf creek joins the Horseneck road.

The oil from the Horseneck field then had to be hauled in barrels to the river at Bull Creek postoffice, now Waverly, and there shipped by boat to Wheeling or Marietta to be refined. This tedious method of transportation was expensive, and also the cost of production was large, each well being an individual job, as there were then none of the modern methods of handling the oil business.

The great Hendershot well, however, created the wildest possible excitement. Jacob Hendershot sold the remainder of his holdings outright to Thomas W. Phillips and Charles M. Phillips, of New Castle, Pa., for the sum of one hundred thousand dollars. He refused to take their check, so they were obliged to go to Wheeling to get the cash or greenbacks. Returning by boat to Willow Island about noon, Mr. Hendershot walked over to his log cabin on Horseneck with the money in his pockets, and the next morning he left, wearing his coonskin cap, with his wife and all his worldy possessions, going to his new home over the river. It is related that after his decease a satchel was found in his home containing several thousand dollars of the original greenbacks received in payment for his Horseneck farm. The bills were so decayed that it was impossible to separate them, and they were sent to Washington for redemption.

Many wells were drilled very near to the Gilfillan well, but none produced more than a few barrels daily, most of them making a great deal of water, requiring to be pumped day and night. The Gilfillan production decreased rapidly, and fell so low that at last it did not pay to work it. But under modern ways of handling the oil business there is still quite a paying production in the Horseneck field, one man taking charge of a large number of wells. On the Hendershot farm and others are wells pumping that were drilled more than twenty-five years ago.

All these were shallow wells, going down only from one hundred to three hundred feet, into the first and second Cow Run sands. The tools used sixty years ago were mere pygmies compared with the massive drills and stems of today. When moving to a new location, the workmen carried them through the woods on their shoulders. The drilling was done with spring-poles, and because of the light weight of the tools deep drilling was impossible. Even at a depth of two or three hundred feet months were frequently required to complete a well. As one old operator remarked, "We did not drill wells in those days; we just worried them down."

S. C. A. Hamilton of Wheeling maintianed that he was the first to use steam in drilling wells in Pleasants county, saying that he put down a well on the Jesse Carroll farm on Cow Creek, using steam power, in 1861. This statement was made at least sixty years after the date given, and it is possible that he may have forgotten the exact year.

Horseneck has the reputation of being the field in which an explosive was first used for the purpose of breaking up the sand and so permitting a more rapid flow of oil. Basil Childers, the father of O. C. Childers, the present assessor of Pleasants county, was the first man to conceive the idea of exploding gun powder in the bottom of a well to crack the rock or earth, and successfully used the method in several wells. This came to the attention of D. A. Roberts, formerly of Pennsylvania but then operating in the Wirt county field. That was in 1864. After seeing the crude method used by Mr. Childers, Mr. Roberts saw a way towards improving it. He employed a tinner of Marietta to make a tin shell, which he filled with gunpowder; on the upper end he fastened a gun cap, one of the old percussion kind, covering it with beeswax and tallow to make it water proof. He lowered the tube into the well with a wire attached to ears on each side of it. Then he dropped a flat-headed iron bar down the hole, and the result was a good explosion and a large increase in the output of oil.

Mr. Roberts is reported to have secured a patent upon the invention, which yielded him a comfortable income; but Mr. Childers is said to have realized nothing for his idea. He died about the year 1890, occupied up to his last moments with inventions.

From the Horseneck field the drilling of shallow wells spread all over the county, but no where else was the producing sand found so near the surface, and in a few years the production was confined almost exclusively to that first field. In the late Fall of 1878 the writer had occasion to pass down Horseneck run to Bull creek, and the scene then was one of great activity. The hillsides of the narrow valley were apparently crowded thick with derricks; everywhere gangs of men could be seen at work, and the atmosphere was charged with the scent of oil.

Outside of that immediate territory there were only two small producing wells at Vaucluse, upon what later became the right of way, and which were kept pumping until the Fall of 1883, when the Ohio River Railroad covered them over. At the foot of the hill by the Oxbow of French creek a well had been drilled and a little oil seeped through the square boxing. From many miles around people were accustomed to travel to this well and draw up oil by means of a tin can attached to a string, using it for medicinal purposes. Attempts were made to find the fluid in the hollow which joins Broad run above the school house, with the only result of giving it the name of "Oil Well Hollow."

It was in the latter part of the decade of 1860 that the manufacture of oil barrels became the leading industry of St. Marys. Absolutely nothing was known then of piping oil; it was all shipped in barrels, and the demand for cooperage became enormous. The whole county seemed to respond to the call. Farmers devoted a large part of their time to getting out oak timber, splitting it into rough staves and hauling them to town, where they were sold for cash to the cooper shops or traded to the merchants for goods. All over the town vacant places were stacked high with rough staves. Farmers who had no means of splitting the staves, brought in "cuts," short logs about the length of a stave. These cuts were quartered, then frows were used to further split them into rough staves and with draw-knives they were bucked down and smoothed into their final shape. From the marshy lands on the river bottom were brought the long, flat leaves of the cat-tail rushes to put between the pieces forming the heads of the barrels, making them practically air-tight.

Later on inventive genius devised a bucking machine operated by horse power, the horse, hitched to a long wooden bar, traveling in a circle as in a cane-mill. The rough stave was fed in on one side and came out on the other side ready for its final dressing down with the draw-knife, while a great heap of coarse shavings fell around. These shavings were used as fuel, making quick and hot fires, especially when to them were added the sawed off ends of the staves. Early on a Winter morning, before dawn, from the chimneys of the houses rose fountains of glowing sparks from the buck-shaving fires on the hearths, giving the impression of a widely scattered display of fireworks.

In 1877 there were eight or ten cooper shops in town. One was at the lower end of Third street, on the east side, where there was a spring or a well; another was on the southwest corner of Lafayette street and Alley A; another on the northwest corner of Second street and George; in fact, they were scattered about everywhere. Most of the men in the town were employed in these shops, every man working according to his pleasure or not at all. The average wage was about three or four dollars a day, but some of the more ambitious made as much as six or seven dollars. To do that, however, they started in at five in the morning and put in from twelve to fourteen hours.

The acme of good cooperage was to make a keg or barrel as nearly air-tight as possible. When the barrel was finished and the bung driven in, a small hole was bored in the side, and through this the cooper blew with all the strength of his lungs. On removing his lips, if the work was well done, the compressed air rushed out with a loud whistling noise. If this did not happen, then the maker must search for the defective place, often difficult to find.

But when it was learned that oil could be cheaply and safely transported from the wells to the refineries in pipes, the coopering business received its death blow, and one shop after another closed its doors. No barrels were needed for land transportation, but still there was a light demand for foreign export. The tank steamer was yet to come. But even that little cooperage was done away with when the export companies began the practice of gathering up the empty oil barrels in Europe, knocking them apart and shipping them back to this country in less space and free of duty because they had been originally manufactured in the United States. And also the large companies began to establish their own cooper shops.

However, the business of getting out rough staves continued for a time, the principal purchaser being the Pittsburgh Stave Company, with shops at New Martinsville. In January, 1883, we find it noted that a shipment of one hundred thousand staves had been made to that company at the rate of $15.50 per thousand.

The oil business was very quiet until 1885, when a well was drilled on Robin's Run, which empties into Cow creek just above the old St. John's Episcopal Church. This was drilled by Frank M. Brown, but as it did not make a good showing another well was commenced on the Russell Hammett farm on McElroy run, and that marked the beginning of the great Eureka-Belmont field. Great improvements had been made in the machinery, and it was now possible to drill much deeper and with greater ease. Gas was struck in the shallow sand of this well and the derrick was burned down. The rig was rebuilt and the work resumed, when the tools were lost in the hole. They were fished out after lying there for a year, and again drilling was begun. At 1200 feet oil was struck. The well proved to be a "gusher," sending out eighty barrels a day. Then it was shot, and the production increased to two hundred barrels. This was the well widely known as "the Burnt Well," which gave new life to the oil industry of Pleasants county.

It was drilled by Frank M. Brown of New York, the location having been selected by George W. Boss, who thereby gained his reputation as an "oil scout." T. N. Barnsdall of Bradford, Pa., bought a half interest in the lease and became an active operator in this field.

APPLE HARVEST IN PLEASANTS COUNTY

CHAPTER VIII

THE FIRST SCHOOLS

Surprisingly little information is to be obtained about the first schools in this county. It is all tradition, and very doubtful at that. Probably here as elsewhere throughout the new Western country the itinerant school master settled for a few months at a time, interested mainly in finding fairly good places for eating and sleeping, with plenty of amusement in the way of hunting, fishing, dancing and drinking. Occasionally, but rarely, some of these traveling teachers were fairly well grounded in the rudiments of the Three R's—Readin', 'Ritin' and 'Rithmetic; and still rarer instances have been mentioned of them having a smattering of Latin and Greek. But always they were rare penmen, making their own quill pens and their own ink.

Under the old Virginia regime there were no free schools. Teachers were employed by the patrons and paid at the rate of so much per pupil. In the case of poor people unable to pay the tuition fee, the State kindly stepped in and paid their share of the charges. but the children of the poor had to sit apart from the sons and daughters of those who could afford to pay. It may well be supposed that a feeling of degradation prevented some children from attending school, and for that reason the percentage of illiteracy in the State was large.

The early log school houses have so often been described that it is needless to repeat the description here. As late as the middle of the decade of 1890 there were still two log school houses in the county, one of them being on Henry Camp run. During the fifties there was a floating school anchored at the head of the Vaucluse Narrows, which was attended in the Summer by children from as far up the river as Grape Island.

After the formation of West Virginia as a State Washington district or township, as it was then called, was divided into three subdistricts, No. 1 above the creek, No. 2 including the neighborhood about St. Marys, and No. 3 extending to French creek. R. P. Caldwell, a young lawyer, was chosen township clerk in 1865, and from his record we learn that in the school election of that year William E. Bier and E. N. Cooke were elected to serve as school commissioners with John M. Strobel, the member holding over. Mr. Cooke failed to qualify, but Mr. Bier appeared and took the stringent oath required at that time. in the last year of the Cvil War. Many citizens of the new State had been Southern sympathizers, and apparently were not yet to be trusted in any form or manner with the government, in fact, under the registration law then in force no one who had aided, abetted or sympathized with the Confederate States was permitted to vote. About one-third of the voters of West Virginia were thus disfranchised, and remained so until the passage of the Flick amendment in 1871. which not only lifted the ban but forbade any further registration of voters in this State. The oath then required, and as taken by Mr. Bier, is here given:

"I. Wm. E. Bier, do solemnly swear that I will support the Constitution of the United States and the Constitution of this State; that I have never voluntarily borne arms against the United States; that I have voluntarily given no aid or comfort to persons engaged in armed hostility thereto by countenancing, counseling or encouraging them in the same; that I have not sought, accepted nor attempted to exercise the functions of any office whatever under any authority in hostility to the United States; that I have not yielded a voluntary support to any pretended government. authority, power or constitution within the United States hostile or inimical thereto. and that I take this obligation freely, without any mental reservation or purpose of evasion.

"W. E. Bier."

For the ensuing term the board elected Mary E. Bailey to teach the school in No. 1 at $25 per month; Ben K. Piersol to teach in St. Marys at $30 per month, and Fanny Cohagan to teach in No. 3 at $25 per month.

The town school was located at the corner of Second and Clay streets, opposite the present railroad station, on ground obtained from Silas Gallaher. the house and lot costing $400. School in No. 1 subdistrict was held in the Bethesda Church, for which a rental of six dollars per month was paid for six months. It seems that a building in No. 3 had been used as a school known as the Dye and Cooke school. and it was ordered to purchase half an acre of land from Col. R. T. Parker, on which the house was situate, for the sum of ten dollars, and that Dye and Cooke be allowed eight dollars each for the building.

E. N. Cooke not taking the oath, the board appointed John F. Taylor to fill the vacancy.

The tax list of the district shows the following names for the year 1865:

John R. M. Agnew, R. G. Bailey, D. K. Baylan. James L. Bailey, Wm. O. Barrick, Wm. E. Bier, Daniel Bailey. Bolden Biddle, Anthony Boley, D. D. Boley. David Boley, Joseph Bookman, John D. Bailey, John Bryson, W. H. Benson. Braden & Co., J. M. Bushfield, Brewer, Berk & Co., Charles Bills, John Boley. Wm. A. Brown, J. W. Baldwin, John Bailey's estate. Wm. Brown, James Bailey, Solomon Bills, Banks W. Broadhurst. Wm. Bennett's estate, Thomas Browse. Walter Brady. Zachariah Cain, E. N. Cooke, I. J. Cooper. John M. Collard. Martha Cooke, Wm. G. H. Core, Timothy Cohagan. Wm. Carroll. R. P. Caldwell. John Cooper, Wm. H. Dye, John Dye, Maxwell Dearth; Jacob W. Dearth, Elias Decker, Dils & Hopkins. Catherine S. Delavan. Harriett Flint, Rachel Ferguson. John W. Gatrell. Silas Gallaher, R. A. Gallaher, Catherine A. Gale. George W. Gale, I. N. Hodgins, Eli Hudkins, Robert Harvey, John Hines, Henry Hess, Joseph Hubbs, D. A. Houser, Rodney Hickman, Thomas Hammond, Wm. Hammond's estate, J. B. Jackson, John Justice, William Jarvis, Amanda Jerard, James Kerwood, Richard Kerwood, John Kelly, George Kelsall, Zadock Knight, Catherine Kimball, Aaron Knight, Rebecca LaRue, Washington Larimore, Wm. Larimore, Harvey Locke, Isaac LaRue's estate, Samuel Logan, Logan & Brother, John McCune, Phillip Meisenhelder, Joseph Mason, I. D. Myers, John G. McCally, Wm. Morehead, Elinor Moor, Wm. P. McKinney, Peter Odenwelder, B. F. Pickens, Powell & Harvey, Josiah Powell, Isaac A. Powell, Jack Powers, Jacob Prunty, Samuel W. Pickens, Hugh L. Pickens, B. K. Piersol, Helen Pickens, Narcissa Pickens, Col. R. T. Parker, Robert Patterson, Jr., George W. Reynolds, G. W. Riggs, Martin Riggs, S. M. Riggs, Wm. Rymer, Nancy Riggs, Sarah Reed, Joshua Ruttencutter, Edmund Riggs, Jr. Rodney Reynolds, Mary Rymer, J. F. Ruttencutter, T. H. C. Reynolds, Isaac Roby, Mary F. Riggs, Thomas Rymer's estate, Daniel Reynolds, Isaac Riggs' estate, Francis Shepherdson, George Shai, John M. Strobel, Absalom Smith, A. A. Stephens, Thomas A. Smith, Abram Samberson, Job Smith, Elijah Scribner, Washington & Hamilton Schmidt, Agnes Smith, John F. Taylor, Toler Oil Co., F. M. Triplett, F C. and Thomas Taylor, Taylor, Nye & Co., J. B. Townsend, Richard Towzey, Joseph Taylor's estate, Michael Weaver (Weber), Isaac Watson, J. B. Watson, Francis Woods' estate and Edward Willis.

In addition we find the following listed in the town:

Samuel Barkwill, A. H. Creel, Wm. Dils, E. S. Haddox, Wm. L. Jackson, Granville Keller, Logan & Keller, John Logan, Meredith Spencer & Co., James Patterson, H. H. Rymer's estate and Edward Johnson, Sr.

The amount raised by levy for teachers fund was $852.69, and the State contributed of its fund $361.71, making a total for the teachers of $1214.40. Some contrast to the fund of the present day.

Teaching school in the sixties and seventies was not taken up as a profession by many men outside of the larger cities, although the remuneration was probably fair enough, compared with the average wages of the period. Many of them went into the profession with the idea of earning enough money to start in some small business or to take them through a course of law or medicine; while in the rural districts the young men found it more pleasurable and profitable than simply feeding the stock all winter, then, the short term of teaching ended, back they would go to the spring work on the farm.

But there were a few exceptions, and among them in this vicinity were Aaron Delong, William Jones and C. E. Slemaker, survivors of the old pioneer school masters. In addition to the regular winter term, they usually gave a six or eight weeks' course in the Spring to "subscription" or pay pupils. Aaron Delong was the most famous of the old-time teachers, and it is claimed that he knew the text-books so well that he could hear any class without having to refer to them. In addition to his talents as a teacher, he himself laid claim to being the ugliest man in the county although his claim was warmly disputed by a Mr. Gorrell of Hebron.

To this day the older inhabitants talk with respect of the abilities of Aaron Delong. His favorite pursuit was mathematics, but he also delighted in polemics, and was a skillful writer. He served a term as county school superintendent in the late sixties, and was succeeded by William N. Jones of Hebron, who held the office until 1872. Our recollection is that Mr. Jones had an inclination towards natural philosophy, as the science of physics was then termed. In his day there was no examining board; applicants for teachers' certificates called at any time on the county superintendent, who propounded a few questions and then, if the applicant created a favorable impression, granted the certificate.

Richard Towzey, of whom mention has been made before, followed Mr. Jones as superintendent, and in 1873 Archimedes W. Gorrell of Hebron succeeded to the office. Mr. Gorrell served several terms, but, curiously enough, none consecutively. He was distinguished for his complaisant and courtly manner, and was greatly admired and beloved by the teachers.

C. E. Slemaker (usually pronounced "Sleighmaker") taught a term or two in St. Marys. It had long been the belief that the school could not be taught successfully without strict discipline, usually enforced with a rod; but the ingenuity of the old time teachers frequently devised other schemes for enforcing order. Physical torture was resorted to by some, such as compelling the refractory pupil to hold a heavy book out at arm's length for a certain time; or stand on one foot; or, with his heels at a certain distance from the base-board, to lean back with his shoulders to the wall until he could no longer stand the strain and fell to the floor. Another teacher carried with him a number of patent clothespins, the kind that close with a spring, which he attached to the pupil's ears. One teacher in St. Marys had a peculiar form of punishment, as related by one of his pupils. About the walls of the room, suspended from the ceiling, he placed a number of straps, each with a small noose at the lower end. The disobedient pupil was compelled to stand with his face to the wall, his thumbs were inserted into the loops and the straps drawn up until the arms were fully extended. His pupil said that it was no uncommon thing to see an entire side of the wall occupied by twitching and squirming penitents.

These methods were not regarded generally at that time as cruel; in fact, we are told that they were not so distasteful as the floggings, and many of the boys delighted in showing their stoicism under punishment, boasting of how long they had withstood the torture before succumbing.

The first teacher of the town school under the new State constitution was Ben K. Piersol, who was then beginning the practice of law. We are indebted to one of his pupils for the statement that Mr. Piersol had plenty of time to read law during school hours and also to consume great quantities of chewing tobacco, adding that he could spit farther and straighter than any one else in the community. This would seem to confirm the opinion of Charles Dickens as to that peculiar skill among the early residents of the Ohio Valley.

Soon after the close of the war John L. Knight, a young veteran of that great conflict, taught two or three terms in the town school, until he was elected to the office of county reorder, which he assumed in 1869, and he is credited with having been a good teacher. P. Gano was employed for a time, also Clinton C. Davis, who taught two terms, during which he qualified himself for the bar.

The population of the town was increasing, and the one-roomed building became entirely too small, so a little building farther down town was rented for the primary pupils until 1876, when a two-story building was erected on the lot purchased from Silas Gallaher. It was the building now occupied by the St. Marys Fruit Company, opposite the railroad station, and was asserted to be the finest school building along the river between Parkersburg and Moundsville. It contained only two large rooms, the upper one for the more advanced pupils and the lower for the primary grades. Later, when it was necessary to employ three teachers, a partition was run the full length of the lower room; and in 1894, when a fourth teacher was employed, the principal's room at the head of the stairs was converted into a class room.

The first principal in this new building was John F. Wayman, of Marshall county, a graduate of Mount Union, Ohio, and his assistant was Greenberry Ruttencutter, a son of J. Frederick Ruttencutter of this county. It was established under the old system which authorized town graded schools, and was directly under the control of the board of education of the district, who employed the teachers and had some direction over the course of study. But in fact at that time there was no established curriculum for any of the common schools in the State. Certain text books were prescribed, but teachers paid little attention to any requirements for their use. The greatest legal obligation resting upon the instructors was to keep school open twenty-two days in each month and to file reports of attendance.

The sub-district or country schools, whose teachers were employed by trustees appointed by the board of education, often had enrolled pupils of all grades, from the infant learning the alphabet to students of higher arithmetic, algebra or Latin, comprising from thirty to forty class recitations daily. At times older pupils were drafted to hear recitations of beginners, while the teacher was employed with intermediary classes.

It is customary among old people to recall with pleasurable emphasis the accomplishments of their youth, and often they comment upon the thoroughness of education in the old days, but it is not reasonable that any teacher who can spare only an average of ten minutes to a class recitation could give thorough instruction. It is more probable that in any case of marked progress it has been due rather to the ability and earnestness of the pupil himself, guided by the precept and example of the instructor.

Education was hampered, too, by the shortness of the school term. In most districts it was only four months, but in Grant district the term was six months, and Washington had five months until 1885, when the term was increased to six months.

CHAPTER IX

THE COMING OF THE NEWSPAPER

Several counties in the new State were without newspapers early in the seventies, and among them was Pleasants. It may be added, also, that at the time very few counties were able to support a paper. The art of advertising was practically unknown and there were comparatively few reading families. Especially in a small county like this the starting of a newspaper required a wonderful hope and ambition, even though the cash outlay for the printing plant was remarkably small compared with that necessary at present.

To the Rev. F. M. Yates, then a young minister of the Methodist Protestant Church, belongs the credit of bringing the press directly into this county. He established "The Watchword" in the latter part of October, 1877, and of that paper the St. Marys Oracle is the lineal descendant, through change of owners and change of names. As the coming of a home printed newspaper may be said to mark an epoch in the history of the town and county, it may be well to take a brief survey of the community at this point.

The entire population of the county was not more than five thousand, and of the town perhaps three hundred. There were only nine postoffices—St. Marys, Grape Island, Raven Rock, Twiggs, Sugar Valley, Hebron, Union

Mills, Schultz and Willow Island. The only villages, outside of the county seat, were Hebron, Raven Rock, Jonestown and Schultz. Looking at the country from the summit of one of the hills it seemed almost like an unbroken forest, just here and there a little clearing being visible.

There were about forty-five dwellings located within the corporate limits of St. Marys, more than two-thirds of them sonth of George street. There were three hotels—the Cain House, the Exchange and the Commercial, but the last named was not in public use, the front section, facing Second street, being occupied by a private family, and the upper rooms on the George street side were tenanted by a few roomers or lodgers, who fitted the rooms with their own furniture, while the rear sitting room was used as the printing office of the Watchword.

The old Methodist Episcopal Church South was in too dilapidated a condition to be used for services, but the Methodist Protestant Church was open for the use of all Christian denominations. The Rev. J. L. Jackson of the Methodist Episcopal Church South and the Rev. F. M. Yates of the Methodist Protestant Church were the only resident ministers who were actively engaged in church work.

Creel was still the business street of the place. There were the stores of Silas Gallaher and George W. Riggs on the south side of the street, between the alley and the Cain House; A. Jackson Watson had a store on the corner of Creel and First street in the building first used by Logan Brothers; George Kelsall's store was on the northwest corner of Creel and Second street. It was originally a one-story structure, but he had added an upper story, which was used for a time as a lodge hall. Opposite to it on Creel street was the shoe shop of B. B. Timmons.

Second street abruptly ended at Creel, being blocked off by the residence of Mrs. Rachel Hall, mother of the late John S. Hall. To the east of the Hall home Parker J. Duff had a drugstore, and in the same neighborhood were two or three saloons, presumed at the time to be out of business, one called "The Indian Queen," exhibiting

Her Majesty painted on a large sign-board. The postoffice was on the east side of Second street on the lot adjoining that of the late Isaac Reynolds, whose house was used as the first court house; it was the building now owned by H. C. Williams. William Carroll, who formerly had a wood yard at Vaucluse, was postmaster, and kept a small general store. On the southwest corner of Second and Lafayette streets was a narrow one-story building occupied as a store by Joseph Hubbs. The Commercial Hotel mentioned above stood on the northwest corner, and directly opposite, in the house now owned by Charles F. Ingraham, a German had started a small bakery. On the other end of this square, the southeast corner of Second and George streets, Joseph Porter had a small general store, and there was a little shop of some sort just opposite where the postoffice is now.

John M. Strobel, an expert cabinet maker, had his shop on the northeast corner of Second and George streets, in which he also conducted an undertaking business, the second story being used as a lodge room by the Odd Fellows and other organizations. This building is yet in good condition. Up on Washington street, then considered far up town, Thomas Huntsman had opened a blacksmith shop; and at the west end of Washington, on the bank of the Thoroughfare, was an old steam grist mill, grinding only occasionally.

Not more than ten or twelve houses stood above Washington street, which then terminated at Third, or rather was continued as the Ellenboro Pike around the foot of the upper terrace and past the cemetery. Three houses were on the court house hill, and four on Gravel hill up to Middle Island creek. All of the upper bottom was then farm land.

Transportation was by boat, and that accounted for Creel street being the center of business, because of its terminal at the wharf. It will be recalled that mention has been made of the county road built about 1850, running down the river in front of the Cain House and through the Narrows. By 1877 this road had been entirely washed away, but there were still traces of it in the Narrows, and well up on the face of the bluff there, above the present railroad track, was the opening of a small coal mine. In the year the Watchword was established there was still quite a large, wide lawn on the river side of the Cain House, and the Thoroughfare at the lower end of the island was not much more than half its present width, the bank from the end of Creel street then sloping gently down to the river.

Between St. Marys and Marietta a small side-wheel steamboat, the Kittie Nye, made daily trips, leaving this port in the morning and returning in the evening. Dode Berry was the captain, Selby Berry the engineer, and Brady Morgan the clerk, all residing in St. Marys. It is a curious fact that very few steamboat men made their homes on the West Virginia side of the river, while Clarington, Sardis, New Matamoras and Newport apparently thronged with them.

The mails were carried by the Wheeling & Parkersburg Transportation Company, two large side-wheel boats, the Courier and the Express, being in the trade. For some reason the general favorite was the Courier, of which Mac Gamble was clerk. The passage between the terminals of this trade required a long day. The boat from Parkersburg usually arrived at St. Marys about ten in the morning and that from Wheeling about six or seven in the evening, so there were two mails every day except Sunday, when the boats laid up. When the steamers could not navigate the mails were brought by wagon or sled in the Winter and by skiff in the Summer.

It was not an uncommon experience for a steamboat to be compelled to tie up to the shore between ports, either by reason of ice or low water, making the trip to Wheeling last several days. But during the tie-up the passengers were taken care of comfortably at the expense of the transportation company, and the time was generally employed in festivities and amusements on board. There was always a piano in the ladies cabin, so there was singing and sometimes inventive geniuses devised vaudevilles and theatricals.

The landing of a steamboat generally drew the entire population to the wharf. On the larger boats liquors were sold, and to that fact was frequently attributed the remarkable haste made by some of the citizens in getting on board, even before the huge stage-plank had been firmly seated on the shore. At any rate the arrival of a boat was a cheerful break in the humdrum life of the village, especially when a drove of cattle was to be put on board. Sometimes the crew was compelled to go far up town to fetch the cattle, keeping the boat at the wharf for an hour or more. Or it might be that there was a consignment of new oil barrels to be shipped, and then the steamer would go up the Thoroughfare about to Lafayette street, where the barrels were stacked, and where wooden troughs or chutes extended down the bank. The barrels were sent sliding down these chutes to the steamer's decks with a great deal of hurrahing on the part of the deck-hands and still more shouting, mixed with profanity on the part of the mate when a barrel bounced out or the chute become clogged. All this was interesting alike to the travelers on the boat and to the inhabitants of the town, the one group having apparently no more active life than the other.

After the departure of the mail packet came the gathering at the postoffice. The sack was usually light, and often Postmaster Carroll himself carried it from the landing to the office, his curling, snow-white hair sweeping his shoulders, a perfect image of a Revolutionary patriot, heading a straggling procession of men, boys and girls.

There were no individual boxes in the postoffice. It was the custom of Mr. Carroll to carefully empty the pouch on the counter, sort out the letters, which he could easily hold in one hand, and then call out the name of the person to whom each was addressed. It seemed that most of them were for the firm of Jones & Haines. As a name was called the recipient, if present, would respond "Here!" as if answering a roll call, and the letter would be passed to him through the crowd. If there was no response, the letter was filed away in one of the boxes. It was all as interesting as the drawing at a lottery. Mr. Carroll had the humorous habit of withholding a letter addressed to William W. Hall, the prosecuting attorney, until the last, and then would call out, "W. W. Hall, and that's all!"

Should the boat be a little late in getting down from Wheeling, the accommodating postmaster nevertheless would open the sack and distribute the mail, even as late as nine o'clock. If the weather was warm, the notables of the town would wait outside of the postoffice for the mail to be brought up from the boat and arranged, sitting upon benches or storeboxes. In passing, it may be mentioned that on the edge of the sidewalk in front of every store in town was a long, heavy plank, usually set in between two locust trees, whereon the loiterers could lounge to their hearts' content. But the bench by the postoffice was the real town forum.

There would gather the lawyers—Colonel Robert Patterson, mighty of frame and so strong that it is reported that once he carried two barrels of flour from the steamboat landing up to the top of the bank, one resting on each hip, holding the chines with his extended hands; in Winter he wore the huge shawl which had been in the height of fashion in the sixties; Mayor James L. Richardson, a younger brother of the late General Richardson of Marietta; John B. Townsend, who had moved to St. Marys a few years before from the central part of the State, a quaint, quiet humorist, who, it was surprising to learn, had once been a sailor and had navigated the Gulf of Mexico, bringing back cargoes of mahogany and other fine woods; he affected a coat with a clerical cut, buttoned square up to the throat; William W. Hall, prosecuting attorney, a veteran of the Civil War who, with two of his brothers, had fought on the side of the Union while three other brothers were helping in the Confederacy; he clung to the fashion of a short cape in cool weather; R. A. Gallaher, an omniverous reader and afterwards for many years editor of the Oracle; Clinton C. Davis, one of the younger members of the bar, just emerged from teaching school, and with intensely intellectual features; John L. Knight, clerk of the circuit and county courts, always on hand, and always looking as if he had just donned a new suit of clothes.

There too would come Parker J. Duff, the wit of the town, who was ever ready with some quaint quip; John S. Hall, a younger brother of the prosecuting attorney, who had lost his sight while serving as teamster in the Union army, later distinguished as "the blind poet of Pleasants" and the first editor of the Oracle; W. G. H. Core, wearing his long black frock coat, an active busi ness man, who had served as a member of the State constitutional convention of 1872; Captain J. R. M. Agnew, an oldtime steamboat man who had retired from the river and opened a drug store in St. Marys; Dr. P. S. Braford, a native of Rockbridge county, Virginia, a man of great size and of very genial nature, a college graduate who still liked to wrestle occasionally with Virgil and other classics, and whose "Quo he" dialect was enjoyed by all; and Richard Towzey, in slippered feet, smilingly issuing his gentle philosophical satires.

It was a little world, but it was an epitome of the bigger world that lay around, containing all the elements which, when developed, make nations powerful and distinguished. And in all probability the actors governed themselves according to the size of the stage they trod. Life was not so strenuous then, and there was plenty of time for argument and personal anecdote.

There were no vendors of newspapers and magazines in the town, all periodicals coming through the postoffice, excepting those sold by the stewards or cabin boys of the passenger steamers. Godey's Ladies Book, Harper's Bazaar and T. S. Arthur's temperance monthly were the principal magazines, and were handed about from house to house until they fell to pieces. The only dailies received here were the Wheeling papers—the Register and the Intelligencer—just two or three copies of each. The favorite weekly was the Cincinnati Enquirer, with the Toledo Blade next in popularity. The New York Ledger, the New York Weekly and the Saturday Night were the famous papers for serial stories of the E. D. E. N. Southworth and Mary J. Holmes stripe, sentimental but far from being vicious; in truth, of a higher literary and moral value than most of those filling the magazines of today.

Joseph Hubbs, who had been a member of the First Wheeling Convention in 1861, was somewhat celebrated for the number of magazines and papers he subscribed for, among them being Harper's Magazine, which he had taken for many years. He was considered rather eccentric. Lying on his back on the counter, his head resting comfortably on a bolt of muslin, his legs crossed easily, and with a book or paper upright on his chest, he spent many a placid hour. It is said that if a customer asked for an article of the value of five cents, he would remark that it wasn't worth the trouble of getting up for it, and proceeded with his reading.

The thirst for newspapers gradually grew with the opportunity for obtaining them. Not many could afford to subscribe for dailies, and when the exchanges began coming in to the new local paper, that office became a popular resort for the men of the town.

In the way of clothes, every man suited his own taste. As noted above, shawls and capes were still worn by men in the Winter season. Ready-made clothes for men were known as "hand-me-downs," and were held in contempt. and if one had to wear them the creases were carefully pressed out before donning them. Men ordered their clothes from real tailors, measured and cut to taste, regardless of the alleged fashionable style, at a cost of twenty-five to thirty dollars. Most of the tailored suits were made by John Messerly of Clarington, who regularly traveled up and down the river taking orders, until he was succeeded by his son, Charles M. Messerly.

Store boots were sold, but most men preferred to have them also made to order, at a cost of nine or ten dollars. Men were then beginning to wear shoes, and could have them made. pegged, including squeaks, for four dollars, or sewed for eight dollars. One pair of shoes was usually considered enough for a year. In fact many fully grown men had the habit of still going barefoot through the Summer.

But in good truth the streets of St. Marys then favored the wearing of boots in Winter rather than shoes, for there were neither pavements nor crossings, and in wet weather the mud was ankle deep. Fortunately most of the fences were built of boards nailed lengthwise to the posts, and by wriggling one's feet along the bottom board while the hands gripped the top board it was possible to get about—a sort of reversal to the methods of our alleged remote ancestors. It may be imagined that shoe polish was not in great demand, most of the men greasing their boots with tallow to keep them soft and to prevent leaking, for rubbers were seldom seen. High topped boots continued to be worn by elderly gentlemen until in the nineties, one of the last to use them being Governor Arthur I. Boreman. who was judge of this circuit in 1894.

What is yet known as the Strobel building, a structure made of upright boards well battened, was erected by John M. Strobel and his son, Christian. The elder Strobel was a Bavarian and had learned the business of cabinet-making in all its finest details before coming to this country. Back in the fifties he had bought the cabinet shop of George Kelsall. He was also an undertaker, making the coffins himself, frequently toiling at the work all night long.

Another industry of the day which should not be overlooked was that of fishing in the Ohio river. This, of course, was indulged in by everybody as a pastime, but it was regularly carried on as a business by John and William Cooper. In the seventies no license was required and there was no restriction as to the manner of catching fish or as to the amount of the catch. All the creeks then abounded with fish, and the angler could always count on bringing home a large string of bass or wall-eyed pike. That was before fish were destroyed by the millions with salt water from the oil wells and with chemicals from the manufacturing plants about the headwaters.

Seining and fishing with trot lines were the usual methods of the Coopers, and it was most interesting to watch them making a haul with their long seines. One end was fastened securely to the shore, and as one rowed the skiff the other deftly let the seine into the water its full length. Then the boat was brought around near to the starting point and the net drawn in, usually heavy with a vast school of frightened, leaping fish. great catfish and spoonfish, sturgeon, silvery drums or white perch as they are called here, bass and herring, with occasional dogfish and other strange denizens of the waters. A favorite place to make a haul was in the little channel between Grape and Bat Islands, which went by the name of Wizard Bay because of the great quantities caught there. In one haul in the Winter of 1888 the Coopers caught 900 pounds of edible fish. The fishermen found a market either on the boats or at Wheeling.

The greatest product of the trot line was catfish, several channel cats weighing one hundred pounds and more having been caught in that manner. One of these we remember having seen borne on a pole thrust through its gills, resting on the shoulders of two men, its tail sweeping the walk.

The initial number of the Watchword was printed in the latter part of October, 1877, the work being done by a printer from Marietta. After getting out this first issue, he went down the river to spend Sunday at his home town and failed to return. Mr. Yates was not a printer, so he could do nothing himself. A week passed, and his few subscribers feared that the first number would be the last one. Then the editor went to New Martinsville and employed the writer of this book to print his paper.

The office nestled in the rear sitting room of the old Commercial Hotel, the door opening on Lafayette street. The plant consisted of a lightly built Day job press, large enough to print one page of a five-column paper. Elisha Baker, father-in-law of Mr. Yates, was the power that ran the press, turning it with one hand by means of a crank attached to the fly-wheel, while with the other hand he pulled the printed sheet off the press, the printer doing the feeding. It was a four-page paper, so it had to be run through the press four times; but as the circulation was only about two hundred the press-work was soon done. There were three cases of news type of the size called Long Primer, and four or five cases of job type. Even this primitive outfit caused considerable comment and questioning, for very few persons in the community had ever seen the interior of a printing office. Some came in, handled the type curiously, and asked the printer if he had moulded them as bullets were moulded.

It seemed an exceedingly barren field. Not a business firm in town was using its own printed stationery; the method of advertising by hand-bills or circulars was unknown, except when rewards were offered for the recovery of escaped criminals or estrayed cattle, and the legal advertising in this small county was negligible. The office had been established four months before the printer had a chance to try his hand on a job, and that was printing an envelope card for John Schauwecker, the tanner.

The Watchword was non-political; in truth, it had a strong tendency editorially towards theological disputation, although the local news columns were well maintained. It had a very slight advertising patronage, and the subscriptions were mostly paid with the products of the farm such as potatoes, apples and firewood. It struggled through the Winter, maintained mostly from the editor's salary as a minister and his receipts from bridegrooms; but in the following Spring the proprietor gave up all hope and taking in the late Rev. John J. Poynter as associate editor, the name Watchword was dropped and that of The West Virginia Methodist Protestant substituted in an attempt to make it a church paper. But in a few weeks that failed also, and the plant was sold to Minos P. Prettyman, who restored the local paper, giving it the name of Observer.

Mr. Prettyman had been a country school teacher, but had a fancy for typography, and came to town early Friday evenings and spent his week-ends in the office learning to set type and run the press, in both of which he soon became efficient. By wonderful assiduity and close management he succeeded in keeping the paper going for a year or two, and then sold out to John S. Hall, who had aided as a writer on the Observer.

Mr. Hall assumed charge in the fall of 1881, and in December of that year changed the name to Oracle, with M. P. Prettyman as publisher. This arrangement lasted a year, when Mr. Prettyman withdrew and the writer was again called to take charge of the paper, January 1, 1883. A complete file of the Oracle has been kept bound from December, 1881, to the present. John S. Hall was owner and editor of the paper until the latter part of February, 1885, when he sold the outfit to Robt. L. Pemberton and W. S. Gallaher. For about fifteen years R. A. Gallaher was editor. then for a year or two John L. Hissom was editor and manager, and from 1902 to the present it has been under the management of the writer, who has been sole owner since 1909. In 1883 M. P. Prettyman bought another small printing outfit and began the publication of a newspaper called the Observer, which managed to exist for a few years, but finally he moved it to New Martinsville, there calling it the New Era.

CHAPTER X

BUILDING THE RAILROAD

Convenience and rapidity of transportation has always had a great deal to do with the growth of communities. While no part of Pleasants county is at a great distance from the Ohio river, yet that stream was not always available, because of the poor roads and also because navigation was frequently suspended for weeks or even months by low water or ice. The carrying of live stock was very uncertain, so that as late as the eighties it was customary to drive cattle overland to Pittsburgh and Baltimore. Nevertheless there were many steamboats on the river and they seemed to thrive.

In the earlier part of the century the boats were given rather fanciful names, such as Lady Byron, Rambler, Mount Vernon, Magnolia, Lady Madison and Reaper. Sidewheel boats were most popular in the seventies, of this type were the Courier, Express, Diurnal and St. Lawrence, broad of beam and imposing with their high wheel houses, the interiors enameled and gilded, so that they indeed resembled floating palaces. There were also fine boats of the stern-wheel class, such as the Andes, one of the largest on the river, the Mallie Ragan and Carrie Brooks. All the tow boats of course were stern-wheelers.

The fare from St. Marys to Wheeling varied from two to three dollars, and this included berth and meals. If for any reason the boat was delayed the passengers were at no extra expense, and it has happened that they have enjoyed the hospitality of the steamboat company for a week without other charge than the regular fare.

Smaller steamboats linked together the small towns in

daily trips, and these could often ply when the larger boats were laid up. One of these was the stern-wheeler Welcome, a very swift boat, owned and operated by Captain Mike Davis, who resided here for a time. Another was the Scioto, owned by Captain Dillon, which made daylight trips between Marietta and Wheeling. It was a side-wheel boat with two decks, and considered the fastest boat on the river. Captain Dillon took great pride in maintaining his schedule of time, and when in a hurry would pay no attention to the frantic gesticulations of would-be passengers at small landings. On one occasion he made the run from Marietta to St. Marys in one hour and five minutes—a record which, we believe, has never been equalled.

In 1882 came the practical development of the plan of building a railroad from Wheeling down the river to Parkersburg, with the further intention of completing it to Cincinnati, whence its first name of the Wheeling, Parkersburg and Cincinnati railroad. It was to be a continuation of the Pittsburgh, Wheeling and Kentucky railroad, commonly called the Pewiky, designed as a part of the great Pennsylvania system, and linked with that corporation until it was absorbed by the Baltimore & Ohio Company.

St. Marys had improved but little in the last five years, yet it was apparent that Creel street was already beginning to be deserted as a business center, The firm of S. Gallaher & Son had moved up town to the northwest corner of George and Second streets, and had built the two-story business house now occupied by E. R. Smith. A millinery store had been established by Mrs. L. G. Brock on the lot now owned by Captain J. C. McLaughlin. The first brick sidewalk in town was built around the Gallaher store. The Cain House and several stores had erected street lights, consisting of oil lamps enclosed in square glass cases perched on top of tall posts.

A summary of the business men of the town was made by the Oracle, showing seven merchants, seven lawyers, three hotels, three physicians, two blacksmiths, two insurance agents, one milliner and one tanner. The cooper shops had entirely disappeared. In those days insurance agents tacked up little tin signs on the insured houses, stating the name of the company in which they were insured. There seems to have been a preponderance of lawyers, but it must be remembered that the cost of living was yet extremely low, there was plenty of hunting and fishing, with absolutely no limit to the bag, and almost every family had a garden and a cow, also a pig to be butchered about Thanksgiving Day. With two or three hundred a year in cash a family could get along very well.

The general cheapness of living may be judged by the cost of maintaining the county government, which was a little less than six thousand dollars a year. Out of this came the salaries of the officers, the keeping up of roads, the building of schools and the pay of the teachers, with but little help from the general school fund of the State. The county levy was 80 cents on the hundred dollars, the teachers fund levy in Washington district 26 cents and that of the building fund 16 cents; but the land valuation was exceedingly light—about one hundred dollars an acre for river bottom land and ten dollars for hill land.

Only a few farmers were in fairly well-to-do circumstances. Their average condition was that of actual indigence, many not being able to afford the slightest luxuries or even to buy school books for their children. There was no convenient market for their produce, so there was very little inducement for them to develop their farms. There was still a slight demand for rough staves, and they could still sell tanbark, but there was no real agriculture, except in a few instances. But they were to receive considerable financial help from the building of the railroad.

Parkersburg men were the chief promoters of the enterprise, under the lead of Colonel W. P. Thompson and Senator Johnson N. Camden. In Pleasants county Major Robert H. Browse took an active part, and was so interested that he traveled the entire distance between Wheeling and Parkersburg on foot, helping to secure the right of way and oversee the surveying.

Preliminary surveys were made in 1882. As in the case of building the Baltimore & Ohio railroad from Grafton to Parkersburg, some business men in Marietta viewed the proposed railroad with jealous eyes, and set on foot again an attempt to construct the railroad on the Ohio side of the river from Marietta to Bellaire. Bernard Rodick of Marietta came even into St. Marys in the Spring of 1882 and attempted to sell stock in the proposed Ohio road. In fact, emissaries on several occasions came to this side of the river and tried to discourage the building of the W. P. & C. road, spreading all sorts of reports, one argument being that the railroad would effectually check the growth of all the smaller towns through which it should pass, as the trains would rush through without stopping, so that people would move to the larger places where the trains would stop.

When the surveyors came to St. Marys the weighty question arose as to how the road should be taken through the town. Already Second street had developed into the main street; it was in a direct line with the survey, but a majority of the citizens objected to permitting its use by the company. The railroad officials professed a desire to comply with the desires of the people, and a sort of unofficial vote was taken, with the result that thirty-one declared in favor of First street, two favored Alley A, five voted for Second street and thirty for Third street.

Major McConnell, in charge of the survey, seemed to be vexed at the indecision of the people and threatened to run the survey at the foot of the hill back of the court house. It is now regretted that he was not permitted to carry out his threat. But at that time the idea was apparently absurd, and almost every citizen raised his voice against it. They did not want the railway station located out in the country. So the town council gave the right to lay a one-track road down the main street.

The residence of W. W. Hall stood on Creel street, exactly blocking the lower end of Second street. From the windows of this house was obtained a clear view of the entire length of the main thoroughfare, and from the porch could be seen all of Creel street. This property was sold to the railroad company, and in 1883 the house was moved to the west side of the track and converted into a temporary station. Active work on the road was begun in 1883, the firm of Garvey & O'Brien getting the contract for grading and construction from the town up to Bens Run, and Mr. Carey the part south as far as Bull Creek, while Halleck Brothers had the contract for building the bridge.

Employment was offered to any one who was able to handle a pick and shovel, and the opportunity was grasped by quite a number of the residents. At the same time, early in Spring, large gangs of Italians were brought in by the contractors and quartered in shanties along the right of way. These men were accustomed to the work, but the natives soon tired and threw up their jobs.

The incoming of the Italians was the first time many of our people had seen real foreigners, and they aroused considerable interest, especially at night, when the strangers gave themselves up to their chief recreations of singing and playing on accordions. And pay days were always exciting times. The offices of the contractors were on Creel street, and on those occasions that little street was filled with a highly excited and gesticulating mob.

Work progressed so rapidly that on November 27 the track was laid through the town, the inhabitants turning out en masse to witness the event. The bridge was not completed, but in a few days the rails were laid as far as the creek and work trains were running constantly to and from Parkersburg. When the river was closed with ice just before Christmas the Ohio River Railroad, as the road was then officially designated, helped the people out by running box cars to Parkersburg to bring up merchandise and mail.

Besides giving to the farmers and their sons an opportunity to earn money by working on the grading, the road offered an immediate and handy market for cross-ties, which were needed by thousands. Subcontractors were scouring the country, negotiating for their delivery along the right of way. Everywhere the hard pressed farmer was again at work felling trees, sawing and hewing them into ties ond hauling them to the river. Winter was spent in making them, and as soon as the roads became passable, which did not often happen then before the first of May, the work of teaming began. The entire county was busy with this new industry. It was a repetition of the former trade in barrel staves.

Getting out railroad ties was a man's job, but the reward was puerile; at least it would so be considered now. Practically the best timber trees on the farm were sacrificed. The demand was for white oak, burr oak, chestnut oak, or any sort of hard wood, sound and solid, for the ties must have at least eight inches face, from sap to sap, be seven feet long and free of all defects. The farmer took this good timber from his land, peeled off the bark, sawed it into proper length, hewed it to get the proper facing, and then hauled it from five to ten miles to some point on the railroad right of way, and for all this he was paid the munificent sum of thirty cents a tie. From eight to ten ties were hauled at a load, and at the best two trips made a good long day's work with a team. And even then most of the farmer's work was liable to be lost through the system of culling. The inspector might discover defects strange to the eyes of the farmer. In such a case, should the latter reload them upon his wagon and have his weary team haul them back for firewood, or should he leave them at the yard? Often he left them, and perhaps those discarded ties for which he had received nothing, would be used in railroad sidings as "seconds," the subcontractor getting paid for them.

So the railroad helped the farmer to ready cash, and it served the citizens of the town a good turn in rainy weather by affording them a fairly good passage from one end of the town to the other. It was not uncommon to see at one time scores of men and women walking in the center of Second street.

The bridge over Middle Island Creek was completed by the first of December, and tracklaying went on rapidly up the river. Then the work was delayed considerably by a heavy fall of snow, followed by rain, and exceedingly cold weather in the first week of January, when the temperature went down to twelve below zero. Then began the great snow which resulted in the flood of 1884. On January 11 snow in the open fields about town was measured and found to be 32 inches deep. There were slight thaws, during which the snow settled down, so that it is impossible to state the amount that had fallen up to the time of the general thaw and drizzling rain that set in about the first of February. Some estimated it at about four feet. From the Oracle of February 15 we take the following account:

The Alleghany ice passed this place on Sunday night, the 3rd instant. The river fell about four feet on Monday. Tuesday it began rising rapidly again, and by Wednesday evening it was quite evident that those living on Creel street would have to vacate their homes. On Wednesday morning news came that the water at Pittsburg was thirty feet and rising twelve inches an hour. The unusual snowfall, which was still in the mountains, the mild temperature and the continued rains indicated a flood of unusual magnitude. On Thursday morning at six o'clock the water was crossing Creel street at Kelsall's corner and was still rising at the rate of four inches per hour, and rain was falling.

The high water mark of 1860 had been reached and there was no sign of abatement. Steadily the backwater crawled up Main street and at 11 o'clock a skiff landed at Riggs' corner, an event which had not occurred since 1852. This was the northwest corner of Second and Lafayette streets at the Commercial Hotel.

Still the same report, four inches an hour. By evening every street and alley was under water, and skiffs, johnboats and every available craft that would float were plying to and fro, moving persons and property to places of safety. All the inhabitants of one-story buildings left their houses, and those in two-story buildings moved to the upper floors. Scarcely any one believed that the flood of 1832 would be surpassed, and many refused to leave their residences until the water was actually on the floor with no abatement in the rise. All night of Thursday was spent in anxious wakefulness. Scarcely an eye was closed, for who could sleep when danger threatened both life and property?

All night long anxious men paddled over the streets and alleys, while their still more anxious families watched from the upper windows. "Four inches an hour!" became monotonous. At midnight the cry became "Three inches an hour!" This, too, in time became monotonous. The water advanced as steadily as before, though not so rapidly, and it was not until six o'clock on Friday evening, February 9. that it was pronounced at a stand. Daylight Saturday morning revealed the fact that a fall of six inches had been made. As the people stood gazing on the receding waters, contemplating the ruin and desolation wrought in their homes, the excitement which for a day or two kept them up gave way to feelings of dismay.

According to old marks the water was three feet and three inches higher than in 1832 at Parkersburg. The former flood was before the existence of St. Marys so no actual comparison could be made here, and in 1884 there were no Government low water marks here. The only guide was the mark set by Halleck Brothers when making the foundation for the railroad bridge in 1883, and the measurement made from that showed the height of the flood here to have been 53 feet two inches, which is probably about correct, as the height at Parkersburg is given at 52.9. Since then Government experts have set a low water mark which is said to be nearly three feet above actual low water.

There was only one spot of ground that was not covered by water, that on which the Episcopal church stands. The water did not quite reach the floors of three buildings—the old M. E. South church, a little dwelling on the opposite side of the street, and a small dwelling on Washington street. The few homes then on the upper terrace were hospitably thrown open to the people, and eighteen families took refuge in the court house. A large gang of Italian laborers took possession of a house belonging to Samuel Barkwill, which stood at the foot of St. Marys hill. He had promised the use of it to some citizens who had been driven out by high water, and when he heard that the foreigners were occupying it, arming himself with a stout stick, he went alone through the night and drove them out.

Several houses on Third street were lifted from their foundations, but not a building was carried off from the town. As in all cases of this kind, the direct losses could not be estimated exactly. The greatest damage to any citizen was that of John Schauwecker, owner of the tannery, who put his loss at about $1,500. The merchants were damaged from $100 to $500.

Saturday and Sunday were devoted to scrubbing and cleaning. Fortunately the weather was mild, so there was no great suffering. As soon as the waters had subsided a little, the Government sent supplies, and, as usual, a large part went to people who had only seen the water from a safe distance. News of the supply steamer was sent out, and people came from far in the interior to get the free flour, coffee, sugar and bacon.

The Ohio River Railroad Construction Company endured the greatest loss, the road-bed being washed away in many places. The large fill in the lower end of town dissolved like brown sugar as the water rose, and the ties hung suspended to the rails. However, it was said that the thorough soaking would make the road settle to a better foundation, and that was probably true, for in very few places has the company been obliged to make new fills since that flood.

The railroad was completed in June, 1884, and after the syndicate had made a trial trip, it was formally turned over to the Ohio River Railroad Company by the construction company. On June 16 regular passenger service was commenced, before the completion of the telegraph system. Three passenger trains were run daily each way, the time from Parkersburg to Wheeling being four and one-half hours. And from that date our people began more largely to explore the outside world.

The former parlor of the old Hall home was used as a waiting room and one of the small bedrooms was fitted up for a ticket office. William E. Hoyt was the agent, and also served as telegraph operator, freight master and general roustabout. When comment was made upon the multiplicity of his duties, he laughingly said that he had gained some experience on a narrow gauge railroad in Ohio, of which he had been general manager, ticket agent, telegrapher, freight handler and at times conductor or engineer. The express business was then distinct, and was handled by M. P. Prettyman, agent of the Adams Express Company. After a few years Mr. Hoyt was transferred to Ravenswood, and later to Walkersville on the Coal & Coke railroad in Lewis county.

CHAPTER XI

STRIVING FOR IMPROVEMENT

Contrary to the dismal predictions of the gentlemen from Ohio who had favored building a railroad from Marietta to Bellaire, and had discountenanced the Ohio River Railroad, St. Marys was not injured by the operation of the latter road, but was rather benefitted by it. No immediate and hurried boom was perceived, but the town and entire county felt the good effects of a rapid and sure means of transportation. It was possible to go as far as Wheeling, transact business, and return home within one day, a trip that had hitherto been difficult to accomplish under forty-eight hours. And the reliability and frequency of the mail service aroused the merchants to greater possibilities, while daily newspapers from the large cities began to supplant the weekly papers.

The younger men were the first to realize the town must grow, and among them was John W. Porter, who went into what was then far up town, away up on the west side of Second street, just below Clay, and erected a store building which he stocked with all kinds of general merchandise. There were people who thought the young merchant had become mentally unbalanced.

But the new spirit of progress had already shown itself in other guise. Some time previously the county commissioners had found it necessary to have the court house repaired, and they had employed C. S. Despard of

Parkersburg to do the work. He found that in order to collect what was due him he had to bring suit, and in the course of that suit it was brought out that the commissioners had come then to the conclusion that the old building was entirely inadequate, and that it would be more advisable to erect a new structure than to repair the old one. They planned to abandon the old site on the brow of the hill and to build a new court house down in the business section of the town, where it would be most accessible. The proposal seems to have met with general approval, but the plan was abandoned when it was learned that such an action would mean an abandonment of the square on which the building stood, and that the land would revert to the heirs or assigns of the donor, Alexander H. Creel. Mr. Despard obtained a judgment against the county for the work he had done.

Although the court house was only thirty years old, even then it had an appearance of great antiquity. While apparently substantial, it had been built cheaply and compactly, without much regard to architectural display and with still less regard to the interior conveniences. The offices of the clerks, on either side of the entrance hall, were so small that not more than two persons could work comfortably at the books. Immediately above them were two other offices, one intended for the sheriff and the other for the prosecuting attorney, but for many years neither was occupied. The stairs leading to these upper rooms were steep as ladders. The greater part of the upper story was divided into two large apartments, one for the grand jury and the other for petit juries.

The court room was on the second floor, back of the clerks offices, with which it had no immediate connection. On either side of the entrance were two tiers of hard wooden benches for the spectators; in front of them was a railing, then more benches, tables and chairs, and the judge's bench, the trial juries sitting to the left of the judge and the grand jurors having chairs on the right.

On the ground floor lived the jailor and his family, and there also were the cells of the jail, happily very seldom used in the earlier history of the county. At that period it was no uncommon thing for the young people to arrange for a party at the jail, meaning that part occupied by the jailor's family.

Though on a most commanding site, the court house was so isolated by the difficulty of getting to it that only those who had urgent business would take the trouble of going there. The sheriff and prosecuting attorney had their offices in the business part of town, leaving the clerk and the jailor the only occupants of the building. Then and for many years afterward there was only one incumbent of the two clerkships, elected and serving as clerk of the county and circuit courts.

The old lane that had been provided, in laying off the town lots of the city, for an approach to the court house, had become neglected, and ran so far out of a direct course that no one deemed it worth repairing. The only direct approach was that of George street, up a steep bluff that was washed by rains into deep gullies. Yet the court house then was the only public building in which entertainments could be given, and was used perforce by the few traveling shows that happened along. It was impossible to get an audience up that hill in a rain.

When home talent decided to exhibit its genius, and in those days that frequently happened, all the material, including the stage and its setting, had to be literally carried up the hill on the shoulders of the young men who were members of the troupe. Furniture, carpets, planks, organs and all the accessories were taken up in that manner, but the extra exertion seemed to add to the enjoyment.

The old building of the Methodist Episcopal Church South was then in a ruinous condition, and the Presbyterians were talking of buying it. Members of the Methodist Episcopal Church were also talking of erecting a place of worship, and Rev. George C. Wilding came here to see what could be done. In the following year, 1885. the Rev. L. D. King was pastor of that denomination here, and through his activities, aided by Mr. Wilding, in May the society bought a lot from Silas Gallaher on Washington street, and contracted with Anderson & Hubbard of Sardis to build a church. The work was completed during the summer, and was dedicated September 18 by Rev. I. C. Pershing of Pittsburgh. The wooden building was 28x50 feet, and cost $1500.

In 1884 the only church in use was that of the Methodist protestants, and it was generously thrown open to all Protestant denominations. In that year the Rev. Joseph Dunn became pastor of it, and at the same time opened a dental office in the Kelsall building, he being the first resident dentist in the county. A trifle uncouth in his manner, with an unfailing geniality, Mr. Dunn was a minister of great energy. One of his first cares was to organize a "mite society," the first society of church women in the community. He had the reputation of being a very successful revivalist, and in January, 1885, carried through what was probably the greatest revival the county had witnessed. The meetings were held in the Methodist Protestant church, and he was assisted by the Rev. Simpson of the South Church, the Rev. King of the Methodist Episcopal Church and the Rev. Spence of the United Brethren Church of Parkersburg. It is recorded that there were 107 conversions, and Mr. Dunn's church gained 80 accessions.

The old custom of the sexes sitting in opposite sides of the church was still observed, the men, as they entered, turning to the pews on the left, while the women turned to the right; but at this time the younger attendants at worship began making breaches in the observance.

Some of our farmers had awakened to the fact that our hills are well adapted to the raising of sheep and cattle, and experiments were made in both lines. Oliver Gorrell, who owned a large tract of land in Union district, took the lead in growing wool, while Edmund Holdren of Grape Island was among the first to introduce a special breed of cattle, stocking his farm with a herd of p lled black Galloways. These were purely individual efforts, for there was no farmers' organization, although occasional meetings of farmers were held and a "Grange" had been instituted, with a store at Union Mills, of which Rev. John R. Shingleton was manager.

But in that year many farmers had other visions of securing rapid wealth. Somebody declared that silver ore of considerable value had been discovered on Bond's

Creek, that assays had been made and that it would yield richly. Nobody seemed to have any authoritative statement, but the story spread and gained credence, so that in a short time the whole county was in a state of great excitement. Farmers searched the beds of creeks, clambered up stony gullies and pried into the crevices of cliffs. Iron pyrites and shining scales of mica led many to believe that the precious metal existed in great quantities on their lands, and they loaded their pockets with specimens to show to the wise men in the town. However, as weeks went by without a "strike," the excitement gradually subsided, and in the course of time the actual worthlessness of the bits of glistening stone became apparent to all.

The age of modern miracles was in its infancy. The old joke about sending paper messages over the telegraph wires still passed current. It was declared that telephones would be established in the large cities, and some enthusiasts went so far as to prophesy that they would some day be in general use, even in the rural districts. A few persons who had traveled had seen the phonograph and had paid ten cents to hear the marvel. Others proudly boasted of having seen electric lights, and it was reported that scientists were working on an electric lamp which could be carried in the pocket.

Some of our citizens were ready and anxious to utilize these inventions. In the Spring of 1885 a serious attempt was made to establish telephonic communication in the county. A few lines had already been constructed in Wood and Washington counties, and those who had tried them were convinced of their practicability. It was proposed to run a line from St. Marys to Raven Rock, stringing the wires temporarily on the railroad telegraph poles. Each subscriber was to pay an annual charge of five dollars, and messages in town were to be delivered at a charge of five cents. It was objected that the rates were too high and that some people would monopolize the wires, so the proposition failed. However, R. H. Browse put up a line between his residence at Spring Run and the home of his sister, Mrs. Edmund Holdren, on the old Browse place, a distance of one mile. This is believed to be the first telephone line erected within Pleasants county.

Teachers institute was held late in the summer. The instructor for that year, 1884, was C. T. Price. The manner of conducting a session then was radically different from the mode of today. The office of instructor was more like that of the moderator of an assembly; while occasionally he lectured, most of the discussions were carried on by the teachers, and the interest aroused in the sessions may be judged by the fact that a resolution carried to hold night sessions in order to have more thorough discussions. Institute attendance was compulsory, but no compensation was granted for attending.

This was a great political year, and memorable here because for the first time the Republicans of the county held a nominating convention. It was called to order in the court house September 6 by A. W. Gorrell, once a superintendent of schools for the county, and Thomas C. Davis of Wasp was named as chairman, with Dudley Smith as secretary. The attendance was small and mostly made up of Republicans from Lafayette and Union districts. It was regarded by many as an unwise experiment in a county which was so strongly Democratic, and argued that it would cause the party lines to be drawn so tight that hereafter no Republican could hope to get elected to any office. The prediction seemed to be verified on October 14, when the State and county elections were held, for the Democrats swept the county by majorities ranging from 49 to 387. The Rev. John J. Poynter was elected to the House of Delegates; Daniel W. Reynolds, sheriff; August M. Campbell, prosecuting attorney; John L. Knight, clerk of county and circuit courts; William Kester, county commissioner; William E. Hammett, assessor, and R. Alexander Gallaher, surveyor.

When in November the returns showed that Grover Cleveland had been elected President, the enthusiasm of the Democrats here was unbounded. A congratulatory meeting was held in the court house, speeches were made and there was much shouting. A big noise was demanded, and S. Kinnard undertook to supply the absence of a cannon by making a bomb. Around a quantity of gunpowder he wrapped a lot of coarse twine, very tightly, making a large ball, from which a fuse protruded. He placed the bomb on the brow of the court house hill, lit the fuse and all hastened to a safe distance. The fuse sputtered; there was a slight hiss, a small cloud of smoke, but no explosion. It was a great disappointment.

Kinnard was one of the curiosities of the time. He was a stroller, dropping into St. Marys at odd times, no one knowing whence he came or whither he went. He was a ventriloquist and an elocutionist, and somehow managed to live from the proceeds of entertainments given at the low charge of fifteen cents. On his few handbills he styled himself "Eskenarde, Facial Artist and Funny Fellow." He was a type of the many strollers of that day who went over the country playing banjos and selling magic recipes, glue, or medicinal concoctions.

During the summer the report of Superintendent E. T. Fleming showed 2,206 children of school age in the county, but the average daily attendance was only 925. The average annual cost was $9.45 per pupil. While Grant district boasted of a school term of six months, in St. Marys and all the rest of the county the term was only four months, and the monthly wage paid to teachers ranged from $20 to $35.

The total cost of conducting the business of the county, including salaries of officers, the poor and road funds, was $17,500, and the financial statement of St. Marys showed that the town government cost only $513.

The total valuation of personal property in the county as given by the assessor was $411,362, and he reported 1,233 white and four colored voters.

William W. Hall, who had served fourteen consecutive years as prosecuting attorney, died September 28, aged 43 years. His death creating a vacancy in the office. Robert Patterson was appointed to finish the unexpired term.

At the January term of the county court, 1885, an order was passed consolidating the magisterial districts, merging Lafayette into Union, McKim into Washington and Jefferson into Grant. This was for the purpose of giving the three back districts the benefit of the railroad tax. The proposition was strongly opposed by residents of the river districts, and when the attention of the commissioners was called to the fact that a proper notice had not been published according to law, the matter was dropped.

Barney Olmstead was a blacksmith, distinguished with a reputation for tempering steel, so that his handicraft was highly esteemed. Axes, hatchets, knives and mattocks made by him were preferred to those sold in the stores, and his brand, "B. O." may be seen on tools still used in this vicinity. He contracted with Aaron R. Doutt to make 1500 mattocks in exchange for a house in the town. Mr. Doutt took the mattocks down the Mississippi where he was well known, and sold them to planters.

Mr. Doutt was a striking contrast to the other residents of the town, with whom, however, he associated freely and enjoyably. His ancestry was of the Pennsylvania Dutch stock, and his peculiar mannerisms interested his neighbors. Because of lameness he carried a stout cane. He dealt largely in tanbark, and made frequent trips by boat to New Orleans.

In February began the second and greatest oil development in the county, but for several years its progress was very slow. It started in the drilling of a well on the Cochran farm near Cow Creek, by John Custer, which filled up with two hundred feet of oil before it was shot, and began pumping twelve barrels a day.

News of this strike reaching the outside world, a few large operators became interested, among them Colonel J. M. Guffey of Pittsburgh, whose agents quietly entered the field. The services of W. E. Hoyt, local station agent, were secured. Mr. Hoyt was a gentleman of uncommon business versatility, with keen perception. He employed James L. Richardson, a lawyer, to get leases on whatever land was available. In the course of the summer many thousands of acres were taken under lease and recorded in a book of printed forms furnished to the county clerk by Guffey & Company. In the following winter H. S. White of Belton came in the interest of the same company and stated that two or three test wells would be drilled to ascertain whether the oil belt of Washington and Bradford, Pennsylvania. extended into Pleasants county. These wells were to be drilled to the "third sand," at a depth of about 2700 feet, at the estimated cost of $10,000 for each well. There seems to be no record of this company drilling such a well, and gradually the Guffey leases were either abandoned or disposed of to other companies.

In the meantime, encouraged by the success of Custer's well on the Cochran farm, Brown & Company of New York drilled in a well on McElroy Run back of Eureka, on the Giles Hammett farm, which came to be known as the "Burnt Well," heretofore mentioned. At a depth of 1100 feet a copious quantity of oil was found, filling the hole to a depth of 100 feet. This was on April 27, 1886. A few days later the well was shot, and for a time it flowed at the rate of forty barrels a day. Unfortunately the rig caught fire, the cable was burned and the heavy tools fell into the hole, where they remained about a year. But this demonstrated the fact that there was plenty of oil from Cow Creek to Eureka, at least.

Up to 1885 Pleasants county had gotten along without an infirmary or poor farm. The care of the poor had been given to overseers, one being appointed for each magisterial district. It was his duty to see that the poor were supplied with needful food and clothing and that they received proper medical attention. It may be imagined that this was a very haphazard way of doing, and often wrought injustice to both paupers and taxpayers.

In the case of able-bodied paupers, it was customary to hire them out to the most responsible bidders; that is to say, they would be bound to some citizen for their board and keep in return for what little work they would be able to do. If they were children of school age it was required that they must be sent to school. In honest and capable families the best of treatment would be accorded, and it sometimes happened that the child grew up as a member of the family, in which it was practically adopted; but occasionally there were instances of ill-treatment, and reports of these condemned the entire system.

Throughout the South this "letting out" of children had always been the custom, but it formed the subject of much bitter comment in the North, where many people were only too anxious to find fault with anything south of the Mason & Dixon line. Yet it was practically the same plan that is in use today in all orphan asylums of the country, in which every effort is made to find comfortable homes for the little ones. Sensational writers for the northern press described the custom as selling the children from an auction block, much in the manner as slaves were formerly sold.

For a long time the county commissioners had under consideration the project of a county infirmary or poor farm, and finally they bought the farm of Colonel Robert T. Parker, below French creek, extending from the river up on the hill, and established the Parker home as an infirmary. Soon after that a few houses were erected in the neighborhood above the infirmary, and the hamlet was called Parkerville, becoming a way station of the Ohio River Railroad. In 1885 its growth was aided by the construction of a government dam in the river, extending from the shore just below the mouth of French creek to the head of Second Brother or Broadhead Island, a work that gave employment to quite a number of laborers.

The dam was very strongly constructed, composed of huge blocks of stone laid between large timbers, the object being to compel a greater flow of water to the west side of the island, scouring out and deepening the steamboat channel. One effect of this has been related in the first chapter, as causing so much silt to be deposited in the still water below the dam that First Brother Island is no longer an island in ordinary stages of the river, the old channel being now part of a corn field.

Another undertaking of the county commissioners at that time met with popular approval, and that was the construction of an approach to the court house. E. B. Park, who had moved to St. Marys the preceding year, was employed to build a wooden stairway up the hill at the east end of George street, making it much easier to reach the court house. This stairway remained until 1924, when the hill was graded to make a driveway to the new court house.

Early in 1885 the St. Marys Silver Cornet Band was organized with Dr. F. V. Cox as instructor. This was the successor of the old brass band, which had managed to produce harmonious sounds from a number of rather battered and bruised instruments which R. H. Browse had purchased some years before for a band at Raven Rock. The new organization, under their efficient teacher and with handsome silver instruments, did a great deal in developing the talent and skill which have made the cornetists of St. Marys famous throughout this section.

John Suck, who had operated a sawmill for several years on Middle Island creek at Delong, purchased the lot on which the Episcopal Church now stands, at the foot of Washington street, which was the site of the first flour mill built in the town. There he set up a sawmill with a planing machine, and also equipped it with a lathe for turning out brackets for telegraph insulators. He operated the mill until April of the following year when it was destroyed by fire, and Mr. Suck removed to Ravenswood.

The absorbing topic of the year, however, was the litigation begun by the heirs of Latimer Bailey concerning the timber which they alleged had been taken from a large tract of land belonging to them in Union District. W. N. Walton, a lawyer of New York, came here as the agent of the heirs, and after investigations extending over a period of several months brought suit against a number of persons. Three of the prosecutions were successful, and the Bailey heirs were awarded damages to the amount of about two thousand dollars.

Walton came here prejudiced against the "hill people," and that feeling increased during his stay. Although he came and went freely, traversing the hills almost daily, he expressed himself as constantly in dread of violence from "the rude and semi-civilized people," as he termed them. He seemed to have some ulterior motives apart from the prosecution of the timber suits. One project was the establishment of a weekly or monthly magazine in which he attempted to enlist the services of the writer, promising his own personal influence with the Lorillards and other wealthy manufacturers to secure sufficient advertising to make the publication successful. From St. Marys he went to Parkersburg, where, without investing a cent, he managed to get credit to lease and equip a large hotel, furnishing it in lavish style, employing expensive aides and serving luxurious meals. He contrived to keep this up for several weeks before the crash came.

In this year came James A. Daugherty from Woodsfield, Ohio, and set up the first jeweler's shop in the town. The business was small, but apparently sufficient to maintain him, for he remained here several years.

School officers were elected in May. E. T. Fleming was a candidate to succeed himself as county superintendent, and O. J. Terry and A. W. Gorrell also entered the race, the latter being elected. In August a special election was held in Washington district by which the school term was increased from four to five months. Conrad A. Sipe of the Fairmont Normal School was instructor at the teachers' institute held here in August.

The ninth annual tournament was held at Bull creek in October. These interesting affairs were managed by Captain C. P. Ross, who came to this county from the Shenandoah valley, where the sport was very popular. The lists were on the level stretch of land east of the railroad on the north bank of the creek, the running course being parallel with the stream and shaded by a grove of large trees.

The knights, bedecked with brilliant silk sashes, their hats adorned with nodding plumes, rode their gaily caparisoned steeds at a rapid pace down the course, along which were a number of posts, from which small rings were suspended. He who succeeled, in a certain number of trials, in carrying off the greatest number of these rings on the point of his lance was declared the victor, and it was his glorious privilege to name the lady who should be styled "Queen of Love and Beauty." Those who most nearly approached him in skill were entitled to select the Maids of Honor.

On this occasion the contesting knights were Ben Sarber, Knight of Rose Hill; C. S. Reed, the Unknown Knight; Burr Sarber, Knight of Glendale; Harry Dornan. Knight of the Ohio Valley; F. Sheets, Knight of St. Elmo; R. Rolston, Knight of River Hill; Robert J. Patterson, Knight of St. Marys; Bert Johnson, Knight of the Red Cross; R. Corbitt, Knight of the Glades; E. Lloyd, Knight of Belmont; Ed Wherry, Knight of Pleasant Grove, and H. MacTaggart, Knight of High Point.

The large crowd, gathered from both sides of the river between Parkersburg and Sistersville, surged against the restraining ropes in their eagerness to note the skill of each knight, commenting volubly and loudly upon the actions of each. Witnessing the scene and the interest of the spectators, the imagination very easily carried one back to the pages of Ivanhoe.

The Knight of Rose Hill vanquished all opponents, and had the pleasure of crowning Miss Mary A. Janes as Queen. The four Maids of Honor were chosen, and as the ladies sat on an elevated tier of seats, with the knights facing them, an eloquent address was delivered by L. N. Tavenner of Parkersburg, replete with the language of old-time chivalry. The evening was closed with a reception by the ladies and knights at the Rose Hill Sanitarium, followed with a dinner and ball, in which chosen guests participated.

In the fall of this year a second attempt was made to establish a paper for the Methodist Protestant Conference of West Virginia, with the Rev. John J. Poynter as manager and editor. The work was done in the Oracle office, but after a career of a few months the effort failed.

In October Will A. Strickler of Ellenboro organized a lodge of the Independent Order of Good Templars here. This order had been quite strong throughout the State at the close of the Civil War, and at this time was experiencing a revival. The lodge flourished here for several years, and undoubtedly was a great help in building up a strong temperance sentiment.

Robert S. Taggart of Tyler county was the principal of the town school in the winter of 1885-6, receiving a salary of forty dollars a month. He inaugurated a movement to prohibit boys from loitering in stores of evenings. The usual hour of closing the stores then was about nine o'clock, but frequently they would be kept open much later, especially if an animated discussion was in progress. All the stores kept general merchandise, embracing hardware, dry goods, shoes, clothing, stationery and groceries; and in addition it may be said that in the evenings and on stormy days they were the forums in which matters of all kinds were discussed by the men of the town, seated on chairs and boxes around the comforing burnside stove. In a way these resorts were alluring and informative, but unfortunately there were frequent lapses into rough language and discreditable tales. and it was to keep the boys from becoming contaminated with these that Mr. Taggart secured the agreement of the merchants to exclude boys from these evening sessions.

In the spring of 1886 J. B. Kigans, who had been managing the Valley House, generally known as the Commercial Hotel, sold it to Thomas W. McClellan, a farmer of McKim creek near Hebron. The new proprietor was a former resident of St. Marys and had for a time served as secretary for the board of education of Washington district. The Exchange Hotel on Creel street was then owned by James M. Wells and A. Furbee, both of Tyler county, Mr. Wells being the manager.

On the 12th of May occurred a great rain anl electrical storm, especially violent on French creek. The water at the forks of the creek rose rapidly to the height of twenty-five feet; several houses were flooded and farms were damaged by the washing away of the soil.

The practicability of the telephone had been demonstrated, and a company was formed at Newport to run a line across the river to St. Marys, but the effort failed. By that time the principle features of the telephone were generally understood, and several kinds of instruments had been put on the market, some of exceedingly simple construction. The Taylor Automatic was the kind in use here; it was shaped like a disk, about eight inches in diameter, with no tube over the exposed diaphragm. By this time several private lines had been strung, mostly through the activities of W. E. Hoyt.

Another invention of the day, then in its infancy, was the typewriter. Very few practical machines were then made, and they were so costly that only large business houses or government departments could afford them. However, as in the case of the telephone, several crude machines were highly advertised at a very moderate price, and one of these was bought by John L. Knight for use in the clerk's office. It consisted of a dial on which rubber letters of the alphabet were placed. By rotating the dial so as to bring the letter wanted immediately over the sheet of paper, and then pressing down, an imprint of the character was made. It was far less speedy than penmanship, and the only virtue it had was that of putting the message into Roman characters with a reasonable degree of alignment.

Not until 1892 was the first practical writing machine brought into the county. That was a "Crandall Visible," and was used for several years by the writer, then a cimmissioner in chancery, in the preparation of legal documents. It was a machine of the "type-wheel" style, and is still in existence.

In the summer a planing mill was built on Spring Run by R. H. Browse and A. S. Vance.

In August the annual conference of the Methodist Protestant Church was held here, largely due to the efforts of Rev. J. J. Poynter. It was the largest gathering of the clergy that had been held in the county. Rev. J. L. Sims was appointed to the charge of St. Marys.

During the summer a mail route was established between St. Marys and Ellenboro, the first carrier being John Watson, father of Dr. Joseph B. Watson, and for many years a constable of Washington district. The mail was carried only once a week, on Saturdays, the carrier leaving St. Marys in the morning and returning in the evening. At the same time three postoffices were established along the route—Gibson, Maxwell and Finch.

Getting out railroad ties still furnished occupation for many farmers, hundreds of thousands being brought in, so that for several months the shipments averaged ten carloads a day. Many were hauled in, but still more were floated down the creek.

Elijah Steele, aged 90 years, died March 1 on Sheets' Run in the upper end of Union district. In his will he bequeathed one thousand dollars for the use of the schools of that district, but the bequest was annulled on the grounds of indefiniteness.

The opening of the Methodist Episcopal Sunday School had cut down the attendance of the Methodist Protestant school, and in 1887 a still further reduction was threatened by the prospect of the Methodist Episcopal South society starting a school of their own. Their building was partially repaired, due to the inspiring zeal of Rev. E. L. Fitch, a young man of remarkable oratorical ability. Concerning his profuse use of descriptive words it was said of him that adjectives rolled out of his mouth as the waters fall over the precipice of Niagara, in a seemingly endless flow. In Autumn he was transferred to Wetzel county, and his work here was taken up by Rev. Elias Kendall.

Pastors of other denominations here at the time were Rev. Miles, Methodist Episcopal, residing at Sistersville; Rev. H. P. F. King, Methodist Protestant, and Rev John F. Wood, a missionary of the Protestant Episcopal Church, who traveled along the Ohio river.

P. L. Taggart of Tyler county had purchased the Valley Hotel from T. W. McClellan. and his son-in-law, J. M. Wells, gave up the Exchange Hotel to become manager of the Wells House, as the hotel was now named. The new management advertised "Splendid fishing, boating and bathing in the world-famed Ohio river, all within two minutes' walk of the hotel. Also magnificent mountain scenery. The great oil and gas wells of Pleasants county are situated within half an hour's drive of the hotel."

This reference to the oil and gas wells carries us back to the middle of January, when William Johnson, drilling for oil on the Green Ruttencutter farm just east of Parkerville struck a large flow of natural gas. The roar of the escaping gas was distinctly heard at St. Marys and the reflection of its light plainly made the streets brighter at night, even at the distance of three miles and with a high hill between. We have not heard that any measurement of the quantity or pressure of the gas was made. It caused great excitement, and crowds from St. Marys, Marietta and Parkersburg went to see the wonder.

Mr. Johnson tried to induce the business men of the town to take up a proposition to pipe the gas to this place, but met with no success. The cities of Parkersburg and Marietta became interested and sent delegations to investigate, with a view of utilizing it, and there was a considerable correspondence with eastern capitalists, but satisfactory terms could not be made.

The Cochran No. 3 came in a ten barrel well, and the tools were gotten out of the Burnt Well on the Hammett, which was then drilled deeper and flowed at the rate of

100 barrels a day. Still the tot l production of the Eureka field was light, being estimated at only 130 barrels daily.

In August a well was drilled on the E. N. Cooke farm on French creek, but proved dry. It reached a depth of 1600 feet, and the log showed that at 265 feet a nine-foot vein of coal was penetrated, and a six-foot vein at 500 feet.

ROBERT HENRY BROWSE

However, the drilling of oil and gas wells in the upper part of Grant district gave Parkerville quite a boom. Early in May Robert H. Browse became interested in the place and bought land there, laid it out into town lots, and changed the name to Belmont. He also built a hotel, of which T. N. Boss became manager. The latter had come here several years previously from the State of New York to take charge of Rose Hill Sanitarium, which he endeavored to convert into a health and summer resort. He was a man of considerable culture and soon took a prominent part in the affairs of the community.

In January, 1887, Newton Ogdin came from Wood county and bought the mercantile stock of Gallaher & Stealey, executors of S. Gallaher, at the same time leasing the building. Later in the year James Stealey formed a partnership with Hugh M. Bookman, buying the stock of Joseph Porter on the southeast corner of Second and George streets, but the firm had only a brief existence. About this time Saul Ankrom of Tyler county, who had been engaged for several years in the lumber and crosstie business, decided to make this place his headquarters and bought a lot on the corner of First and Clay streets, on which he built the house now occupied by D. W. Dillon.

Daniel Reynolds died on April 3 at his home on Middle Island. He was born April 27, 1801, and married Sarah, daughter of Isaac LaRue. who, with his brother Jacob, had made the first settlement in this county. In 1830 Mr. Reynolds moved to his farm on the island, where he resided until his death. As has been noted. he took a very active part in the formation of Pleasants county, and was a man of strong personality. It is said that he had caused his coffin to be made several years before he died, keeping it in his home. It appears that this was not an unusual thing in the early days, when cabinet makers were scarce and there were no undertaking establishments outside of the large cities.

The first undertaker in St. Marys was George Kelsall, who came here soon after the formation of the county and opened up a cabinet making shop. Then John M. Strobel came from Stuttgard. Wurttemberg, and bought the business, which he carried on until his death. Mr. Strobel was very skilful, a real artist in his workmanship, and many samples of his cabinet making are still to be found here. He also made caskets, or coffins, as they were commonly called then.

Early in 1888 Dr. Leander B. Maxwell, president of the county court, who had been traveling in the West, decided to locate in Kansas, and resigned his office. R. A. Gorrell was appointed in his stead, and John R. Shingleton was promoted to the position of president.

The slow growth of the town was shown by the fact that only 116 pupils were enrolled in the school, but while no street in the town had yet been paved, there was a noted improvement in the sidewalks on Second street.

The community was still lacking in social entertainment for the young folks. Exceedingly few cared for dancing, or indeed knew how to dance, still fewer could be pleased with cards, and the old-time frolics had been discontinued. Sometime in the year 1884 a club had been formed by several young men and women, known as the Scott Reading Circle, which held a session one evening each week at the home of some member. A literary selection was there read and studied, and in the course of time papers were written and debates engaged in, which were doubtless profitable. This society was kept alive for two or three years.

Early in 1888 a debating society among the young men of the community was formed, the sessions being held weekly in the school building. It developed into a practical parliamentary body, the presiding officer being styled the Speaker, while the members assumed the titles of senators representing the various States of the Union. Bills were presented, and put through the regular course of readings and amendments. The game was so fascinating that older men joined and soon all the lawyers and politicians of the neighborhood were members. The perfect freedom of selecting one's own side in a debate was a great attraction, putting it far above the old-fashioned system of choosing debaters. The Assembly endured two winters, and was perhaps responsible for arousing lyceum activities all over the county.

This was another year of great political activity. The Democrats were anxious to re-elect Grover Cleveland as President, while the Republicans strained every nerve to bring their own party back into power. Early in February the Democrats organized local Jeffersonian clubs all over the county, and their opponents endeavored to stem the tide by organizing clubs on their side. Another method of arousing political ardor was by raising poles, each party striving to erect a higher pole than the other, perhaps actuated by the old saying that "the longest pole knocks the persimmons." The Republicans raised a pole on the court house lot that towered to the height of 126 feet, but in October, after two days of strenuous labor, the Democrats raised one on the same lot that reached upward 140 feet, and was claimed to be the tallest hickory pole in the State. To the top of this pole was run a lighted lantern covered with a red bandanna handkerchief, the Democratic emblem of the campaign in honor of Allen G. Thurman, candidate for Vice President.

This political fervor was also responsible for the starting of two small weekly papers, each of very short life. In March Mahlon D. Hanes and Alva B. Moore brought a small printing plant here and began the publication of the Gazette. professedly independent, which endured about four weeks, when the plant was taken to New Martinsville. In April a Republican paper called the American was started by James A. Oldfield and the writer, and managed to exist until December.

Notwithstandng the utmost need of a united front when facing the enemy. the Democrats waged an exceedingly bitter conflict among themselves in their nominating convention on August 4. The chief interest centered in the battle for the sheriffalty nomination, John W. Porter and Ralph A. Gorrell having divided the convention almost equally between them. The voting was so close that ballot after ballot gave first one side and then the other only a fractional vote in the majority, the rules requiring a majority of at least one whole vote. The balloting continued until midnight, amid a perfect babel of confusion, partisans leaping on tables to get attention, motion after motion being vainly made, all on the verge of a sanguinary conflict. Finally an adjournment was made until the following Tuesday, when a compromise was effected, Mr. Gorrell receiving the nomination for sheriff.

In the November election the Democrats carried the county. A. B. Fleming was given a majority of 116 votes over General Goff for governor; R. A. Gorrell was elected sheriff over W. E. Bier; G. D. Stout defeated J. F. Brammer for assessor; Robert G. Hammett defeated Newton Ogdin for the Legislature, and Job Smith was elected county commissioner over Frank M. Triplett. In the same election an amendment to the State constitution prohibiting the manufacture and sale of intoxicants was defeated in this county by a majority of 340. The total cost of this election to the county was only $119, or about $17 for each precinct.

Reports of the oil business from the Eureka field were made at irregular intervals. In February the Burnt Well was said to be pumping at 45 barrels a day; another well on the Russ Hammett farm was given in at thirty barrels, while No. 4 on the Cochran farm was shot and made fifteen barrels. Altogether the production was placed at about 125 barrels daily; but in April the Burnt Well was shot in a lower sand and for a time made 225 barrels a day.

Men interested in oil were gradually gathering here, and as there was also great activity in lumber, cross ties and staves, the hotels did a very good business. Abraham Ruttencutter was managing the old Exchange on Creel street and George W. Brown had taken charge of the Wells House on Second, changing its name back to the old one of "Commercial." Isaac O. Reynolds reopened the old Reynolds inn, heretofore mentioned as the building in which court was first held, and called it the Central Hotel.

Few other matters of general interest occurred this year, among them the stopping over night of April 7 at the Wells House of Paul O. Boynton. the famous swimmer, who was then swimming down the whole length of the Ohio, which was still cold with cakes of floating ice.

The postoffice of Cluster in Bull creek was established in April, and in the following month Josiah, just below Bens Run, was made a postoffice, getting its name from the first postmaster, Josiah D. Riggs.

The M. P. Wells, a stern wheel boat. began making daily trips between New Matamoras and Marietta, taking the place of the Ida P. Smith.

The Silver Cornet Band, which had languished for lack of an instructor, was reorganized, with Professor W. L. Skaggs as teacher, thirteen handsome new instruments having been obtained.

The year 1889 opened with talk of a new railroad to be known as the Ohio & West Virginia Southern. It was to begin at Marietta, cross the river at Willow Island, thence go up Cow creek and through Ritchie county to tap the coal fields of Gilmer county. Several tentative surveys were made, with the usual excitement, but the road got no further than the paper stage.

Change in the National administration, Benjamin Harrison having been elected President, brought corresponding changes of the postmasters of the county. Theodore Clovis succeeded G. H. Hudkins at Hebron; George M. Williamson became postmaster at Raven Rock, and Mary Craig at Grape Island. In October Newton Ogdin succeeded George Kelsall as postmaster of St. Marys, the latter having served in that capacity since the death of his father-in-law, William Carroll, in 1881.

April 30 was the one hundredth anniversary of the establishment of the United States government, and the event was celebrated in the M. E. Church, patriotic addresses being made by Revs. H. P. F. King, J. H. Doan and W. W. Kelley.

Fifteen ministers of the Parkersburg district of the Methodist Episcopal Church held a conference here in the spring, the session being presided over by Rev. J. A. Fullerton.

In the May election Leander A. Ellis was re-elected superintendent of schools, defeating R. L. Pemberton for the second time.

Thodore W. Hanes bought the Exchange Hotel, and Hugh M. Bookman erected a store building on Second street, where the St. Marys Hardware Company's store now stands.

The lumber business broadened out considerably, and there was a great demand for rough staves for oil barrels. Ogdin Brothers had a large saw mill on Schultz Fork of French creek, and Callahan had many men getting out staves near Nine Mile, producing more than 200,000 during the summer. Lumbering brought out the fact that there were still rattlesnakes as well as copperheads in the back end of the county. John Harris reported killing eight rattlesnakes on French creek. They were mostly found sheltered under piles of tanbark, and occasionally one was picked up by a workman while tossing an armful of bark into the wagon.

Winer & Kaminsky, the first Jews to enter business in St. Marys. opened a store in September in a small buildisg belonging to Green Haddox on Second street. They dealt exclusively in clothing, and continued in business until the fall of the following year, when the store and its contents were destroyed by fire.

In the spring of 1889 William Johnson drilled in another fine gas well, this being on the land of Absalom Smith at Belmont, and again tried to dispose of it to the local people, but failing, the whole property fell into the hands of the Standard, through a subsidiary company.

The oil business still centered in the Eureka field, where Barnsdall & Moore drilled in a well on the John Hammett farm, getting a production of 200 barrels a day, which soon increased to 300. It went by the name of the Big John well. In November Cochran No. 6 was drilled in, making about 200 barrels. Operators, scouts and scalpers flocked into the county during the year, with a tendency to lease land in a northeast direction from the Eureka field, some arguing for a 30 degree line and others for 45 degrees. Nearly all the farms about St. Marys were leased, several large bonuses being paid. Joseph Story held some leases on Green run and drilled a well on the Smith farm, getting a small quantity of oil at 440 feet.

CHAPTER XII

THE BELMONT OIL BOOM

The first week in January. 1890, was remarkable for its warm weather. The buds on peach trees swelled until ready to burst into bloom, and near Maxwell a pear tree was reported in full flower. Immediately following this warm wave came the first general spread of influenza, then termed "la grippe," a name which originated in France, where the epidemic is said to have first broken out, the pains having been described as the gripping and twisting of the muscles by a powerful hand. In a few weeks the disease spread through the county, many deaths being attributed to it.

Political reforms also swept the country, one of them being a new system of balloting with what was then known as the "Kangaroo ballot," because it was first tried out in Australia and New Zealand. Up to this time each political party had furnished its own ballot, a narrow strip of white paper on which were printed the names of the candidates. The new system took the preparation of the ballots out of the hands of the different parties, excepting so far as requiring the names of the nominees to be certified, and county officials caused all the tickets to be printed in separate columns on one ballot, of which samples must be published in the newspapers both for the public information and as a preventive of fraud. All this to be done at the expense of the county.

This was assumed to be a panacea for all political ills, but the few who opposed it maintained that the more secrecy there is placed about the ballot box the greater opportunity there is for fraud. However, a majority of people seeming to favor the plan, the Legislature enacted it into law so that it would go into effect in 1892.

Hon. Oliver Gorrell was a farmer of progressive ideals, and it was constantly his endeavor to bring the farmers of the county together in a union, or organization of similar character. arguing that only by doing so can the farmer expect to hold his own in competition with men in other lines of business. He succeeded this spring in organizing a farmers institute for Union district. himself being president, J. Emory Galloway vice president, Thomas C. Davis secretary, Leander C. Hanes assistant secretary, and M. L. Gorrell treasurer. In March a similar organization was formed at St. Marys for the entire county, Oliver Gorrell being chairman and Amos Smith secretary.

There were 156 pupils attending the town school, rather crowding the three roomed building, and showing a gradual increase in the population, due chiefly to oil operators moving in. To meet this growth, the heirs of Silas Gallaher marked out a number of building lots north of Clay street and west of the railroad, which were soon sold at prices ranging from $200 to $300, the lots being 80 by 160 feet, to correspond with the lots of the old town as staked by A. H. Creel.

The decennial census was taken this year, the enumerators for the districts being E. B. Steere of Grant, A. B. Core of Jefferson, Isaac Wagner of Lafayette, R. A. Anderson of McKim, J. D. Riggs of Union, and A. H. Cole of Washington. Their report, which was not published until the ensuing year, gave the entire population of the county as 7,539, and St. Marys as 520.

Aside from oil, the chief enterprise of the year was the organization of the Middle Island Creek Boom Company. with a permissible capitalization of $250,000. Most of the incorporators were residents of Tyler county, but the principal office was at St. Marys, Saul Ankrom being its head. The company was empowered to construct booms across the creek and to deal generally in all kinds of lumber. As it was calculated to handle all the lumber produced in Doddridge, Tyler and Pleasants counties, it was expected to do an immense business.

An important business deal was the sale of the Gallaher store building, then the largest and finest in the town, to Joseph Strickling of Newport for the sum of $1800. It was occupied by Newton Ogdin, who gave up possession in the fall and moved his goods and the postoffice to the Joseph Porter building, on the corner diagonally opposite.

Rev. Exline, pastor of the South Church, had succeeded in having the building repaired so that services could be held in it. The members of the Methodist Protestant Church prepared to erect a new building, moving the old one to the rear of the lot, where it was used until the new one was finished the following year. J. F. Barron erected a two-story frame building adjoining the Strickling store, using the upper floor for law offices. In March I. O. Reynolds closed the Central Hotel because of other business. At about the same time Captain Will Roe put his new boat, the T. N. Barnsdall, into the Raven Rock and Marietta trade. This little stern-wheel steamer became very popular, and was frequently used for Sunday excursions.

The Democrats were again successful in the fall election. W. G. H. Core defeated E. B. Steere for the Legislature; J. L. Knight was elected circuit clerk over A. H. Cole; J. W. Porter defeated R. H. Boyd for county clerk, and John W. Morgan defeated M. M. Wells for county commissioner, the majorities ranging from 121 to 205.

Early in the fall an attempt was made to establish a branch of the Parkersburg Young Men's Christian Association in St. Marys with H. M. Bookman as president and Robert H. Boyd secretary, but the effort was soon dropped from lack of interest and also of funds.

The rapidly increasing oil development brought the usual demands for higher prices in the stores and higher wages for employes. A plea was made in the Oracle for increased wages for household help. It seems that the customary amount paid to a housemaid was one dollar a week, but it was argued that under the changed conditions the wage should be doubled.

Everybody was now talking of oil. The development that began at Eureka had extended up the river to Belmont and thence to Vaucluse and the Green run neighborhood, and the "strikes" were mostly notable ones. Johnson & Brockunier drilled in a 700 barrel well on the William T. Locke farm at Belmont, and on First Brother Island and at Vaucluse wells were drilled in that made fifty to one hundred barrels daily.

The Cochran No. 7 in the Eureka field, which reached the sand in the latter part of January, showed up for 600 barrels. It was within three hundred yards of the Big John, and brought the production of that field up to 1,500 barrels a day. In April the daily production of the entire field was put at 2,000 barrels. Another well on the Russ Hammett farm, drilled by McCullough, came in a gusher, and a three-fifths interest in the lease of fifty acres sold to the Standard for $40,000. On March 18 the Mc-Cullough No. 2 came in a gusher, flowing one thousand barrels a day, and was proclaimed the largest well in the State. Near the same time the Russ Hammett No. 5 was drilled in and started off at 500 barrels.

These were gushers, in which the oil was forced out of the sand by the tremendous gas pressure under it, and as the power of the gas lessened the output of the well declined, sometimes very rapidly. A gusher of five hundred barrels or more in a few days ordinarily settled to one hundred barrels, and in the course of several weeks it was often found necessary to pump out the oil, the gas pressure having become exhausted.

But the excitement was intense. Oil men from the "upper country," New York and Pennsylvania, rushed to this section, leasing everything that was available, often paying large bonuses. The leasing extended up the river above St. Marys and also up Middle Island creek. The whole county was assumed to be underlaid with rich oil sands, and every well was expected to start in with at least one hundred barrels. All below that were considered poor wells, and if the production was only ten or fifteen barrels they were abandoned as if they were mere "dusters," and perhaps the territory was condemned as valueless.

Above town a well was drilled on the Charles W. Bills farm and started off with twenty barrels. At Spring Run the Browse well was put down 2085 feet, getting no oil but encountering a good supply of gas, which Mr. Browse utilized in heating and lighting his home.

Many of the largest operators came to this county, and it seemed that St. Marys would become the leading depot of supplies for oil operators within a radius of many miles, but the result fell far short of expectation. It is true that the population of the town increased, but it was little more than normal. There was no sudden accretion of great wealth; there was no rapid erection of large business blocks.

One reason given for this is that the residents did not make any especial efforts toward encouraging operators to make their homes here; but perhaps the logical reason is that the development extended for several miles up and down the river and the railroad. Materials were delivered at points through the whole length of the county. Below St. Marys were the shipping stations of Waverly, Willow, Salama, Eureka and Belmont, while above the town were stations of Grape Island, Raven Rock and Bens Run, so there could be no concentration in the matter of delivering materials. It was not until the development of the oil regions of Long Run, Broad Run and up Middle Island creek that the town began to feel the thrill of a rapid growth, but by that time the greatest interest was being diverted to Sistersville, where an abundance of oil was found in the town itself. It is true that there were supply shops here—the National, the Jarecki and the Oil Well Supply companies all had stores here.

The little village of Eureka early took advantage of the boom. A hotel of thirty rooms was built, and every available apartment in the place was tenanted. Belmont also felt the impetus. Two hotels were built there, many dwellings were erected and large stores of general merchandise opened by T. N. Boss and R. G. Caldwell. Every house in the village had lodgers. From Wheeling and Parkersburg excursions were run every Sunday during the summer to the great oil field. There was much carousing on the steamboats, and occupants of shanty boats along the river shore did a thriving business dispensing liquors on the "speakeasy" plan.

Almost daily new strikes were made, most of the wells producing hundreds of barrels at the start. Barnsdall & Boyd drilled in a 700 barrel well on the county poor farm in June, and then came in Island well No. 2 at 400 barrels and No. 3 at 350 barrels. No. 8 Russ Hammett came in with 400 barrels.

The general trend of production was northward. At Belmont Johnson got a 600 barrel well on the Shingleton farm, Duncan beat that with a 900 barrel on the Taylor farm, and the Emery Oil Company topped that by drilling in a 1,000 barrel well on the same farm. A well on the Jones land on the river bank just above the mouth of French creek produced 40,000 barrels in ten weeks.

Competition became so strong that derricks were built almost touching each other, making the field resemble some of the later densely crowded oil sectors of Texas or California. Even the railroad right of way was not ignored in the wild enthusiasm, and from Belmont station to French creek were two rows of derricks, one row on the railroad property and the other bravely defending the boundary of the private landowner.

The average daily production had increased to 3,000 barrels, and to take care of it the Eureka Pipe Line Company began laying the great system of pipe from Eureka to Mannington, running in an almost straight line over the hills. The company paid twenty-five cents a rod for the right of way.

Several small producing wells were drilled in the neighborhood of Vaucluse; some venturesome operators tried French creek, but with little success, and the fever laid hold of many conservative citizens of St. Marys, so that companies were organized and a little drilling done in the Cooper Hollow section, but no fortunes were realized. The most notable instance of "wildcatting" this year was that of Hanna Brothers, who drilled near the mouth of Shawnee run, several miles east of development, and got a small producer in the deep sand.

There was not so much activity in the oil business in 1891. No great strikes were reported in the Eureka-Belmont field. The Little Gulch well below town made 100 barrels a day for a time, and several small wells of 15 to 25 barrels a day were brought in on the Riggs farms and on Middle Island. The attention of the larger operators was centering on the Sistersville field, which now began a remarkable career of production.

What was known as the Tomcat well, on the Bier farm at the mouth of Alum Cave run, was shot in two different sands, but produced no oil. However, it became a great gas well, with such pressure that the roar of the escaping gas was distinctly heard in St. Marys, four miles distant. Again a vain effort was made to interest the people of St. Marys and have the gas piped to town.

Away up on Sugar creek another wildcat well was drilled, far from any development, with no particular result except to find a strong flow of warm water at a depth of 1300 feet.

In the beginning of 1891 members of the M. E. Church South organized the Sunday School that had long been discussed. Attorney Aug. M. Campbell was superintendent and A. C. Imlay secretary, with James Patterson, Mrs. A. M. Campbell, Mrs. A. C. Imlay, Miss Annie Imlay and Miss Jenny Patterson as teachers. In the course of the year Mr. Campbell was admitted to the ministry of the church and licensed to perform the marriage ceremony.

Newton Ogdin, Republican, of Pleasants had received a small majority in the election of the preceding November for the State Senate, but his election was contested by William W. Morris, Democrat, of Tyler county, who was his opponent, and the State Senate declared that Morris was entitled to the position.

High water in the latter part of February assumed the proportions of a flood, reaching its height on the 20th of the month, at a stage only seven feet and ten inches below the crest of the 1884 mark. While no damage was done in St. Marys the oil operators in the river bottoms suffered severely, their loss being estimated at about $100,000.

John Suck, who had formerly operated the sawmill here, returned and became the partner of R. H. Browse in the flour mill. The grinding was then done with stones, but in July rollers were installed and a fine quality of flour was produced.

Moses A. Ruckman, who had been associated with W. H. Sheets in a general store at Borland, this year bought his partner's interest and soon built up a large business.

Another business enterprise in the country was the establishment of a general store at the fork of French creek by George and John R. Stanley. It proved to be a good business stand, and a postoffice was created there called Calcutta. Another postoffice established that year was at Pleasants Mills on McKim creek, named Selection, with C. L. Barron as postmaster. Belmont suffered a severe loss in May by the burning of the hotel and store of R. G. Caldwell.

In St. Marys there was quite a building boom. Work was begun on the Odd Fellows building on the corner of Second and Washington streets; the new Methodist Protestant church was well under way; George Kelsall put up a new store building on Second street, to be used as a millinery shop, and several dwellings were constructed.

This year marks the beginning of bicycles in Pleasants county. This curious device for self-propulsion was very slow in developing, and although it had been used in America for about thirty years, but few of our people had seen one. That was probably owing to the poor condition of the roads, for the pneumatic tire had not then been invented and driving a narrow and hard tired wheel over rough roads was a weary task. To R. A. Flesher perhaps belongs the credit of bringing the first bicycle into this neighborhood, a "safety" in which the pedals actuated a ratchet in the rear wheel. Two citizens, John Harris and H. B. Gabbert. made machines from their own designs, but they were not practical. It was not until 1896 that a great impetus was given to the use of the machines, pneumatic tires then being general.

At this time the Junior Order of American Mechanics spread rapidly throughout the country, and in this county the order soon became very strong. One specialty indulged in by the order was to present flags to the public schools. The presentation of one to the St. Marys school was made an occasion for a holiday, the ceremony taking place on the grounds of the M. E. Church South. Rev. A. M. Campbell delivered the address, and the response was made by Rev. W. Mack Williams.

Two other affairs worthy of mention as happening this year were the building of a new bridge over French creek

145

and the establishment of a weather bureau at the court house. Clerk John L. Knight had agreed to attend to the weather reports without emolument. Besides keeping a record of the weather he was required to display flags of various designs showing what sort of weather could be expected.

In 1892 the oil business was more quiet than in the preceding year. Barnsdall drilled a few wells on French creek, getting several gas wells and one small oil well in the Alum Cave run neighborhood. A few other wells of little importance were drilled along French creek, but no gushers were reported. However, leasing continued, the trend being towards the Shawnee territory.

That the population was increasing was shown by the enrollment of 179 pupils in the town school, all confined in the three rooms of one building.

Silas A. Gallaher, who had been appointed to make an assessment of the lands in the county, reported the value of real estate at $798,825, and the leaseholds at $128.848.

The Odd Fellows Hall was completed in Spring and on April 26 was dedicated to the purposes of the Order by Grand Master John Beckley of Raleigh Court House, assisted by Grand Warden Septimius Hall of New Martinsville. The usual evening banquet followed the dedication.

Aithur P. Riggs, who had been residing for several years on the Pacific coast, returned and became manager of the old Exchange Hotel on Creel street, succeeding James M. Wells.

Dunn Chapel. occupying a commanding site on the Ellenboro Pike, looking down the valley of Broad Run, one of the most picturesque scenes in the county, was dedicated May 29, the sermons being preached by Rev. M. M. Everly and Rev. Aug. M. Campbell.

This was the year of another hotly contested political battle, in which Grover Cleveland was elected President for the second time. In Pleasants three political parties held conventions. The Demorcrats nominated Robert G. Hammett for the House of Delegates, D. W. Reynolds for sheriff, J. C. Noland for prosecuting attorney, A. B. Core for assessor, B. F. Seckman for county commissioner and Clyde B. Johnson for surveyor. The Republicans named

George W. Boss for the House of Delegates, Newton Ogdin for sheriff, Charles N. Matheny for prosecuting attorney, T. E. Fleming for assessor, W. S. Scott for county commissioner and F. M. Triplett for surveyor. The Prohibitionists formed the third party. naming Rev. J. H. Doan for House of Delegates, Green Ruttencutter for sheriff, J. M. Snively for county commissioner and Henry Steele for assessor.

In the election of November the Democrats elected their entire ticket, but for several days there was doubt as to the sheriffalty, Reynolds getting the office by a small majority.

This was the first election held under the Australian ballot system. The first ballot commissioners were John L. Knight, R. L. Pemberton and William E. Reed. The system was new and seemingly intricate, a great deal of trouble arising because of the different methods in which voters marked their ballots.

The first county Sunday School convention was held August 26 and 27 in the M. P. Church, Robert H. Boyd being chairman and Miss Annie Bookman secretary. Two days later the teachers institute was held, with Major J. M. Lee as instructor.

Early in the year 1893 the county commissioners decided to build a bridge over McKim creek near its mouth. This improvement was very greatly needed. Frequently residents of the entire eastern part of the county could not reach the county seat except by walking, crossing the streams in small john boats. The roads leading from the creek to the Ellenboro Pike were very steep and rough, as they remain to this day. Down the creek the only outlet was by fording and then crossing an exceedingly steep road leading from the Cunningham farm over the hill to Middle Island creek at Porter's ford. In all its length within the limits of Pleasants county there was not a wagon bridge over McKim creek. The proposed bridge was built and a new road constructed around the foot of the hill. This road is now part of the State road which is to connect St. Marys and Middlebourne by way of Meadville, and is destined to become one of the leading roads of the county.

In the Spring D. W. Reynolds bought the lot on the corner of Second and George streets from Charles W. Bills and erected a small office building on the lower half, which still stands below the brick postoffice. When in May James M. Wells was appointed postmaster to succeed N. Ogdin, he moved the postoffice into this building. Among the postoffice changes resulting from the election of a Democratic President the preceding year, the office at Raven Rock was given to C. Perry Barker and that of Grape Island to Robert Goerder, the latter, we believe, retaining the office to the time of his death.

It was in the days of the nefarious Star Route contracting system, when the postoffice department favored certain firms in contracting for the carriage of mail over many different routes, presumably letting them out to lowest bidders. Under color of this system, a few paying routes more than made up for a deficiency in several small routes; and even at that the contracting firms often found persons who would carry the mail for considerably less than the price they were getting from the government.

From St. Marys to Ellenboro, a distance of sixteen miles, the mail was carried twice a week, and the job was secured by Lloyd Bailey, then living on Willow Island Run. For this he received the munificent sum of $108 a year, or a few cents over one dollar the trip of thirty-two miles, furnishing his own horse. A little ready money was a great thing then, but when, in a few years, Bailey became comparatively wealthy with the discovery of oil on his farm, he willingly gave up the business of carrying mail. But he was a bluff, hearty man, whom prosperity could not spoil, and was probably no happier after good fortune had come to him.

A. J. Huggins of Shawnee made a better contract, getting $115 a year for carrying the mail from Shawnee to St. Marys twice a week, the round trip being about twenty-four miles. Samuel King carried the mail from Calcutta to the county seat, the round trip being about seven miles, for which he received thirty-five cents the trip.

But everything was low then, even oil in the month of May bringing only 59 cents a barrel, although in June the price rose to 64 cents. The cheapness of oil was the main reason why small wells were not considered worth pumping; besides, at that time, pumping a string of wells with one engine was not much practiced or understood.

Another instance of the high value of money then might be cited in the election for county superintendent of schools. The salary was only $150 a year, and the term only covered two years. Robert Anderson, the incumbent, was a candidate for re-election, being opposed in the Democratic convention by M. L. Barron. The clerks of the convention made an error in counting fractional votes, and the convention adjourned without making a nomination. The executive committee took the matter in hands and, deciding that neither aspirant was entitled to the nomination, gave the honor to Coleman L. Shingleton, who had not been a candidate. In the meantime, Anderson had caused a calculation of the fractional votes to be made which showed that Barron had really received a majority of one vote. But the committee refused to recede, so the friends of Barron induced him to run independently. The election resulted in favor of Shingleton after as much excitement as is usual in a Presidential election.

This was the last May election, the law being altered so that all school officials should be chosen at general elections held in November. At the same time the term of the superintendent was extended to four years and the salary raised to $200. Robert A. Armstrong was instructor at the teachers institute held late in the Summer, and a teachers association for the county was formed, with C. B. Johnson as president and Miss Kate Gallaher secretary.

In the Fall John W. Porter, who had been elected county clerk, sold his store and lot on Second street to Saul Ankrom, who had for several years been at the head of the lumber and tie business of Middle Island creek.

The great financial panic of 1893, which caused so much distress in the United States, affected Pleasants county very little because of the large sums paid out monthly to the farmers as rentals for oil leaseholds. Leasing went steadily on, but drilling was negligible. A few wild cat wells were obtained, mostly producing ten to twenty barrels, the most notable strike being a well on Alum Cave Run drilled by Barnsdall & Company, making 85 barrels.

But 1893 is memorable in the annals of the town by reason of the introduction of natural gas as a fuel and an illuminant. The citizens had declined the propositions of William Johnston, but the Mallory Brothers and T. N. Barnsdall literally forced the people to use gas by bringing it to their very doors.

The Mallorys operated under the name of The Mountain State Oil and Gas Company and the rival firm was known as the Barnsdall Company. The franchise of the city to lay pipes was granted to each of them, and each had a list of consumers. Early in the Fall many homes were supplied with natural gas, and on November 1 street lights. in the nature of flares or torches, were erected, the Mountain State Company furnishing eighteen and Barnsdall twelve.

For several months the service was poor because of the ill condition of the mains leading from the wells. Often in cold weather water in the lines froze and shut off the gas. The rate to consumers was one dollar per month for one fire, regardless of the amount of gas consumed, so that frequently fires were roaring in the stoves and grates while doors and windows of the overheated houses were thrown wide open. No economical burners were used. The customary plan was to heap the fireplace with broken bricks coated with whitewash and then turn on the gas until they became red hot.

The rivalry between the two companies was ended early in the following year by the Mallorys buying the Barnsdall interests, and in the Summer the name was changed to the River Gas Company, with William Reese as manager. A line was laid across the river and the town of Newport was also supplied.

On December 7 died John L. Knight, clerk of the circuit court. He was born in Ohio in 1847, and when scarcely more than a child had entered the Union army in the Civil War. Coming to Pleasants to teach school, he was elected county recorder or clerk in 1868, serving in that office twenty-two years, and also as circuit clerk twenty years. His son, Earl D. Knight, was appointed to fill the office until the next general election.

The Summer of 1894, like that of the preceding year, was very dry, and corn on the hills was a failure. Farmers living on the ridges had to haul water from the creeks, where a few pools could be found. The river was perhaps the lowest ever known, some of the timbers of the old stone-barge at the quarry across the river showing above the surface. Failure of the crops caused a feeling of despondency in spite of the income from oil rentals.

Cross-ties, staves and lumber were still marketed, but there were only two manufacturing industries in the county outside of the oil business. They were the Schauwecker tannery and the mills, which made flour and meal and also sawed and planed lumber, each operated with only a few employes. Along the Thoroughfare in the upper end of town W. F. Johnson of Long Reach had started a boat yard the preceding year, which gave occasional employment to several.

The county commissioners helped, however, by contracting for two bridges over Middle Island creek, one at Arvilla and the other near its mouth. Both bridges were completed this year and paid for without a bond issue.

A great reunion of veterans of the Civil War was held at Hebron August 22, continuing three days. It was estimated that two thousand persons from the neighboring counties attended.

The blue ribbon temperance movement, which had been started in the East by Francis Murphy, former saloon keeper, reached St. Marys, and in April a series of meetings was held in the M. P. Church, creating a wave of enthusiasm. Most of the sessions were conducted by William Murphy, but on one evening his father, Francis Murphy, came up from Marietta and took charge.

For the first time the Republicans were successful in the November election. Charles McKnight was elected as member of the legislature, R. A. Flesher circuit clerk, R. L. Pemberton county superintendent, F. M. Triplett county commissioner and Dempsey Wells surveyor. The pluralities ranged from one to 67.

On December 5 A. L. Johnson of Belmont started with a load of forty quarts of nitro glycerine into the country back of Newport. The weather was cool and he got down from the wagon to walk. The horses became frightened at something and ran off. Johnson dropped to the ground, and in a moment there was an explosion that shook the buildings in St. Marys. Johnson was not injured, but it was said no remnants of either team or wagon could be found.

The only noteworthy incident in the oil business in 1894 was drilling in a well by Bettman & Watson at the ox bow of French creek that made 125 barrels; but in 1895, with a slight increase in the price of oil from $1.10 to $1.20, came a renewed activity. The general trend of operation during the year was northeast.

In February Mallory & Barnsdall got a small producer on the John Boley farm on Broad run, and soon after several other wells were put down to the east of that, opening up one of the most productive fields in the county. L. H. Ballard got several small wells on the Job Smith farm. On another part of that farm Mallory & Barnsdall drilled in a well that flowed 60 barrels a day, and the same firm was fortunate in getting another on the William Brown farm that flowed 100 barrels. Ballard's No. 2 on the Core farm pumped at the rate of 20 barrels a day, but in November it broke loose as a gusher, flowing at the rate of 100 barrels. It was supposed that shooting other wells in that vicinity had opened a crevice in the rock, causing oil to flow into the Ballard well.

From Broad Run the field extended over the ridge to Willow Island Run, rival companies fighting along farm lines, as they did a few years before at Belmont. Wildcatters kept drilling far ahead of development, and often with good results, a well on the J. G. Smith farm near Hebron being drilled in the following year and producing 200 barrels a day, also one on the Givens farm in the same neighborhood yielding 145 barrels, while a good well was reported on the Mahan farm on Sugar Creek.

In the meanwhile active operations were still going on in the Eureka-Belmont field. Mackey & Braden drilled down to the Berea grit on James Hammett's farm on McElroy and struck a flow of 700 barrels. This well was 1675 feet deep, or 200 feet below the same sand at Belmont. Operators again rushed to the scene and frantically paid bonuses of $500 to $1000 an acre for leases.

The old school house in St. Marys was found insufficient. Four teachers were employed and used three rooms as well as they could. In the general election of 1894 a bond issue of $13,000 had met popular approval, and in the Spring of 1895 contracts for the new building were let. The ground was secured from the Samuel Barkwill farm, extending from Washington street to the Ellenboro Pike, and the plan was to construct a building with six rooms and a basement. The contracts were let mostly to local bidders, and the total amount of the brick structure was not to exceed $11,705. The building was completed in December, 1896, and the Winter term began the first week in January with 176 pupils, R. A. Gallaher was president of the board of education during its construction. The old scohol house and lot were sold to A. P. Riggs. who converted it into a hotel. It is now occupied by the St. Marys Fruit Company.

By 1905 the new building was overcrowded, there being 330 pupils, and an election was held for a bond issue of $7,000 to provide four additional rooms. The question carried by a large majority, and the addition was completed in 1906.

The pastors of the several church societies in St. Marvs in 1894 were R. C. Dean of the M. P. Church, R. B. Ward of the M. E. Church, S. T. Mallory of the M. E. Church South, and G. P. Somerville of the P. E. Church, services of the last named society being held in the M. E. Church every fourth Sunday. In October the Rev. A. W. Owenby came as pastor of the M. E. Church.

Mr. Johnson, who had been in charge of the flour mill, withdrew and O. C. Sweeney & Company took charge. Stanley Brothers, who had been doing a successful business at Calcutta, opened a store in town on March 4, under the management of George C. Stanley, while John R. Stanley remained at the Calcutta branch. The town store was in the building formerly occupied by H. M. Bookman on Second street, afterwards replaced by the brick building erected by E. R. Smith and now occupied by the St. Marys Hardware Company.

George Bartrug, who had been employed in the flour mill, now turned his attention to coal mining and opened up a three-foot vein of fairly good coal on the Kelley farm above the creek. The demand, however, was so small that it did not pay to work it, and after a few years the mine was abandoned.

In November began the long continued fight between the gas company and the consumers. The company raised the price from the original fixed rate of one dollar per fire to $1.80 for cook stoves in Winter and $1.35 in Summer. Heaters were charged at the rate of $1.50 per month for the first, $1.50 for the second, and one dollar for each additional stove. Stores and large buildings were charged by the floor space—$2.50 for the first 500 square feet and fifteen cents for each additional space of 300 square feet. The increase aroused loud complaints; many householders and nearly all the merchants went back to the use of coal, but the company maintained its new rates. These continued in force until the Fall of 1897, when under plea of a shortage in the supply of gas the company increased the rate on cook stoves and heaters from $1.80 to $2.50 per month, and further gave notice that after the end of the year meters must be used. Citizens contending that the use of meters meant another increase in the price of gas, the company installed several as tests, the result demonstrating that it was actually cheaper to use meters than to pay a flat rate per fire.

However, the demonstration was not convincing to all, and on December 27 the town council granted to Ed. H. Morrison a franchise to lay and operate gas lines, his charge to be a maxmium of $1.50 per fire in the Winter and one dollar in the Summer, stores and large buildings to get the fuel at two dollars per month, regardless of area. So far as the records show, Mr. Morrison does not appear to have made any physical effort towards putting in the proposed lines.

At that time the rule of the gas company was that all bills must be paid on the 10th of the month, no payment tendered before that time being accepted. On January 10, 1898, consumers brought in their payments and all were notified that unless meters were immediately installed the gas would be shut off. The company proceeded to carry out its threat, when the council procured an injunction, tying up the hands of the company for twenty days. In February the injunction was dissolved, and the River Gas Company was victorious in the matter of using meters. The rate was fixed at twenty cents per thousand cubic feet, with a discount of two cents per thousand if paid by the 10th of the month.

The first St. Marys Gun Club was organized March 24, 1896, with Sid T. Mallory as president, Dan A. McGillis secretary, and R. A. Gallaher, E. F. Hobbs and John Richey as trustees. Some ground was leased from the Gallaher estate, adjoining the present Odd Fellows Cemetery, where yet may be seen the trench in which the shooters stood.

John W. Porter, clerk of the county court, died February 11 in his 38th year. The county court appointed Wm. E. Reed, who had served as deputy clerk, to succeed him until the next general election.

After using the old Hall home on Creel street as a station for twelve years, the Ohio River Railroad Company built a new station on Clay street, Zach Taylor of Parkersburg doing the work. It was completed in June, and was then pronounced the best station on the road except that at Parkersburg. After nearly twenty-two years of service it is still used. W. C. Dotson was then station agent.

Moving the station to the upper end of town gave quite a boom to that section, while land and buildings in the lower end suffered a corresponding depreciation. What would have been the effect had the railroad company carried out their threat to put the station at the foot of the hill on the Ellenboro Pike?

A few houses had been built in the Gallaher Addition north of Clay street, but when the depot was moved every lot was sold and built on. Lots also were staked off and rapidly sold on the east side of Second above Clay and on Barron street.

Judge Arthur I. Boreman, the first governor of West Virginia and one of the first members of the Pleasants county bar, died April 19. At the time he was judge of the Pleasants county circuit court. Realizing that death was near, he had suggested that Lewis N. Tavenner be appointed to succeed him, and his wish was carried out.

O. H. Suck, who had established a large business in hay and feed, added a bicycle agency to his several activities this year, and created an intense enthusiasm for the wheel among the young folks. Pneumatic tires made riding possible over the rough dirt roads, and frequent long distance races were held. Many farmers were almost up in arms because their horses were frightened by the new vehicle.

This was the year of Bryan's first campaign, and again the political feeling ran high. The Republicans started a campaign paper called the Advocate, which closed its career after the election. Then an independent paper was started by a preacher, aided by C. E. Copen, a school teacher from Wirt county, and the plant was finally bought by Joe Williams, who came down from Sistersville and gave the new paper the name of the Leader, making it the organ of the Republican party.

There were five tickets in the field, and the result of the election was rather mixed. Bryan had a plurality of 34 in the county. The Democrats elected George Kelsall for member of the Legislature, A. B. Core for sheriff, W. C. Dotson for county clerk, W. M. Curtis for county commissioner and Jacob M. Copenhaver for surveyor; while the Republicans got C. P. Craig for prosecuting attorney, R. A. Flesher for circuit clerk and J. T. Sullivan for assessor.

GEORGE KELSALL

In 1897 the Pleasants County Bank was founded, marking a distinct advance in the business interests of the county. Heretofore the banking business had all been carried to Marietta or Parkersburg, the banks at those places having agents here who negotiated loans at higher rates of interest than the law prescribed, and and also, in order to avoid the trouble of going to those cities to dispose of notes or orders, the holders often sold them to individuals at a large discount. The opening of the State bank put an end to both those practices here.

D. W. Reynolds and his brother, Isaac O. Reynolds, were the actual promoters of the enterprise. The incorporators were A. S. Grimm, Newton Ogdin, I. O. Reynolds, John Schauwecker, C. C. Schauwecker, George Gale and D. W. Reynolds. They received a charter and on January 11 the stockholders organized by electing N. Ogdin, A. S. Grimm, R. H. Browse, C. C. Schauwecker, D. W. Reynolds, George Gale, John Schauwecker, R. M. Corbitt and R. A. Gorrell directors. At the first meeting of the directors N. Ogdin was chosen president and I. O. Reynolds cashier. The bank began business in March with a capital of $25,000 in the frame building on Second street adjoining the postoffice. Edward A. Sayre was employed as bookkeeper, retaining that position until the death of I. O. Reynolds, when he became cashier.

The first county board of health was organized under the State law in April, and was composed of Dr. Joseph B. Watson, George Kelsall and Wm. E. Reed, acting with the prosecuting attorney and the president of the county court.

On May 31 a rather severe earthquake was experienced in this and the adjoining States. It was so forcible that the walls of the new school building were slightly wrenched, and a report rapidly spread that the entire south wall had fallen in. This was the third shock in this county of which there is a record. The first was September 19, 1884, which was very slight and only noticed by persons within doors by the tinkling of dishes. The second was known as the Charleston earthquake, because it centered near that city in South Carolina. It occurred at 10 o'clock in the evening of August 31, 1886, the vibrations lasting several seconds and being plainly noticeable; but no damage was done here.

A. H. Cole, a veteran of the Civil War, became postmaster in St. Marys on July 1, succeeding James M. Wells, whose term had expired. At Schultz, Thomas H. Core, also a veteran of the war, was appointed postmaster.

It was in this year of 1897 that the many Baptists in the vicinity of St. Marys seriously talked of the necessity of having their own place of worship. Getting together, they appointed Amos C. LeBaron, Rodney Reynolds and G. D. Stout as trustees. Mr. Stout, who had served a term as county assessor, at the time resided at Belmont, where he conducted a hotel.

A lot was obtained from Samuel Barkwill, on Pike street, adjoining the school grounds, and a handsome frame building erected, which was completed in 1901 and dedicated May 26, the officiating ministers present being Rev. Harvey Cofer, pastor of the congregation, Dr. Carter, Rev. J. S. Stump and Rev. J. F. Cost. The society was greatly strengthened by this act, and has grown rapidly in numbers. A few years ago a basement, to be used as a room for the Sunday-school and as a community hall, was completed.

A law creating county school book boards went into effect this year. Up to this time the text books for free schools had been selected by a State Board, insuring uniformity throughout the State. It had long been claimed that certain publishers had dominated the State officials, and this law was perhaps an effort to fling off that influence. The effect was to create great confusion all over the State, utterly destroying the uniformity in education that had been desired, and making it burdensome on families moving from one county to another, because of the difference in text books. The county board was composed of six members, one from each magisterial district, besides the county superintendent, who was ex officio the secretary of the board. August M. Campbell was elected president of the board. To the great regret of many, the old series of McGuffey's Readers was discarded and Stickney's substituted.

This year, 1897, occurred another drouth, one of the most serious ever experienced here, no rain falling for several weeks until October 24. In the meantime the river again became exceedingly low, almost as low as in 1894. A complete survey of the channel and shallows was made by a corps of Government surveyors, establishing a new low water mark. Among the many rumors created by this survey was one that a dam was to be thrown across the river from Middle Island to Ferguson's landing, and that the lower end of the island was to be cut away.

At Hebron a roller flour mill was built by Theodore Clovis, J. M. McKinney and J. C. McGregor.

In 1898 came the first genuine attempt to establish telephone lines. As has been stated, several short private lines had been erected, but there was no communication between the different sections of the county and people seemed slow to acknowledge the utility of the invention. In the Spring the Mallory Brothers ran a line from St. Marys to the Whiskey Run oil field, where they were operating, and connected with lines that had been installed by E. R. Smith at Schultz and the Stanley Brothers at Calcutta. The habit of using these lines by the public increased to such an extent that it was finally realized that the time for a general public line had arrived. On May 11 the McKim Telephone Company was organized, with R. H. Browse as president, L. A. Ellis secretary, Arlando Eddy treasurer and William C. Dotson superintendent. A construction committee was appointed, composed of W. C. Dotson, John B. Watson, Amos Smith and J. W. Martin. The company proceeded to erect a line from St. Marys to Hebron, by way of Delong, Gibson, Maxwell ond Shawnee. The terminal at St. Marys was in the drug store of Watson & Watson, and at Hebron in the store of J. C. McGregor, where connection was made with Ellenboro and Pennsboro.

After several years of service the McKim Telephone Company was absorbed by the United Telephone Company, which was organized in 1900. This latter company originated along Cow Creek. It was incorporated May 29 of that year by E. P. Nole, J. W. H. Cornell, J. C. Ruckman, E. W. Williamson and O. C. Childers, and soon developed from a few straggling lines in the lower part of the county into a strong corporation, with chief offices at St. Marys, giving night and day service. A few years ago it formed a business alliance with the Bell system, enabling its subscribers to send long distance calls. J. L. Hissom served as secretary and general manager for several years, and the last president was S. V. Riggs. At the time of its sale to Mr. Harold V. Marsh in 1928 the company had 450 telephones on its list.

The Citizens Telephone Company was another local affair, organized in March, 1910, with a capital of $10,-000. J. H. Garrity was elected president, A. D. Hannen of Belmont secretary, John White treasurer, and C. T. H. Cain manager and line superintendent.

CHAPTER XIII

THE OIL BOOM AT ST. MARYS

There was a resumption in oil activities in 1898, the field rapidly extending to the northeastern section of the county. A well producing 200 barrels a day was drilled on the Tarleton Hanlin farm near Hebron, and Edwards drilled in a one hundred barrel well on the Asa Wagner farm on Sugar Creek. While a few small wells were obtained near the mouth of French Creek, it was ascertained that the neighborhoid of Calcutta offered the best inducements, and then began the great production of the Virgin, Bills and Reynolds farms. The Broad run pool was pretty thoroughly exploited, and the field had crossed Willow Island run and extended to Middle Island Creek on the G. K. Roby farm. The price of oil ranged from 95 cents to $1.19.

On March 25 the river reached an unusually high stage, estimated at 51 feet above low water, and caused great destruction to property in most towns along its banks, but very little here excepting the damage done to derricks and tankage on the lower bottoms.

The declaration in April of war with Spain aroused some enthusiasm, and about a dozen young men of this county volunteered into service under Lieutenant Parfit of Williamstown. There seems to have been some technical irregularity in the enlistments, however, so the volunteers scattered and re-enlisted wherever they could get in. A complete roster of the volunteers from this county is not available, but among them were Robert W. Patterson, Earl D. Knight, Joseph A. Ruttencutter and Earl Reed. The war was so brief that very few men were needed, and not many of them saw actual service. Admiral Dewey's May-day victory at Manila was celebrated with great vigor, the town being a mass of flags and bunting, with a great parade and speaking in the evening.

On July 26 many from this county crossed the river to attend the hundredth anniversary of Newport, which was the third permanent colony in Washington county, Ohio.

In November the Democrats elected their entire ticket by majorities ranging from 70 to 164. R. A. Gorrell defeated W. S. Allen for Legislature; A. W. Locke defeated W. E. Clovis for school superintendent; and Jacob L. Varner defeated John W. Gorrell for county commissioner.

The building activity which had started auspiciously in the preceding year went on with still more vigor. C. W. Bills employed F. M. Triplett to mark out town lots on a part of his farm, and immediately there was a rush to that section, which soon became known as Billsville. In all about forty new homes were built in various parts of the town, and among them was the parsonage of the Methodist Protestant Church, largely through the efforts of the pastor, Rev. E. J. Wilson.

The population was increasing, and Postmaster Cole was gratified with the information from Washington that on the first of the following January the salary of the postmaster would be increased to $1,100. A vision of a greater St. Marys was entertained, and at the town election held in the first week of January, 1899, a proposition was submitted to the voters to include the Gallaher Addition along First and Clay streets. However, the voting was 56 for and 56 against, so the proposition failed.

The months of January and February, 1899, are memorable for their extremely cold weather. On January 2 the temperature was eight below zero, and changed but little during the four following weeks, until on Friday morning, February 10, the mercury went down to the unprecedented mark of 30 degrees below zero. The weather was so calm that not many realized how cold it was. Workmen in the oil field suffered greatly. Orchards were seriously damaged, and even large limbs of forest trees were killed. The temperature varied, in some localities being reported at 34 degrees below zero, and in others at 26 below.

Development of the shallow sands went on more rapidly than ever in this year. The Calcutta and Willow Island run fields reached their height, and operators were flocking to the Shawnee, Bens Run and Sugar Creek pools. This interior development naturally made St. Marys a distributing point, and consequently the town was filled to overflowing with men more or less connected with the oil business. Notwithstanding the large number of houses that had been built, there was not accommodation enough for the increase. Many crossed the river to Newport to secure lodgings. In St. Marys men were offering undreamed of prices for rooms furnished or unfurnished. A few years before a small cottage and a garden could have been rented for five dollars a month, and a dollar a week for a furnished room in the town was considered bountiful. The price was raised, not so much by the residents, as by the oil men themselves, anxious to secure accommodations. From one dollar a week for a room it rose to five and then to ten. Stables, barns, anything that had a roof on it, could be rented for lodgings. Two teamsters considered themselves fortunate in getting possession of a rather large coal shed, which they fitted with a stove, a bunk and a couple of chairs, using a store box for a table. Looking down any of the alleys one could see stove pipes thrust out from the side or the roof of many a building that had not long before harbored a cow or horse.

And, unfortunately, it became more like a frontier town in another respect. Along with the oil men of the better class there came a leavening of the coarser element, demanding saloons and gambling rooms. These they could not have lawfully, but several saloons were opened in violation of the law, and for a few years, backed by powerful influences, ran their course openly. The police reports for 1900 show that six "speakeasies" existed in the town, besides several gambling resorts. Many arrests were made and fines imposed, but the breaking of the law continued. The town authorities decided to legalize the traffic, hoping thereby to put some restrictions upon it; but the county commissioners resolutely declined to sanction the business and would issue no licenses.

The saloon men had a majority in the town, and held it for years in spite of the sickening increase in the list of homicides and suicides. The better element of the new comers joined the old residents in an attempt to purify conditions. On April 21 a mass meeting of citizens was held in the court house and a "Law and Order League" was formed, John S. Hall being president and Joseph E. Cochran secretary. Committees were appointed to investigate and to prosecute, but although many indictments were found by the grand juries, it was almost impossible to convict for lack of direct evidence.

However, business affairs in the town and throughout the county were good, and 1899 was another year of building and enterprises. D. W. Reynolds had completed the brick building on the corner of Second and George streets, and the ground floor was occupied by H. J. Williamson as a grocery, also by the postoffice, Charles N. Matheny having succeeded A. H. Cole as postmaster. Brown & Graham of Clarksburg purchased the general store of S. Ankrom, and Rolla McMahon came here as manager of it, buying the business a few years later with W. H. Guth as partner. The stock was confined to that of men's and women's furnishings, and the firm continues today as W. H. Guth & Co., Mr. McMahon having withdrawn and entered business at Huntington.

Harry H. Dawson had a stationer's shop in the Grimm building; there were several tailors here then, among them F. C. Abel, Joe Goldstein, Frederick Gabbert, Gerber and Waxelbaum, all doing a good business. Frank Grimm was the town plumber. C. R. Dulin had a furniture store in the same building now occupied by Ruttencutter & Son. The new Howard Hotel was completed and Frank S. Clark was manager. The Bell Telephone Company opened an exchange in the Barron building on the east side of Second street, with Mrs. Lizzie Thompson as operator.

W. Burns McGregor of Highland, Ritchie county, aroused interest in the establishment of another bank, and J. F. Barron, B. F. Standiford, W. B. McGregor, Saul Ankrom and W. C. Dotson applied for incorporation. The application was granted, and on October 3 the stockholders of the First National Bank met and elected S. Ankrom, R. H. Browse, H. G. Feller, Rodney Reynolds, J. F. Barron, John F. Mallory, T. F. Campbell, E. T. Martin and A. T. Smith as directors. The officers chosen were J. F. Barron president, Saul Ankrom vice president, and W. B. McGregor cashier. On October 24 L. P. Walker was employed as book-keeper. The bank began business, with a capital of fifty thousand dollars, in the Barron building on the west side of Second street. In the following Summer W. B. McGregor resigned as cashier and F. C. Percival was appointed to the position. In October, 1899, the directors made a contract with P. Q. Shrake of New Matamoras to construct their present fine building on the corner of Second and Washington streets, the site of the old home of Samuel Barkwill, which was moved to the rear and is now occupied by the Pleasants County Leader.

Lone Star Lodge No. 13, A. O. U. W., was organized in the Odd Fellows Hall on October 6, with W. S. Allen as Past Master Workman, C. B. Johnson as Master Workman, and Frank Grimm recorder.

The Gallaher heirs marked out town lots on upper Second street, extending to the Bills line, and sold all of them before the end of the year. Early in 1900 they also marked out lots on Dewey Avenue and Fourth street, selling them immediately. Previously a few lots had been sold and built upon a short distance above Tannery Hollow, where the lower glass work are, and a part of the Barkwill farm near the court house had also been divided into building lots, so that by this time it seemed that the suburban population exceeded that of the town itself. An enumeration was taken by the postoffice department, early in 1900, showing a total population of 1715. In June of the same year the decennial United States census gave the town a population of 825, and of Washington district 2406, while the entire county was credited with 9,345.

In view of the large increase in the suburban population, which for various reasons it was desired to add to the town, an election was held on March 8, 1900, in an effort to include within the corporation all that territory extending northwardly from Cooper's Hollow along the foot of the hills to the creek, down the creek to the railroad, and with the railroad to the Gallaher line, thence following a ditch to the Thoroughfare, and with that and the river to the beginning. The measure carried in the town with a vote of 98 for and 58 against, but it was defeated by the suburbanites, 86 of them voting against it while 79 voted in favor.

The chief argument used in favor of taking in more territory was that of providing a water system. The taxable property inside the town was held to be insufficient. In June, 1899, a bond issue of $7,000 had been voted for, under the recommendation of F. R. Porter, of Marietta, who had estimated that sum to be sufficient, the water to be obtained from drilled wells. However, the question of sewerage also entered into the proposition, and it was evident that the sum voted for was inadequate, so no action was taken by the council except to put down a test well at the corner of George and Third streets.

The question of paving Second street also came up that year, and the Ohio River Railroad Company agreed to pay one-third of the cost, besides furnishing the sand and gravel necessary for the whole paving, but no further action was taken for several years.

A revaluation of land was ordered by the State Board of Public Works and the task assigned to J. W. Morgan, who filed his report in December, giving in 83,758 acres in the county, the land and buildings valued at $929,077. In St. Marys the value of real estate was $80,671.

The matter of greatest interest in the oil business was the sale by the Mallory Brothers & Stewart of their leaseholds in this county to the American Oil and Gas Company for $180,000.

Eearly in 1900 the town council abandoned the idea of municipally owned water works, and in March granted a franchise to John Duffy, of Washington, Pa., to construct a water system and to operate it for a period of 25 years, the town reserving the option of purchasing the plant at the end of that period. Although Mr. Duffy organized a company with an authorized capital of $50,-000 nothing was done, and the council again decided to construct and operate a plant for the town. On August 11 another bond issue of $12,000 was carried by a vote of 156 to nine, and the first bond issue was declared void. A contract was made with H. P. Day & Co. of Bellaire, Ohio, to build the system for $13,120.10, the town to furnish two Westinghouse engines at a cost of $2,282, two Worthington pumps for $1,800, and to pay about $4,000 for sewerage making a total outlay of about $21,000.

The price of oil decreased from $1.68 in February to $1.10 in October, but despite the decline in price, the business of drilling was active, especially in the Long Run and Calcutta fields. One of the largest operators then was Joseph C. Trees, who sold his lease on the Haddox farm on Long Run for $100,000.

It became more and more evident that the court house was inadequate and unsafe. The commissioners, F. M. Triplett, J. L. Varner and William Curtis talked seriously of erecting a new building, with the intention of paying for it out of the county funds and with a slight additional taxation. They traveled to several places to get ideas as to the proper architecture and cost. Still, not feeling warranted in taking all the responsibility upon themselves, in the following year they caused inquiries to be made in the several districts as to the desire of the people. The returns indicated that all the districts except Washington opposed a new building. However, the commissioners in August, 1901, proposed to carry out their design and to pay for the construction with county orders issued in multiples of fifty dollars, bearing interest at six per cent; but this very sensible plan was blocked by its apparent illegality. The people of other parts of the county were resolved to oppose any movement toward a new court house until the sale of intoxicants should cease at St. Marys. This was shown in 1904 when a petition was presented signed by 743 voters asking for the removal of the county seat to Belmont The lax condition in the town was such that at the January term of circuit court, 1901, the grand jury found 533 indictments for misdemeanor, nearly all of which were for illegal selling.

In the meantime the town was bustling with business. It was now the center of a largely extended oil field and money was plentiful. O. C. Ogdin had bought the large furniture store of C. R. Dulin; H. P. Boyd had started a machine shop in the upper end of the town; Allen H. Stanley was now manager of Stanley's Bargain Store; McCormick & Co. had opened a large shoe store, with Scott Gainer as manager; C. A. Traugh had bought W. J. Towzey's bakery on upper Second street and was making deliveries in a wagon. About this time grocers generally began to deliver merchandise to the homes of their patrons, but nearly all employed boys for the purpose.

Newton Ogdin had recently erected a three-story building on the east side of Second street, the third floor being fitted for a Masonic Hall. It was dedicated to that purpose October 29 in the presence of 250 Masons. William F. Adkins came down from Sistersville and started a boiler shop; the M. E. Parsonage on the corner of Second and Cherry streets was built, also several of the larger residences in the town. The Episcopal Church had been finished but not dedicated, and on April 24 and 25 the Northwestern Convocation was held in it, Rev. J. F. Woods presiding as dean.

The M. E. chapel known as Bethesda, at Grape Island, was burned to the ground on March 12, and on July 18 fire destroyed the old log house built by Joseph Bills about sixty years previously. It stood near the railroad bridge along what was formerly the county road.

This was the year of William Jennings Bryan's second campaign for the Presidency, and Theodore Roosevelt was running for Vice President on the Republican ticket with William McKinley. Political excitement reached a high pitch all over the land, and was heightened by the speaking tours of both Bryan and Roosevelt. On October 17 was the greatest feast of political speaking ever held in St. Marys. The Democratic rostrum stood at the corner of Second and George streets, while the Republicans held forth on the lumber piled for the building of the First National Bank, a square farther up Second. John H. Holt, Democratic candidate for Governor, delivered his almost unrivaled oratory at the former stand, and Congressman Bynum of Indiana and Charles T. Caldwell of Parkersburg spoke from the Republican stand. Toward evening Colonel Roosevelt and Colonel Guild Curtis of Massachusetts addressed the populace.

On November 6 the Republicans carried the election, with the exception of R. E. Bills, who was elected prosecuting attorney over James A. Oldfield. L. J. Murphy was elected to the House of Delegates over D. W. Reynolds, B. F. Riggs defeated Arlando Eddy for sheriff, J. T. Sullivan was re-elected assessor over O. C. Childers, D. R. Dunn county commissioner over M. A. Ruckman, and F. M. Triplett defeated Oliver Gorrell for surveyor.

The question of issuing saloon license had been put before the people and was defeated by a vote of 1011 against 660.

W, G. H. CORE

W. G. H. Core died August 23 at the age of 72 years. He had long been a prominent business man in the county, was a member of the State constitutional convention of 1872 and represented Pleasants one term in the Legislature. It is reported that, taking offense at some act of the town council, he purchased a tract of land just below the Vaucluse Narrows with the intention of founding a town there that should rival St. Marys. He built the house now occupied by Mr. Oscar Goetgeluck, caused several dwellings to be erected near by, including a general store, and constructed a stone wharf along the river. He called the embryo town Forest City, and the locality is yet known by that name.

In January, 1901, the newly elected town council ordered another election, to be held on the 28th of that month, for the purpose of taking in the Gallaher and Barkwill Additions, but the election was not held. Shrewd advisers showed that a safer and surer way to secure the result desired was to apply to the Legislature, then in session, for a special charter; so the order for the election was annulled.

The Legislature enacted the charter, subject to the approval of a majority of all the voters included within the proposed boundaries, and it was ratified at an election held March 25 by a vote of 279 for it and only 82 against. The charter provided corporation lines which included Gallaher and Barkwill Additions, and also took the licensing power out of the hands of the county court by creating an excise board, composed of three citizens, which should have supreme licensing power. The first election under the new charter was held April 2, Tim Penwell being elected mayor. The excise board, elected at the same time, issued license to six saloons.

A temporary organization of firemen had been made and the council purchased 800 feet of hose and two second hand reels. Almost the first use they were put to was at the fire which destroyed the old Commercial Hotel on the corner of Second and Lafayette streets. The hotel was managed by a Mrs. Slater and was full of guests. At two o'clock on Monday morning, April 22, flames started from a defective gas connection and spread rapidly to the entire building, which was two stories in height. When the guests on the upper floor were aroused the stairways and the long, narrow corridor were enveloped in flames, and the only means of escape was by dropping from the windows to the sidewalk. Four persons perished in the fire, John, a young son of Mrs. Slater, Harry Robinson of Marietta, Samuel Cunningham of Rexford, Pa., and John George, also from Pennsylvania.

At the time of this fire there was a late fall of snow on the ground, and the Ohio river was at a flood stage, being only a few feet lower than the flood of 1898.

Immediately afterward two companies of firemen were organized, one known as the Citizens Hose Company and the other as the John F. Mallory Hose Company, so named because Mr. Mallory had donated a considerable sum towards equipping it. Almost every able bodied man in town was a member of these two companies, and for several years they were the means of arousing considerable civic pride. On Independence Day both companies united in a parade, joined by most of the business firms with decorated wagons, while the town officials rode in finely bedecked carriages.

Up to this time merchants kept their places of business open of evenings so long as there was a customer, but now a strong appeal was made by some for regular hours. Accordingly an agreement was signed, fixing upon 8:30 in the evening as the time for closing. At first this caused great complaining among the citizens, but soon all became accustomed to it; and since then the closing hour has been gradually brought up to six o'clock by the grocers and to 5:30 by the dry goods stores without appearing to create any hardship. Those who were in business at that time, signing this agreement, were Holly Simmons & Co., groceries, Ankrom & Bills, shoes, Hendrickson & Co., dry goods, Ogdin & Riggs, general store, Strickling Brothers, general store, Stanley's Bargain Store, general store, Rosenberg Brothers, dry goods, Cutler & Pomeroy, millinery, O. C. Ogdin, furniture, George Kelsall, groceries, J. C. Cotton, furniture, E. T. Martin, hardware, W. E. Reed, hardware, Oil Well Supply Co., National Supply Co., Jarecki Manufacturing Co., T. A. Davis & Co. and H. J. Williamson, groceries.

The council erected a city building at the foot of George street, which a few years after its completion, was moved to its present location on the spot where the

Commercial Hotel had stood. The work of grading the Washington street hill was also begun, and late in the year a curfew ordinance was passed to keep the children off the streets at night.

In the preceding year, 1900, a baseball club was formed whose achievements are still mentioned with pride by the enthusiasts of this day. The team was composed of Ray Haddox, catcher; P. Hall, pitcher; L. Johnson, first base and captain; H. J. (Chalky) Flading, second base; J. Johnson, third base; Sapp, short stop; C. Hall, left field; Wyant, center; Jackson, right field; with Charles Haddox and Robert W. Patterson as substitutes. During its first season, playing up and down the Ohio valley, this team, like the famous Red Stockings of Cincinnati in 1869, won every game, and in the season of 1901 only lost one game, and that to Parkersburg while playing a series which St. Marys won. In the local annals of baseball there has been only one event that has aroused so much enthusiasm, and that was the famous game played at New Matamoras by a team from St. Marys early in the 70's, when live balls were used and before the art of throwing curves had been discovered. We are told that the score on that occasion was 26 by the New Matamoras team and 149 by that of St. Marys. It is doubtful if that record has ever been equalled. ,

The Pleasants County Tile and Brick Company was incorporated this year, with the intention of developing the clay found on the Z. T. Riggs farm and of making pressed cement brick from the sand of the river bottoms. A small shop was set up along the railroad in the upper part of town, but after making a few thousand pressed bricks the charter was surrendered.

A board of trade was organized in November, with John R. Stanley as president, John Schauwecker vice president, O. H. Suck secretary and I. O. Reynolds treasurer. The executive committee was composed of L. J. Murphy, N. A. Ogdin, W. C. Dotson, R. T. Browse and George W. Wentz.

In 1900 the population of Pleasants county reached its highest mark, and from that time began a slow decline, due to emigration. The great tile and pottery industries in the neighborhood of East Liverpool, Ohio, sent out calls for laborers at attractive wages, and many of our people responded. Their successes induced others to follow; the certainty of receiving money every pay day, coupled with the allurements of life in cities, where every comfort and luxury was easily obtained, proved an irresistible temptation to abandon the rough hillside farm, the meagre sustenance and the comparatively rude accommodations of the average farm home. We feel safe in saying that had it not been for this movement the population of the county would be nearly or quite double its present number. So large was the exodus that one could not travel in any direction through the county without seeing many deserted homes.

And even while new development in the oil fields here was yet bringing in operators and workmen from Pennsylvania and New York, the great strikes made early in 1901 in the Beaumont field of Texas drew some of our oil men into that section, and the successive opening fields of the Southwest have led a steady stream of workers and operators from Pleasants county, thus further depleting our population. It is surmised that probably more oil men from this county are now in the western fields than remain in Pleasants.

Oil operations in 1901 continued in all parts of the county, with increasing production in the northern and eastern fields. At Adams Ford on Middle Island Creek two wells of 100 barrels each were drilled in by Zahnizer. The best well of the year was that of Bartlett & Stancliff on the Morrison farm of Rock Run, which started in at 150 barrels. Some of the leading firms operating here in the year 1901 were Schlegel & Fried, M. L. Zahnizer, Bartlett & Stancliff, Trees & Benedum, Millicent & Browse, Kennedy, Lawrence & Griffith, Dinsmoor & Co., Benninger & Neely, Franchot, Cadwalader, W. S. Edwards, S. Y. Ramage and Joseph H. Ellsworth.

In 1902 there was a steady advance in the price of oil, beginning with $1.15 in January and closing at $1.51 in December, this despite the great gushers of Texas. The industry was very active, pay sand being struck every where in the county, but the greatest event was a well drilled by the Three Joes Company—Joseph C. Trees, Joseph H. Ellsworth and Joseph C. Brown—on the Elroy Wagner farm near Hebron, which started in at 900 barrels and settled down to 400.

A curious formation was reported by Schlegel & Fried, operating in the Bens Run field. While drilling a well on the farm of Edward Massie an oil bearing sand was struck at the depth of 18 feet. The stratum was twelve feet thick, and oil in considerable quantity found, but no estimate was given of the amount, and since the company drilled down to the deeper sands it is supposed that the quantity of oil was really negligible.

After thorough investigation the county commissioners declared that a court house and separate jail could be built for sixty thousand dollars, and in March accepted plans for the two buildings with the assurance that they would not cost more than fifty-four thousand dollars. It seemed such a reasonable proposition that they submitted a bond issue to the voters at the November election, but so strong was the sentiment of the rural voters against the saloon features of the St. Marys charter that they voted almost solidly against tne project. The vote was 421 for and 772 against.

In February a company was formed for the purpose of erecting a theater, and was capitalized at $20,000. The incorporators were O. H. Suck, W. C. Dotson, R. A. Flesher, R. W. Clendening and R. T. Browse. The western half of the Commercial Hotel lot was secured and the building erected, called the Auditorium, with a seating capacity of about 600. It was opened September 18 with the comedy "Our New Minister," and for several years furnished many good acting plays. However, as a theater it did not pay, and finally it was purchased by H. H. Robey of Spencer and is now chiefly used for moving pictures.

The village of Belmont had been steadily growing, a machine shop there giving employment to several hands. The old school house of Mount Olive on the hill, half a mile back, was abandoned and a new two-story house built in the village, equipped with a fairly good library. A new union church was also completed, and was dedicated July 20 by Rev. Brown of Harrisville, Rev. J. J. Poynter, Rev. J. P. Varner and Rev, J. H. Doan. The postmaster of Belmont was D. W. Boss, and John A. Griffith had been commissioned postmaster of the newly created office at Styron on Cow Creek.

Four buildings in the county were destroyed by fire in 1902. The home of Robert H. Browse at Spring Run was burned January 27; John Schauwecker's tannery in St. Marys was totally destroyed May 28; the Gravel Hill Bakery on Upper Second street, owned by James S. Smith, was burned August 13, and on August 15 the home of M. L. Hedleston at Salama was burned, a young son of Mr. Hedleston losing his life in the fire. In August of the preceding year the store of Clovis & Wagner at Hebron was burned.

In the way of education it may be noted that the salaries of teachers in the town schools had been increased, D .W. Dillon, the principal, receiving $70 a month, Ella Klinzing $50, and the other teachers, Annie Smith, A. G. Lamp, Epsie McVay and Dollie Triplett $40 each. The attendance had increased to 286, and in November the citizens voted for an eight months' term.

In the November election the Republicans elected Thomas C. Davis to the Legislature, R. A. Flesher clerk of the circut court, and J. F. Brammer county commissioner; the Democrats elected W. C. Dotson county clerk and A. W. Locke county superintendent.

The most important business changes of the year were the formation of McMahon & Company by J. R. McMahon, W. H. Smith and H. B. Crow, and John L. Hissom retiring from the Oracle and entering the lumber business with Stephen M. Riggs.

In 1903 the price of crude oil rose to $1.90. Operations were steady, but the richest fields were the Calcutta on French Creek, the Big Knot near Hebron and the Bens Run sections. The Vespertine Oil Company, of which William Seymour Edwards was manager, drilled two wells on the F. K. Bills farm at Calcutta, each starting off at 200 barrels.

Rev. H. C. Cox of the United Brethren Church came to St. Marys and began the erection of a church on the corner of Dewey avenue and Locust street, doing much of the work himself. It was completed in the Fall, and services held in it for a few years, but not receiving sufficient support it was abandoned and finally sold to the Catholics. It was dedicated by Bishop Donahue of Wheeling October 12, 1913.

Under the pastorate of Rev. O. E. Thorne the old M. E. South church was torn down and a new building erected. This old church had been built about the year 1851; Rev. Samuel Black was the first pastor and William Rymer was the first superintendent of the Sunday school. The cornerstone of the new edifice was laid June 10, 1903, by the Masonic fraternity, E. M. Turner, Grand Master, placing the stone, and Judge L. N. Tavenner, Past Grand Master, delivering the address. Rev. M. D. Helmick, Grand Chaplain, assisted at the ceremony. The trustees at the time were A. C. Imlay, E. P. Scott, Moses Gorrell, William Outward and William E. Hammett. The building was completed in that year and dedicated December 13 by Rev. Sims, Presiding Elder of Kentucky. The cost of the structure was about $3,500.

On March 4 Hazen Post No. 66, G. A. R., reorganized at the court house, electing A. C. Virden commander, A. C. Gorrell senior vice commander, Henry Steele junior vice commander, A. H. Cole quartermaster, E. P. Scott adjutant, Henry Reed officer of the day, J. M. Snively guard, George W. Meanor quartermaster sergeant, I. B. Myers chaplain, and J. T. Morehead surgeon. All of these men are now deceased.

For sometime the construction of an electric railway through the valley had been discussed. There was already a line from Parkersburg to Williamstown and also one from Sistersville to New Martinsville. Electric lines were then regarded as the most convenient method of travel all over the country, being more cheaply built and maintained than steam roads, besides being able to overcome steeper grades. It was confidently expected that a continuous line would be made from Parkersburg to Wheeling. Two rival companies were formed, the Ohio Valley Electric Railway, headed by P. H. Anderson of Friendly, and the Williamstown & Moundsville Railway, of which G. A. Wagner was president. The rivals fought strenuously for the right of way, and in October Anderson's company erected a few poles along Dewey avenue, promising that the road would be completed in 1904. There the matter ended, the death of the project perhaps hastened by the persistent reports of the growth of a new vehicle of travel called the automobile, which had already made its appearance in several parts of the United States and had been seen by a few of our citizens.

This year the Stanleys moved their store into its present quarters in the Odd Fellows building, and, deciding to specialize in dry goods and clothing, disposed of their grocery stock to Amos Smith and his son, E. R. Smith, who bought the old Stanley building. In 1908 E. R. Smith, who succeeded to the business after the death of his father, moved the old building to Third street and erected the large brick now occupied by the St. Marys Hardware Company.

A great step in the development of St. Marys was the opening of the Fairplains Addition. This comprised about thirty acres on the upper bottom, purchased from the Gallaher heirs by the St. Marys Improvement Company. It was marked off into town lots and at an auction held November 5 by Colonel Morrow of Pittsburgh 130 lots were sold at prices ranging from $110 to $410.

On March 30 died James W. Williamson, near Arvilla, at the age of 94. Captain Williamson was a recruiting officer in the Civil War, a member of the Wheeling convention, a member of the first State Legislature, and served for sixteen years as justice of the peace.

In 1904 Dinsmoor & Company bought the oil properties of Mallory & Stewart. The firm then was composed of John C. Dinsmoor, his two sons, James D. and Lyell E. Dinsmoor, his nephew, L. D. Dinsmoor, and Dr. E. M. Sellers. At about the same time a French oil company, under the title of Compagnie Francaise de Petrole, headed by Charles Verbeke, entered the field. This company bought most of the holdings of M. L. Zahniser, but was involved from the beginning in unfortunate litigation. Captain Leon Goetgeluck, a former Belgian officer, was in charge for about a year and was succeeded by Marcel Daly.

In this year the Presbyterians organized a church society, the result of a meeting held at the home of Dr. R. W. Douglass on January 16. The organization was completed at a session held in the Episcopal church April 28, and began with a membership of eighteen. At this first meeting Rev. R. H. Rogers of Buffalo, N. Y., Rev. D. R. Francis of Parkersburg and Rev. E. A. Brooks of Waverly were present. Later the Rev. W. D. Harrell was secured as pastor. The society held services in the Episcopal church several years, but in 1912 began the erection of a building of their own on Washington street. The corner stone was laid October 10 of that year, with Masonic ceremonies, Frank Wells Clark of New Martinsville acting as Deputy Grand Master. An address was delivered by Rev. G. I. Wilson and a poem by Jonn S. Hall. On September 21, 1913, the building was dedicated by Rev. G. I. Wilson and Rev. E. V. Black. The cost of the structure was $3,800.

Within the last two years an addition has been made at a cost of more than $6000, providing a large school room and hall for general purposes.

The first primary election held in the county was that of the Republican party on August 16, 1904, at which 762 votes were polled. The same party was successful in the November election, getting every office. C. P. Craig was elected to the Legislature, Lafayette Pethtel county commissioner, M. O. Swallow sheriff, M. L. Barron prosecuting attorney, T. R. Birkhimer assessor and F. M. Triplett surveyor.

Another attempt was made in this election to get a bond issue for a new court house, but it was again defeated. At the same time a proposition to move the county seat to Belmont was voted upon and defeated. It was a bitter fight between the prohibitionists and the saloon men. The former vowed that they would oppose any court house proposition so long as license was granted in the town. and when the question of a new building was again submitted in May of the following year it was defeated by a vote of 965 to 224, so the commissioners were forced to be content with making such repairs as were absolutely needed.

In January, 1905, Joe Williams, editor of the Leader, was installed as postmaster in St. Marys. The question of paving Second street came to a head, and the council awarded the contract to C. Skidmore of Parkersburg at $1.18 per square yard. The work was completed late in the Summer. This was the first street paving done in the town.

In March came the annual Spring freshet. one having occurred every year since the high water of 1901. The crest of the flood reached St. Marys March 23, and was forty feet above low water mark. All trains on the railroad were stopped for several days.

A notable advance was made this year in the valuation of real estate in the county. The revaluation was made by James A. Oldfield as commissioner, who made it $2,593,293, more than double the amount reported in 1904, which was $1,064,168.

A few important business changes had been made recently. In 1904 Mrs Ella Watts had opened her china store; early in 1905 Alexander Russell started a machine shop; N. J. Williamson & Co. bought the Palmeter and Weber buildings, consolidated them and opened a general store; C. A. Wernecke came from Middlebourne and started a jewelry store, and the Sparks Hoe Company was organized, with a shop along the railroad above town. In a year or two this company shared the fate of other enterprises that were not backed with sufficient capital, although the product was a very good and substantial one.

The year 1905 marks the forming of the first social club for men in the county—the Arbutus Club, having rooms over the Simmons grocery. The object was purely for enjoyment, and the room was fitted up with games of various sorts. However, it served as a bond among the enterprising young men of the community and they were successful in bringing several plays and operas of a higher class to the Auditorium.

The progress of the times was also shown in two other matters in the same year. One was the introduction of the phonograph, then a wonderful novelty, but offered to the public at low prices, so that in a short time it would seem that almost every house in the county possessed this means of amusement. The other was the coming of the automobile, the exhibition to our people of the first machine of this kind being due to George B. Phillips, who brought a Yale car to the city—a manufacture that has never been heard of since. This vehicle had no top, no doors, no windshield, no headlights; but it could move of itself, and was long the admiration of the public. The roads then were miserable and could only be used by such a machine in dry weather. On one occasion Mr. Phillips drove in it to Marietta and it happened that he started from the landing on the other side of the river just as the steamboat Virginia was leaving St. Marys for the same port. The time of the trip is not remembered, but the Virginia was far from being a fast boat, yet Mr. Phillips is still proud of the fact that he reached the Green street corner of Front street in Marietta just before the steamboat pulled in to the wharf.

In the following year John C. Dinsmoor brought the second car to town. By 1909 the number of cars in the county had increased to seven, and it is true that, proportionately to the population, Pleasants county exceeded nearly every other rural county in the Union in the number of its cars. In 1914 a census showed that there were thirty-five cars owned in the county, and the business indicated such signs of growth that in that year W. E. Clovis and R. H. Triplett formed a partnership for the purpose of handling Ford and Overland cars and doing repair work. It was not long before other garages sprang into existence, and the number of car owners was so large in 1921 that an automobile association was formed, with James D. Dinsmoor as president and George R. VanValey as secretary. At present there are about eight hundred motor cars in the county.

CHAPTER XIV

INDUSTRIAL ENTERPRISES

In 1906 the price of crude oil was fairly steady, starting at $1.58, rising to $1.64 in May and declining to the former price at the end of the year. While drilling proceeded steadily in all parts of the county, the leading activity was in what became known as the Spindle top field—the name being an adaptation of the "Spindel Kopf" of the South African Boer war. This was in the neighborhood of Federal postoffice, between McKim and Sugar creeks, and credit for its development is usually awarded to Edward W. Frink. Quite a number of fine wells were obtained, perhaps the best being that drilled by Edmunds and Schauwecker on the Schultz farm, which started in at 250 barrels.

Spindle Top may be classed as the last of the great pools that have been developed in Pleasants county. Although since there have been fine developments on the head of French creek, in the Maxwell neighborhood and about Cave Run, none of these have created the general excitement and interest that accompanied the opening of the Spindle Top section.

Yet, notwithstanding the rich strikes, it was evident that the oil business alone was not sufficient to insure steady prosperity to this section, so a meeting of the business men was held at the court house early in January to discuss means by which industries could be located here. It was felt that the high price of natural gas a fuel was a great obstacle. The lowest price offered by the River Gas Company to factories here was 12 cents per thousand cubic feet, while in other towns in the State the price was so low as five cents per thousand. A committee composed of John R. Stanley, M. O. Swallow and W. C. Dotson was appointed to investigate, but no report seems to have been made.

The matter of good roads also came before the people this year. It was yet before the day of the motor car, but all realised the necessity of having serviceable roads for farmers and teamsters. A meeting was held in the Auditorium on March 19, largely attended from all parts of the county. Dr. A. S. Grimm presided, and addresses were made during the day and evening by Colonel W. H. Moore, president of the National Good Roads Association, and Colonel T. P. Rickey of Missouri. A local association was formed with Dr. Grimm as president.

Property valuations in the county were mounting rapidly. The realty valuation was put at $2.621,630; personal property at $1,961,212, and public stilities at $1,695,672 —more than six and a quarter millions in all.

Ed Hammett was the only Democrat elected in November, defeating Frank Triplett for county commissioner; C. P. Craig was elected to the Legislature over W. S. Sparks; and A. L. Baker defeated Clarence T. McCullough for county superintendent.

The contract for paving Washington street from Second up the hill to Fourth street was let to C. Skidmore of Parkersburg for $6.101.18.

The growth of the congregation of the M. E. Church made a larger building necessary. The old one was removed and the corner stone of the present brick edifice laid May 22 by Elder S. P. Crummett of Parkersburg. The building was erected by C. S. Booth of Sistersville at a cost of $8,600, and was dedicated November 18 by Elder Crummett and Dr. Arbuthnot of Clarksburg. A large basement for church social purposes has been completed since then.

Rev. M. F. Kiger was pastor of the Baptist Church, Rev. C. A. Isner of the M. P. Church, Rev. J. P. McDonald of the Presbyterian Church, Rev. C. A. Dowell of the Episcopal Church, and Rev. J. H. Spence of Parkersburg of the United Brethren Church.

Members of the G. A. R. in 1906 were George W. Meanor, Thaddeus Oldfield, Henry Howell, William R.

Shepherdson, John B. Oldfield, Samuel White, Joseph Kiggins, George W. Dinsmoor, Esau P. Scott, William H. Cooper, Abner C. Virden and John Boley.

On New Year's day, 1907, a meeting of the members of the Church of Christ was held to consider building a church at this place. C. T. McCullough was chairman and H. L. Riggle secretary. It was proposed to buy the L. S. Varner lot on Second street adjoining the Bills farm, now owned by A. H. Stanley, but finally the location on the corner of Dewey avenue and Second street was selected. The ground was purchased from the Gallaher heirs, and the building erected in 1909, the dedication taking place October 10, Evangelist J. M. Caleb officiating.

Opponents to the saloons were not inactive. They succeeded in getting a bill through the Legislature striking out the excise clause in the St. Marys charter, but their triumph was brief, for the courts soon decided that in certain cases, such as existed in St. Marys, city councils had the right to grant saloon privileges, irrespective of the county commissioners. However, the fight was continued, and when in the following year the council granted license to August Martin, the prohibitionists obtained a temporary injunction, which was dissolved by Judge Homer B. Woods on the ground that under the law the council was within its rights.

Again, in 1911 a bill was passed in the House of Delegates taking away from the council the privilege of granting saloon license, but failed to pass the Senate for the peculiar reason that the Legislature had not the power to amend the charter of any town of less than 2,000 population. However, in 1912 the temperance people won in the city election, and saloons ceased to exist in St. Marys on June 30 of that year, two years before the State prohibition amendment went into effect.

Rev. E. D. Fellers. who was pastor of the M. E. Church, became interested in the need of an organization at Clay Point, together with a place of worship. Lloyd Bailey donated the ground and the old M. E. Church in St. Marys was torn own and rebuilt at that place. The church was dedicated November 17 by Rev. S. S. Klyne and Rev. E. D. Fellers.

In the Summer of 1908 there was a long drouth, the river getting lower than it had ever been known. and Middle Island creek had dwindled so that in several places it could be stepped across. The first rain fell on October 1.

The Republicans won most of the county offices in the November election, E. C. Goodno being elected to the Legislature, R. L. Griffin clerk of the county court, W. R. Carson clerk of the circuit court. W. E. Clovis sheriff, I. E. Brammer assessor and F. M. Triplett surveyor, while the Democrats got G. D. Smith for prosecuting attorney and J. R. Mason as county commissioner. William H. Taft for President received a majority of 66.

In 1909 a new industry sprang up along the river. This was the gathering of mussel shells to be shipped to pearl button factories. Not only in gathering shells was there profitable employment, but it was found that sometimes the shell fish contained pearls of considerable value, several being obtained that were priced at one hundred to one hundred and fifty dollars.

There was a possibility that a factory might be established here where the shells were so abundant. so the Board of Trade opened a correspondence with Harvey Chalmers & Sons of Amsterdam, New York, who owned a number of factories in the Ohio Valley region. The negotiations resulted in the erection of a button factory here. The sum of $4,000 was donated by the citizens for purchasing the site along the railroad in the north end of town and for the erection of the buildings.

Early in 1910 the factory was in operation. employing a number of workmen who cut out the blanks, which were shipped to Amsterdam to be finished. The factory afforded employment for from fifty to one hundred men at good wages, the work being reasonably steady the year round. However, this factory is now a thing of the past. Acids released into the upper waters of the Ohio softened the shells, utterly ruining them for the purpose of button-making, and, in addition, it is said that deepening the water of the river has prevented the propagation of the shell fish. This theory is based on the fact that the mussels lay their eggs in shallow water, preferably on sandy or shingly bars, where they may be hatched by the warmth of the sun. Deepening the water by making a nine-foot stage has covered the bars so that the sun's rays cannot penetrate it to warm the eggs, and as a result mussels are rapidly disappearing. Shipping the shells from western streams was too costly, so the company was compelled to close the works here, and early in the Summer of 1928 the factory was shut down permanently.

The bridge over Middle Island Creek at Arvilla had become unsafe, owing to a defective pier, making it necessary to rebuild. This work was done this year by the York Bridge Company at a cost of $4.400, while W. A. and J. B. Wilson rebuilt the stone work for $4.000. This bridge is very important to all residents in the upper end of the county, and especially helpful to the oil operators.

On June 3 was laid the corner stone of the M. E. Church South at Eureka. Grand Master Frank Wells Clark of New Martinsville laid the stone according to the Masonic rites, and the principal address was delivered by Clyde B. Johnson. Other speakers were Rev. J. H. Jackson, who had been in charge of the St. Marys circuit more than fifty years before and was now the presiding elder, and Rev. W. M. Givens of New Martinsville.

Another building of the same denomination was started at Sugar Valley. the corner stone being laid September 27.

The county went Democratic in the November election, only one Republican being elected—C. L. Farnsworth, who was chosen county school superintendent over C. M. Bailey. Robert L. Pemberton was elected to the Legislature, Marion Hart county commissioner for the long term, and John R. Shingleton commissioner for the short term.

The charge for natural gas to domestic consumers as fixed in 1898 was 20 cents per thousand cubic feet with a discount of two cents per thousand if paid by the tenth of the month. In July, 1911, the Hope Gas Company, which had bought the franchise of the River Gas Company, served notice that the rate thereafter would be 22 cents with a rebate of two cents, making the price twenty cents net. The council through its attorney, G. D. Smith, objected to the increase and obtained an injunction from Judge Nesbitt of the First Circuit. The gas company appealed to Judge Homer B. Woods of this circuit to dissolve the injunction, but the application being dismissed, the company carried it up to the Supreme Court, which also decided against the company, holding that the old franchise rate still held.

In the meantime Dinsmoor & Company, declaring that they would furnish gas at the former rate, applied for a franchise to lay gas lines within the limits of the city, and the privilege was granted.

In 1919, the terms of the former franchise having expired, the Public Service Commission fixed the rate to the domestic consumers in St. Marys at 23 cents net, but that 28 cents net should apply to the city water works.

Many have forgotten the warm weather of 1911. The average temperature was higher than that of any other year since the weather bureau began keeping a record, forty-two years before. The warm wave extended all over the northern hemisphere, and set scientists to disputing and the commonalty to wondering what great change was taking place in the solar system. Many attributed it to renewed activities in the sun, while others thought the internal fires of the earth had a great deal to do with it. But the long hot drouth ended August 17, and from that time on copious rains fell and the unusual spectacle of high water in September was the result.

The city school was growing rapidly, almost every year the board of education finding it necessary to employ an additional teacher. In the Fall of 1911 the teaching corps consisted of C. N. Wagner, principal, Dan B. Fleming, assistant, Lucy Stacy, Effie Gorrell. L. S. Campbell, Nina L. Ashley, Edith Gallaher, Glenna Dotson, Lilian Cotton, Opal Core, Ethel Flesher and Hattie Graham. In the high school department two literary societies were formed—the Hall and the Pemberton—and an organized system of athletic contests also begun. The school was made so popular that the district school of Green Run was abandoned.

In the following May the first field meet of the high school was held in what was then known as Weber Park, the local contestants defeating the Ravenswood team by a score of 68 to 28 points. Athletic enthusiasm waxed strong, the St. Marys school taking a high rank, in 1915 winning second place in the State field meet at Charleston, and in 1917 taking first place in the Ohio Valley Athletic Meet. In literary contests with other schools the local boys and girls were also generally successful, and all these added much to the honor of the school, increasing the attendance so that a new school building became imperative. On June 5, 1917, while the World War was going on, the proposition for a new high school building was laid before the voters of Washington district and was carried by a vote of 322 to 194.

The board selected five acres from the farm of James and Solomon Bills, adjoining the city, and after some litigation effected the purchase for $8,000 in 1919, and completed the building in tne Fall of 1920.

Going back to the year 1911, the hottest Summer of which there is record, it will be best remembered, perhaps, because of the extraordinary quantity of chestnuts produced by the native trees. It is possible that the warm, dry Summer had something to do with it. Farmers throughout the valley hauled the nuts to market by the wagon load. For some time they were paid the low price of 75 cents per bushel, but the market became so glutted they could not even obtain that later, so they carried the nuts back and fed them to their hogs.

Robert Alexander Gallaher died at his residence in St. Marys August 12, 1911, aged 68 years. He was a son of Silas Gallaher, and came here from Marshall county in the early fifties, practiced law, was county surveyor and editor of the Oracle for many years. He was probably the best read man in the county.

During the Summer of 112 the feasibility of establishing an oil refinery in St. Marys was talked of. Several public meetings were held and addressed by gentlemen from Pennsylvania. On October 31 a company was organized at Sistersville, to be known as the High Grade Petroleum Products Company, and incorporated with a paid up sub-

ROBERT ALEXANDER GALLAHER

scription of $20,000 and a limitation of $300,000. L. A. Reed, of Bruin, Pa., was elected president, R. W. Douglass vice president, E. A. Sayre secretary and L. P. Walker treasurer. The superintendent of the pipe lines was W. F. Miller.

The construction of the refinery on the Barkwill land south of the court house was begun in February, 1913, and also the work of laying pipe lines to several sections of the county. The first run of oil was made December 9 from a tank of the West Virginia Limited Oil Company on Middle Island, a premium of five cents being paid for the oil, the Standard price being $2.50 per barrel. Distillation began January 1, 1914, the capacity of the works being then 400 barrels daily. Co-incident with the opening of the refinery came a steady fall in the price of oil, until at the end of the year it sold only for $1.35. In July of that year the company went into voluntary bankruptcy, naming Evert L. Burk receiver.

The works were sold by decree of the court in March, 1916, to the Reno Oil Company of Sistersville, and in the following month turned over to the Ohio Valley Refining Company, organized by T. B. Gregory, H. T. Crawford and S. Miller of Emblenton, Pa., James D. Berry of Oil City, Pa., and S. G. Messer of Sistersville, with a capital of $250,000. Mr. Messer was chosen president and J. P. Flynn vice president, while P. S. Tarbox was put in charge of the works as manager. Under this organization the business has succeeded and has become one of the best finanrial assets in the community.

The company has always taken a great interest in the welfare of its employes, a notable instance being the erection of several handsome dwellings on Sycamore street. After the retirement of Mr. Tarbox the position of super intendent has been filled by J. Bruce Northrop, under whose administration many considerable improvements have been made in the machinery as well as several large additions to the plant, making it now one of the largest in the United States.

In the election of 1912 the county went solidly Republican as to county officials. A. B. Flesher was elected to the Legislature, S. V. Riggs sheriff, M. L. Barron prosecuting attorney, J. W. Grimm commissioner, W. H. Myers assessor, Guy C. MacTaggart school superintendent, and John Triplett surveyor. It was the year in which the National Republican ticket was divided, Theodore Roosevelt running for President on an independent platform against W. H. Taft, the regular nominee. In this county Taft received 493 votes, Roosevelt 364, and Woodrow Wilson 796.

In the same election the vote on the prohibition amendment to the State constitution was submitted. There were 1251 votes for the amendment and 303 against. In Lafayette district there were only two votes against it.

Oliver Gorrell died May 15, aged 73 years. He had taken a prominent part in the affairs of the county, served as sheriff, two terms as member of the Legislature, and is especially remembered as having repeatedly striven to organize the farmers.

Another distinguished citizen who died in October was Francis M. Triplett, aged 75; a member of one of the oldest families of the county, many times elected surveyor and serving one term as county commissioner. He was a major of the Pleasants County Home Guards during the Civil War, and served as lieutenant colonel of the regiment which marched to Ellenboro in 1863 to repel the threatened attack upon Harrisville by the Confederates under General Jones. The Confederate forces were withdrawn without an engagement.

On March 29, 1913, rose to its height the greatest flood that has occurred here within the memory of man, following a series of great storms from the West. It was immediately preceded by a terrible storm which had cost the lives of more than two hundred people in Illinois and other mid-western States, and which brought a downpour of rain over Ohio and Western Pennsylvania, approximating eleven inches within twenty-four hours. The Alleghany and all other streams from the north poured a sudden flood into the Ohio. Fortunately the rainfall was slight in West Virginia and there was no snow in the mountains. This led old residents who had passed through several floods to say, even when the waters had risen almost to the height of the flood of 1884, that it could not equal the high water of that year. But they had not taken into full consideration the tremendous rainfall and the large drainage of the Muskingum river, whose system covers more than half of eastern Ohio.

The water poured out of that tributary into the Ohio at Marietta in such volume and force that its current was only stayed by the West Virginia shore, and people at Williamstown said that the cross-current stood like a wall, several feet above the waters of the Ohio. It was this damming and holding back of the latter river that raised it to such an unusual height to a distance of about fifty miles up. Farther up, the mark of the 1884 flood was not reached, but the crest increased rapidly towards the mouth of the Muskingum. At St. Marys the height was four feet and three inches above that of 1884. All the ground of the lower town was covered, but there were so many homes on the higher bottoms that everyone was taken care of comfortably; and, in fact, while the losses were great, they were much more easily borne than the comparatively slight damages done in the former flood, and in an incredibly brief time after the water subsided the normal condition of the town was restored.

The water of the city was pumped directly from the river without filtering, and was usually so filthy that it could not be used for domestic purposes, while the gritty sand made sad havoc with the pumps. In the latter part of 1913 a well was drilled on the water works lot, and at a depth of 95 feet a flow of 35 barrels an hour was obtained. This encouraged the council to submit a bond issue of $12,000 for the purpose of putting down more wells and also to construct a reservoir. The question carried by a vote of 145 to 89 on March 12, 1914, and that Summer Foreman & Putnam of Marietta were awarded a contract to construct a reservoir with a capacity of 380,000 gallons on the hill southeast of the court house for the sum of $6,894. The work was done in the following year, other wells were drilled and an air pressure system installed. It was not, however, until several years had passed that the river water was entirely abandoned. Now there is an abundant supply of wholesome water from the wells, pronounced by State authorities to be perfectly safe.

With the coming of more automobiles there was an increased demand for better roads, and acting on a petition the county commissioners submitted a bond issue of $60,000 for Washington district on December 16, which included the town of St. Marys. The vote was favorable beyond expectations, being 368 for and only 58 against. W. C. Dotson, R. L. Pemberton and J. L. Hissom were appointed by the Board of Trade to select an advisory committee to act with the county commissioners in building and paving the roads, and they selected T. J. Taylor, E. R. Smith, James D. Dinsmoor and W. R. Carson, this making a very fair representation over the district.

The river road above the creek was not included in the proposed work, but the commissioners wisely removed it from the low and dangerous location along the bank of the Thoroughfare and made it wholly above the railroad, so there should be no crossing.

Convict labor from the State Penitentiary was largely employed in grading the roads, and the contract for concreting given to W. A. Wilson of St. Marys. The work was completed to the Zadock Pethtel farm on the Ellenboro Pike, to Green Run and to Samberson's Narrows on the creek, in all nearly five miles, and October 27, 1915, Mr. Wilson reported that after finishing the work he had on hands about $9,000 in cash and machinery to the value of about $10,000. These roads are now controlled by the State Road Commission, and of the fifty million dollar bond issue of the State, Pleasants county has been awarded about $350,000. With this sum a little over a mile of concrete has been laid on the Ellenboro Pike, part of Barkwill street in St. Marys has been concreted, a covered sewer on Third street, Ellenboro Pike graded and graveled, the river road graded and graveled its entire length of eighteen miles, together with culverts, and some grading and graveling has been done on the road up Middle Island Creek to the mouth of McKim.

One of the largest expenses in constructing roads is the forming of culverts. This is especially true in Pleasants county, where there are so many small streams to be crossed. While William H. Steere of Grape Island was a member of the county court, in 1924, it happened there was a sale of the dismantled tow boats of the Pittsburgh Coal Company at West Elizabeth, Pa., and the commissioners seized the opportunity to buy the boilers for the purpose of converting them into road culverts. These huge boilers ranged from 14 to 30 feet long and were 38 and 40 inches in diameter. They were shipped to the landing above Raven Rock in care of H. A. Carpenter and there cut to the proper sizes by W. F. Adkins. They were then hauled to different parts of the county.

Mr. Steere informs me there were six boilers from the steamer Boaz, seven from the Tom Dodsworth, seven from the Raymond Horner, three from the Duquesne, two from the Sam Clarke, and two "nigger" boilers from the Alice Brown, together with steam drums, mud drums and other "nigger" boilers. These boats, especially the first three, will be vividly remembered by older inhabitants of the valley as the best of their class, towing acres of coal in barges down the wide bosom of the Ohio on every rise of the river.

The county commissioners have taken the Cow Creek road out of the water and made a good grade for it on the north side of the creek, and the Bens Run and Calf Creek roads have been improved by grading; while the districts of McKim and Lafayette have united in levying a special tax to improve their roads. So it would seem that the time is near at hand when any part of the county may be easily reached in any sort of weather.

The year 1913 was marked by two business changes. In February the St. Marys Hardware Company was organized by W. E. Clovis, R. H. Triplett and the latter's son, H. C. Triplett, and was established in the three-story brick block erected by E. R. Smith. In the following year Mr. Clovis and the elder Triplett withdrew to establish an automobile business, and the hardware company was continued by the three Triplett brothers, Harry, Ralph and Guy, later branching out into other lines.

In June John L. Hissom bought the interest of his partner, Stephen M. Riggs, in the lumber mill, and moved it to its present location on Barkwill street, near the court house. Mr. Riggs was the last of the stalwart sons of Isaac Riggs, mentioned so often in the diary of Thomas Browse. For the greater part of his life he had dealt in coal, cross ties and lumber, but after his withdrawal from the partnership with Mr. Hissom he lived quietly at his home on Third street, until his death at the age of 83, September 24, 1926.

On the first of August O. C. Sweeney took charge of the postoffice of St. Marys, which was enlarged by adding to it the store room on the corner which had been occupied by H. J. Williamson.

It is worthy of menton that the deadly rattlesnake had not yet been exterminated in Pleasants county, for in July of the year 1913 Arch Nichols killed one on Carney Fork of Cow creek which measured four feet eleven inches in length. The rattlesnake is said to avoid the haunts of man, but unfortunately that is not the rule of the copperhead, whose poison, while not so deadly, causes great and long continued suffering.

The necrology of 1913 includes several men of prominence. On January 7 died George W. Dinsmoor, an oil operator, and although only 66 years old at the time of his death, was a veteran of the Civil War.

Frederick Ruttencutter, aged 94, died May 1. The son of a German immigrant, Daniel Ruttencutter, his entire long life had been passed in this neighborhood and he was known far and wide for his genial qualities.

James M. Ruckman, once a county commissioner, died at his home on Cow Creek June 21, aged 68; and William M. Curtis, who had also served as county commissioner, died at his home on Middle Island creek July 14, at the age of 66. Martin L. Dotson, a veteran of the Confederacy, a member of Company G, Twentieth Virginia Cavalry, died July 28 aged 67; and Greenberry Haddox died September 3 at the age of 67. The last had been very active in local affairs, and bore the reputation of being an excellent carpenter and builder. His chief work was the construction of the interior of the Episcopal Church.

The first chautauqua held in St. Marys was in July,

1914. It was the Lincoln management, with a fine six-day program, but the shortage in attendance and receipts was so large that the guarantors declined to make a contract for the following year. However, in 1916 the big tent was again pitched on the school grounds, and every Summer since has witnessed its arrival, of late years the Redpath bureau getting the contract. When the price of admission to the entire series of lectures, musical performances and plays is considered it is indeed astonishing that so much can be given for so little. Even the numbers given in the course of the high school lyceum cannot compare with it for variety and low cost.

In the Fall of 1914 a fund was raised by citizens of the town and from the country to aid in bringing to the county C. Claude Anderson, the first County agricultural agent. It may be recalled that at first there was considerable opposition to such an official, but as time passed on and the effects of a competent helper were realized, that feeling has entirely worn away. The good work of Mr. Anderson and his successors, I. S. Middaugh, French L. Miles and G. B. McIntire has been recognized by all. With their aid the Farm Bureau has been established, organizations of farm women have been effected, boys and girls clubs and other organizations of an inspiring nature. Mr. Anderson was instrumental in bringing about the first county agricultural fair, which has been held annually since 1915, and which has repeatedly demonstrated the great farming and gardening resources of the county.

In the election of November, 1914, the Republicans won the honors for every office. Dr. J. R. McCollum was elected to the Legislature, Friend Wagner county commissioner, G. C. MacTaggart school superintendent, R. L. Griffin county clerk and W. R. Carson circuit clerk.

Of those who passed out of this life in 1914 may be mentioned Dr. Edgar Humphrey, dentist, whose death occurred September 9 at the early age of 35; also Miss Nannie P. Hall, who died the following day, aged 78. She was a sister of William W. Hall and John S. Hall, and most of her life had been spent as a teacher in the public schools, in church and Sunday school work, and in the cause of temperance.

A county high school had been talked of, and in 1915 a petition was presented to the county court asking for a bond election for that purpose. The court ordered the election, the sum to be $50,000, but it becoming apparent that the majority was opposed to it, the order was rescinded. Another matter proposed and abandoned by the commissioners was that of dividing Jefferson district between Grant and Washington. This had been suggested because the low valuation of property in Jefferson would not enable the people of that district to make needed improvements in roads and schools.

The old flour mill, which has had many different owners, again changed hands early in the Spring of 1915, John B. Locke buying a third interest from Charles F. Ruttencutter, the new firm being Locke, Griffin & Carson, with Mr. Locke as manager.

H. C. Humphreys resigned as superintendent of the Washington District schools, and was succeeded by Dan B. Fleming, who held the position five years, together with the principalship of the High school, thereby establishing the record for continuance in that office.

Robert G. Hammett, aged 69, died April 7. He had long been prominent in business and political affairs, and twice had been a member of the Legislature. David Q. Steere, who had represented the Wood-Pleasants District in the Legislature, died May 25 at the age of 77, and George Kelsall, who had also served a term in the Legislature, died December 1, aged 87. He was born in Baltimore, came here in 1851 as a cabinet maker, but most of his life was spent as a merchant.

In 1913 C. A. Wernecke had installed a small dynamo in the rear of his jewelry shop on Second street, where the Central Drug Store now stands, and proposed to furnish the town with electricity. He was granted a franchise and began operating on a small scale, supplying the city with sixteen street lights, and furnishing lights to several stores and churches. Three years later his plant and franchise were bought by E. W. Mallory, for $2550. Mr. Mallory put up a concrete building on the corner of Barron and Gallaher streets, but later moved the plant to Barkwill street, adjoining the refinery. With more powerful machinery he was enabled to give good service, and the city installed boulevard lights on Second street. In 1923 Mr. Mallory sold the outfit to the Monongahela West Penn Public Service Company, which strung a high power line from Weirton to Parkersburg.

R. S. Giese of Charleroi, near Pittsburgh, came here in September, 1916, with a proposition to erect a plant for the manufacture of glassware. The idea pleased the business men, as it was apparent that a large number of persons would be employed, so the bonus required was soon subscribed and a site purchased by the citizens on the south of the refinery. The buildings were erected in the following year, and in the Winter of 1916-17 the plant began to operate, turning out fine art ware which was taken to Charleroi to be finished. It was suggested by Mr. Giese that this finishing should be done here, so as to save carriage. In 1919 the Board of Trade raised six thousand dollars and an additional structure was built. Before it was fully equipped the firm was declared bankrupt, and since then one of the buildings has been used until recently by the St. Marys Glass Company, V. J. Kuntz manager, and the other occupied by the Automatic Glass Company, whose specialty is the manufacture of electric bulbs.

Another attempt in the glass industry was the erection of a large building by the Western Glass Company on ground purchased from the Bills farm, adjoining the button factory. This building is now owned and operated by the Paramount Glass Company.

The county reversed itself politically in the election of 1916, giving President Wilson a majority of 23. The Democrats elected G. D. Smith to the Legislature, O. C. Barkwill sheriff, E. R. Smith commissioner and G. A. Reed assessor, while the Republicans got J. C. Powell as prosecuting attorney and John Triplett surveyor, neither being opposed.

Older citizens dying in 1916 include John Wesley Morgan, who passed away February 15 at the age of 79. He had served as county commissioner, was a native of Wetzel county and a member of the celebrated Morgan family descended from Morgan ap Morgan. Samuel White, a veteran of the Civil War, died October 19, aged 77, and on December 30 died Mrs. Mary Brooks, on French creek, reputed to have reached the age of one hundred. It is said of her that up to within a short time of her death she attended to her household duties with the regularity and ability of most women only half her age. She affords an instance of the wonderful longevity sometimes attained in this section, many having passed the age of ninety and a few reaching that of one hundred.

In July of 1917 Hoily Simmons, who had been engaged in the grocery business in St. Marys for nearly twenty years, sold his stock to Arch Way, and moved to Point Pleasant. Another business change of the year was the purchase of Wm. H. Hague's drug store by John McComas, who in a few years moved it from the Grimm building into the handsome brick block adjoining the W. H. Guth block.

Thomas H. Hart, a son of one of the oldest settlers, died February 24, aged 72 years; Jonathan Powell, a leading farmer of Lafayette district, died March 16, aged 85; George D. Stout, aged 77, who had served a term as assessor, died March 26; and James M. Hammett, aged 86, a soldier of the Confederacy under Stonewall Jackson, died December 14.

The numberless activities of the great World War engaged the attention of our people in the years 1917 and 1918, and the latter year was especially bare of business enterprises. The necrology includes Edward Nellis of Cloverdale, who died January 8, aged 75; Rodney Reynolds of St. Marys, a son of Daniel Reynolds and Sarah LaRue, dying January 19, at the age of 86; I. Bud Smith of Green Run, who died January 23, aged 80; William E. Hammett, a former assessor, died April 19, aged 85, and Dr. Joseph B. Watson of St. Marys, who had practised medicine many years, died October 18, at the age of 79. He was a fervent member of the Methodist Protestant Church, and had rarely missed a conference since his early manhood.

In 1919 was built the new bridge over Bull creek, the counties of Wood and Pleasants uniting in its construction. The great war was now over, and the steady growth of St. Marys seemed to warrant a general plan of home building. For that purpose the St. Marys Improvement Association was formed in September, with Oran C. Ogdin as president, E. L. Burk secretary and George B. Phillips treasurer. Land was bought from the Samuel Barkwill farm adjoining the refinery, and five small cottages erected, also two or three larger houses on Barkwill street. These homes were soon sold on reasonable and easy terms, but the Association, organized solely for the purpose of helping the community and not with the design of profit, decided to abandon the project, and a few years later sold the remaining lots at public auction.

The feasibility of an ice-making plant was broached, and as the service in this line from other cities seemed inadequate, a company was formed by Charles F. Ruttencutter and Oliver C. Barkwill for the purpose of handling coal and manufacturing ice, but later these two projects were separated into the St. Marys Coal Company and the St. Marys Ice Company, to which was added the St. Marys Milling Company. To take care of these several enterprises a large brick building was erected adjoining the railroad yard, on Gallaher street, in which the equipment for the manufacture of ice was installed and to which also the machinery of the old flour mill was removed. Later Mr. Ruttencutter withdrew from the firm to take care of the furniture and undertaking business which he bought from O. C. Ogdin in the Fall of 1925, the management of the flour mill was taken over by C. L. Douglass, the ice business by J. R. Locke and sons, and the coal business by O. C. Barkwill.

Death made sad havoc among the older citizens this year. The first to succumb was John Schauwecker, January 4, aged 74. He was a native of Germany, but for forty-nine years had resided in St. Marys, where he operated a tannery until it was destroyed by fire, and after that engaged successfully in the oil business.

Other deaths noted are those of George A. Locke, February 19, aged 68; Reverend John R. Shingleton, August 28, aged 87, for many years an elder in the Baptist Church, serving as a county commissioner, and prominent in business matters; Esau P. Scott, August 9,

JOHN R. SHINGLETON

aged 74, a veteran of the Civil War and formerly a boat builder, contracting for the building of barges for the firm of Jones & Haines in the prosperous days of that company; Abraham Samberson of Broad Run, September 14, aged 65, a native of Philadelphia, whose mother, buried in the old Samberson cemetery, died at the age of 104; Amos Wagner of Hebron, October 27, aged 66; James Patterson, November 17, aged 80, a son of Colonel Robert Patterson; James E. Robinson of Cloverdale, November 19, aged 82 and Theodore W. Hanes, November 28, aged 78, a veteran of the Civil War.

Early in 1920 the Auditorium was sold by W. C. Dotson to H. H. Robey of Spencer, who made it one of his chain of motion picture theaters. George R. Clarke was appointed County Road Engineer, succeeding L. V. Carpenter, and the making of roads was put upon a purely scientific basis.

This was a census year, and Joseph M. Murphy of Parkersburg, supervisor for the Fourth District, appointed Arch B. Hammett, O. C. Childers, W. D. Williamson, Isom H. Mott, Fred A. Minter and Frank J. Barron as enumerators of Pleasants county. Reference has been made elsewhere in this work to the decrease in population and the causes, but for the purpose of comparison a table is here given of the three enumerations of 1900, 1910 and 1920:

	1900	1910	1920	Decrease
Grant District ..	1214	959	951	263
Jefferson	1415	1190	969	446
Lafayette	953	791	649	304
McKim	1281	1123	791	490
Union	1901	1605	1427	474
Washington	2581	2406	2592	* 11
	9345	8074	7379	1966
St Marys	826	1368	1648	* 822

* Increase.

It will be noted that the population in every rural district decreased, while that of Washington in which St.

Marys is situated, showed a slight increase, and the population of St. Marys had almost doubled. The large increase in the population of the city in the first decade is accounted for by the enlargement of its corporate boundaries. There is little doubt that the census of 1930 will show that the city has a population of 2500 to 3000. At the last election, 1928, it cast considerably more than one-third of the entire vote of the county.

In the year, 1920, two more fine brick buildings were added to the city—the large garage of W. E. Clovis on Washington and Third streets and the handsome terra cotta brick of the Phillips drug store on Second and Washington. Two companies were operating just below town in getting out large grindstones to be used in grinding wood into paper pulp.

The mortuary list of the year includes John Cooper, January 7, aged 80, for seventy years a resident of the vicinity and celebrated as a fisherman; George W. Meanor, February 4, aged 73. a veteran of the Civil War and a boat builder; James L. Davis, February 23, aged 77, a farmer of Federal; John R. Mason, April 2, aged 79, once county commissioner; Isaac H. Mott, April 17, aged 75, a farmer of Union district; George E. West, July 13, aged 56, oil operator; and William H. Shingleton, September 11, aged 68, a farmer of McKim district.

In 1921 George Zipf & Son added to the number of substantial brick business blocks in the city by erecting one on Washington street, using it for their hardware business. John W. Zika bought the old city bakery and added extensive improvements, and the first attempt was made to establish an omnibus line between this city and Marietta, by E. R. Smith, with Ed Heilman as driver. The first trip was made May 16, with A. C. Imlay holding the honor of being the first passenger. The trips were soon discontinued.

An important help in postal matters was the establishment of a rural route from Hebron to the Rock Run territory. In December S. V. Riggs succeeded O. C. Sweeney as postmaster in St. Marys.

That people had faith in the future of the community was shown by the rapid sale of lots in the Morgan addition, at an auction held July 23 by the Bowman Land Company. Five and one-fourth acres had been staked off into 38 town lots and were sold for the aggregate sum of $11,440.

Deaths of the year were: John H. Rolston, February 6, aged 74; Daniel W. Wiley, March 29, aged 87, a Civil War veteran; James M. Hammett, May 28, aged 82, noted as inventor of farm implements; George W. Varner, June 15, aged 82, prominent farmer and laborer in the Church of Christ; E. M. Hall, October 27, aged 69, for many years a constable; Charles Wesley Morgan, December 17, aged 78, Civil War veteran; Joseph Wright, December 19, Civil War veteran, and Leander A. Ellis, December 15, aged 75, once school superintendent and a teacher for many years.

Very little demanding a place in a history occurred in the year 1922, but it may be mentioned that in this year the firm of Core & Smith introduced into the county that marvelous achievement of recent years, the radio, which has since then helped so much to beguile the tedious hours and also to entertain with songs, music and addresses. But by this time people were well sophisticated, so they were surprised and astonished at nothing. The radio did not create so much astonishment as did the talking over a piece of twine attached to two tin fruit cans forty years before.

There was talk of a community hall, meetings were held, committees appointed and plans discussed, but nothing came of it.

The year is remarkable because of the great mortality among the older people, and only a few of the deaths are here recorded:

Willis Park Crouse died January 4 at the home of his daughter, Mrs. R. E. Bolles, in St. Marys, aged 96, and Jerry McCune of Point Lookout died the following day, aged 89. Mr. Crouse indulged in his favorite occupation of gardening to within a year of two of his death, and Mr. McCune is remembered for his many quaint sayings, frequently sending items with the suggestion that they be published "as a matter of history."

Edward A. Sayre, for many years cashier of the Pleasants County Bank, died March 23 at the age of 68; Ephraim W. Seevers, a member of a pioneer family, died April 23, aged 87; Francis H. Morgan, a veteran of the Civil War, died at Hebron May 4 at the age of 82; Robert G. Anderson, well known as a teacher and county superintendent, died at Corona, California, June 12; John Franklin Barron, for years the leading lawyer in the county, died September 26 at the age of 66; Charles Ward Bills, merchant and farmer, died October 1, aged 84, and on December 2 died William Edwin Reed, aged 74, the first merchant in St. Marys to specialize in one class of merchandise, that being hardware.

In 1923 the merchants of St. Marys organized the Advertising Club, with the design of following the Golden Rule or Neosho plan of doing business, cultivating a greater intimacy between the rural communities and the city. The general plan was to put on special sales twice a year, each merchant advertising a certain line of goods to be sold at low prices, at the same time the club was to distribute as prizes articles of great value, and an auctioneer was to be employed to sell any articles that the farmers or citizens might wish to dispose of. With some variations this general plan has been carried out every year, with apparent success, since the first sale May 15, 1923.

Michael Eddy died at the age of 85 in February, noted as having carried on as blacksmith in his shop at Nine Mile more than fifty years; T. R. Birkhimer, aged 72, once assessor, died at Cloverdale March 31; William F. Locke, an old time teacher, died at Belmont June 7, aged 81; John S. Hall, aged 78, died September 25, and George M. Williamson, aged 88, a Civil War veteran, died November 21.

John Sebastian C. Hall, whose death is noted above, deserves rather more than a mere mention, because of his genius and his activities towards the betterment of the community. The youngest son of Samuel and Rachel Hall, born in Laporte, Indiana, but reared in Ritchie and Pleasants counties, he passed through the greater part of his life under the serious handicap of total blindness. During the Civil War, unable to enlist as a soldier because of his youth and the refusal of his widowed mother to assent, he secured employment in the army as a teamster. In Tennessee he was stricken with typhoid fever, and his recovery, after many weeks of delirium, was blemished by the bursting of his eyeballs.

JOHN S. HALL

He attended a school for the blind in Columbus, Ohio, returned to West Virginia, studied law and was admitted to the bar after an examination by the Supreme Court of Appeals, but never engaged in the practice of the profession. However, he taught school for a time and then became editor of the St. Marys Oracle, which he established. In early life he wrote a novel, which was published in the newspapers, and later he indulged a taste for poetical composition, producing a number of excellent poems which were published in book form under the title of "Musings of a Quiet Hour." The celebrity of his verses secured him the beloved designation of "The blind poet of Pleasants."

He was active in Democratic politics, a fervent advocate of temperance, and a devoted member of the Presbyterian Church. In all things it may be said he exercised his talents for the help of mankind.

The year 1924 is memorable in local annals by the building of the new court house, described fully hereafter, and by the formation of the Kiwanis Club. This organization, which has done so much to bring about a better acquaintance among the business men of the community, was formed April 28 by Jeff Bailey of Birmingham, Alabama, and R. U. Adams of Sistersville, the complete organization being effected May 1 by the election of Beryl A. Dotson as president, Dan B. Fleming secretary and Robt. L. Pemberton treasurer. The charter presentation occurred May 28 in the Methodist Episcopal Church, Kiwanians from Sistersville, Parkersburg and other places being present. This club has sponsored and supervised many movements in aid of the community, and has been especially interested in creating a good feeling between the farmers and the city. That Fall the club began the Halloween celebrations which have been maintained since, and followed that up with a community Christmas tree.

It is a pleasure also to note that a Pleasants county lad, Leroy Kohler of Willow, was selected to represent West Virginia at the National Dairy Show in Milwaukee this year, and that there he and another boy from the West were chosen as the two leading Four-H boys in the United States.

B. Franklin Standiford, aged 87, died June 13. He was a soldier in the Confederate army and had been largely interested in the steamboat trade.

In the mortality list of 1925 are Arza W. Powell, county commissioner, who died April 6, aged 63; Martin Riggs, who died July 11 at the age of 90, and Abraham R. Ruttencutter, brother of Frederick, mentioned above, who died November 24, aged 90.

CHAPTER XV

THE WORLD WAR

In 1917 the United States was drawn into the vortex of the great European war, which became designated, from the number of contesting nations, the World War. It had been going on since the first day of July, 1914, the first nations engaged being Austria and Germany on the one side against France, Russia and England on the other. Later the former powers were joined by Turkey, while Italy took sides with her ancient enemy, France.

American shipping had suffered, many American lives had been lost by the action of German submarines, until the patience of our Government was exhausted, and finally on April 5 President Wilson issued a declaration that a state of war existed between this country and Germany. Loyalty and ratification meetings were held all over the country. In St. Marys a great gathering of citizens was held in the auditorium in the evening of April 6, pledging support to the Government.

On the recommendation of the President Congress passed an act to draft soldiers for the war instead of calling for volunteers. In accordance with the plan Governor John J Cornwell of this State appointed conscription boards for each county, that for Pleasants being composed of Sheriff O. C. Barkwill, County Clerk R. L. Griffin, Dr. J. R. McCollum, William C. Dotson and William C. Butcher. Mr. Dotson was chosen president of the board and Mr. Griffin secretary.

On June 5 all male citizens between the ages of 21 and 30 were registered, the number in this county being 482. Each man was given a number, and the drawing of the numbers was done in Washington. The first drawing was

July 18, when 51 men of Pleasants county were selected for examination. The first man on the list was Herbert T. Bailey, No. 258. Physical examinations were made by the local board in August, and only one man in every four was found of such sound body that he was pronounced fit for service.

In the meantime, even before war had been declared, many young men of the United States had enlisted in Canadian regiments or had entered the navy in the expectation of seeing active service. Among the latter was Donald Core, a son of William L. Core of St. Marys and a grandson of Alfred H. Cole, a veteran of the Civil War. It happened that Core was assigned to the battleship Mongolia, under command of Lieutenant Bruce R. Ware, and it also fell to Core's lot to be a member of the firing squad on that ship which discharged the first gun fired against the enemy.

Every effort was made by the Government to fill up the quota of soldiers required, and also to utilize every resource in prosecuting the war. Every able bodied citizen, man and woman, was expected to take a part, either bearing arms, aiding in hospital and field work, or producing sustenance and supplies. To this purpose the Legislature passed a vagrancy act, which went into effect June 18. This law provided for the arrest and employment at some public work of any physically fit man who was not engaged in some useful vocation.

The Young Men's Christian Association and the Red Cross Society prepared to devote their energies in taking care of our soldiers both at home and abroad, and for that purpose requested donations of cash, assigning proportionate sums to each county. The first calls were made in June, and in each instance Pleasants county subscribed more than the amount assigned to it, giving $503.82 to the former and $4,632.16 to the latter. Societies were organized among the women in various parts of the county for the purpose of making surgical dressings and bandages, also knitting woolen caps, vests and socks to be worn by the soldiers in the Winter season. Many of these articles could have been manufactured better and cheaper with machinery, and countless thousands of them were so crudely done that they were never sent across seas, so that the time and labor were wasted. But hysteria was rampant throughout the whole country.

The first contingent of conscripted men from this county was sent on September 5 for training to Camp Lee, near Petersburg, Virginia. They were Olin S. Hissom, Arja Morgan and Ralph Core. This was five months after the declaration of a state of war. On the 19th twenty more men were sent to the same camp—Raymond L. Sunderman, Henry M. Davis, William C. Kelley, James W. Farren, Frank H. Hayes, Arland D. Wernecke, Dale Scott, Harold V. Dawkins, Grover C. Seckman, Harry C. Bailey, L. Cecil Hanes, Wesley D. Bailey, Floyd C. Abel, Paul Mercer, Ernest J. Fauss, Peter J. Kurtz, Loman D. Hadley, Fred A. Minter, Willard E. Noland and Harry K. Curtis.

A third contingent was sent October 3, eleven men going to Camp Lee. They were O. L. Gregory, Ralph Gardner, Thomas A. Robinson, Roseman L. Skaggs, Frank E. Russell, George M. Joseph, David A. Butler, Alfred O. Griffith, Samuel J. Brewer, George W. Cunningham and Noah Burga.

Besides these several had gone to the officers' training camp, Fort Benjamin Harrison, in Indiana, among them being J. C. Powell, Homer W. Grimm and Lyle VanValey. Charles Locke of Eureka had volunteered in the navy as an electrician; S. E. Outward was a machinist in the aviation corps in France, and Ralph Rife was also in France.

In October Olin Hissom was made corporal of Battery A, 314th Field Artillery, Fred Minter and Arnold Wernecke sergeants in Battery C, L. C. Hanes a sergeant in Battery D, and Corporal Floyd Abel second bandmaster of his company.

The Government needed funds with which to prosecute the war—not merely millions, but billions of dollars. To our allies we were not only giving sympathy but we were also giving money, loaning it, as it was supposed, in staggering amounts. The country was prosperous; the credit of the Government was unquestioned, and when loans were requested on what were called Liberty Bonds and War Savings Stamps the response was generous. At every call the people of Pleasants cheerfully made up more than the required quota. This was greatly aided by the rapid rise in the price of crude oil, the production of which was still the leading industry of the county. At the beginning of 1917 oil was quoted at $2.85; at the end of the year it was $3.75, going up to $4.00 in February, at which price it remained until after peace was declared.

The activities of the Government in the prosecution of the war were not limited to the field of operations, but were also directed towards a control of the citizenry. Councils of Defense were organized in every county in the United States and committees appointed to see that the rulings issued at Washintgon should be carried out. Dennis M. Gibbs of Belmont was chosen as president of the Council here, and Ross Wells secretary.

While many of these rulings were undoubtedly wise, yet some savored of hysteria. Despite the great aid that newspapers were to the Government in disseminating orders from Washington, in every instance gratuitously, they were subjected to many unnecessary restrictions, such as cutting down the size of their issues and being forbidden to send copies to persons and firms who were not bona fide subscribers. In the midst of the extremely cold weather all places of business were required to do without heat on Mondays, and limitations were placed upon food supplies, special days being set apart as "fasting days" with regard to certain sorts of food. But for the most part the people bore these regulations cheerfully, feeling that by every self-deprivation they were aiding in the war.

The Winter of 1917-18 will long be remembered as one of unusual severity, ranking as one of the three worst seasons experienced since the formation of the United States. Throughout January the temperature in this vicinity ranged about zero, sometimes going to twelve degrees below. The continuous steady cold penetrated deep into the ground, freezing water mains so that for weeks one-third of the town suffered for lack of water.

On January 29 the following recruits were sent from this county to Vancouver: Okey J. Hawkins, George N. Mercer, Bruce Cronin, John T. Cronin, Daniel P. Scadden, Jonathan F. Gilmore, James C. Sunderman, Freeman Wright, William C. Shingleton, Ode J. Samberson, Tice Harris, Thomas Sparks, Hobart Flowers, Earl Shingleton, Jacob Wells and Clyde Lancaster.

Others sent to Fort Leavenworth on January 31, were Bernard L. Wagner, Clyde M. Cunningham, Lawrence Little, Wayland F. Williamson, Clyde T. Ingraham, Roy C. Seckman, George Lane, Charles A. Cramblett, John W. Bailey, Robert B. Little, Chester A. Deems, Donald B. Riggs, Richard Little and Ira Myers.

A few days later, February 5, Otha Wilson, George C. Cox, Thomas E. Brewer, Thomas Brock, Wiley Sloan, Dewitt Poynter, Harrison Boley, Okey S. Buchanan, Dennis A. Locke, John I. Scadden and Emory B. Morris were sent to Vancouver.

Such was the patriotism of our citizens that on February 27 Pleasants county was commended by the National Food Administration as being the first county in the nation to abandon needless feasting.

The Government was rushing men across the sea as rapidly as they could receive an initial training and be supplied with arms. The large training camps were now fully equipped, the railroads had been commandeered for the easy and quick transfer of troops, and there was no confusion in the handling of recruits. In the course of a few months four more contingents of soldiers were taken from Pleasants county.

On March 4 the following men were dispatched to Camp Greenleaf in Georgia: James A. Bradford, Alpha Taylor, Ed D. Hughes, Asa C. Smith, Claude M. Bonner, Tom J. Johnson, Floyd C. Howell, Martin L. Higgins, Ola Weekly, William H. Feeney, George B. Barnhart, Everett H. Rodgers, Frank M. Bailey, Charles Anders, Homer E. Pollard and William E. Wherry.

April 25 Kenneth C. Russell, William J. Oldfield, John O. Elliott and Clarence Northcraft were sent to Camp Meade.

May 25 twenty-seven left for Camp Lee: Floyd L. Dotson, William A. Cross, Peter W. Highley, Raymond M. Meyer, Lee Wells, Michael R. Malone, George Hashman, Glenn Gatrell, Charles H. Morrell, Dan C. Markley, Howard M. Dearth, John E. Wilson, Ira C. Roby, Howard E. Hupp, William E. Horner, Donald Triplett, Abraham Ingraham, Bernard Wayne Defibaugh, William C. Matheny, Alva T. Hart, Charles H. Colvin, John L. Campbell, James H. McCullough, Leo E. Flowers, William E. Adams, Charles E. Williams and Robert E. Kester.

August 20 the following were called to the service: Samuel F. Bailey, Fred DeLong, Alonzo G. Barron, Roy Dewey Carpenter, Willard L. Graver, Ben A. Winland, John W. Riley, Henning R. Reynolds, Albert C. Mercer, Alva B. Oliver and Wiley M. Williamson.

The last contingent to leave the county departed on September 8 for Camp Lee, and comprised Clifford R. Bailey, Bishop Stewart, John William Trembley, Roy M. Gregg, Ernest Lee Wise, Hobart Pethtel, H. Eugene Carroll, Wm. R. Wright, Truman M. Gardner, Lawrence E. Dunn, George E. Cornell, Paran DeLong, James W. Ingraham, Brady Janes, Everett S. Boley, Ernest Underwood, Abe B. Samberson, Homer B. Smith, Clyde Brammer, Michael L. Eddy and Robert H. Bell.

Other Pleasants county boys who entered the service were Clarence Ankrom, Moses Adams, Harry Atkinson. John Quincy Adams, George Black, Earl B. Barker, David J. Blouir, Frank J. Barron, Earl K. Barkwill, Brady B. Barnhart, Pearle Raymond Butcher, Lawrence Brammer, Pearle Brewer, James F. Cunningham, Fred M. Cramblett, James E. Cornell, Leroy Cross, Benjamin Cumblidge, Fern Carroll, Herman Carroll, C. Allen Carson, Henry W. Campbell, Frank Cramblett, Donald Core, Henry Dearth, John Henry Dennis, Bernie Wesley Doty, Wm. C. Dotson, Jr., Roy Doty, Harry G. Dotson, Benjamin Ellis, Brooks F. Ellis, Leroy C. Fauss, Ervin V. Flesher, James Wm. Farson, Wm. Garrison, Henry C. Griffith, Kenney Ross Gardner, Roland Graver, Herbert L. Gard, Truman Greenwalt, Harley Greenwalt, Herbert Clyde Hescht, C. W. Hall, W. A. Hall, Albert P. Hoy, Harry Dean Hughes, Donald H. Harper, Benjamin H. Hines, George Haddox, Howard Ingraham, Kenneth P.

Imlay, James B. Jordan, Ernest Kester, Charles Edwin Kerns, Arthur M. Kiester, Charles W. Locke, George A. McFadden, Charles McKnight, Okey O. McKnight, Alfred W. Martin, Frank Mercer, William R. Morris, Harvey Maston, Kencil Myers, Harry H. Morgan, Harry Noland, Robert H. Outward, Stephen E. Outward, Richard V. Outward, Corda Owens, James Arthur Pethtel, Bert Patterson, Earl E. Poynter, Reese Asa Poynter, Richard Pethtel, Elmer E. Riggs, Howard C. Riggs, Ferris Riggs, Lynden E. Reynolds, Harry M. Roby, Walter Otha Robinson, Daniel Lester Ryan, George F. Roberts, Jr., Frederick W. Riggs, Arthur Rogers, Ralph A. Rife, Andrew Gale Riggs, Howard T. Sweeney, Wm. H. Simonton, Ingle S. Smith, Joseph B. Steere, Lawrence Schultz, John Randolph Seckman, Franklin Luther Tice, Howard L. Trautman, Leon Albert Tarbox, Earl Underwood, G. Wallace VanValey, Dustin Vincent, Samuel Ray White, Ronald R. Walker, Arza E. Wiley, James P. Wiley, Jesse Wright, John Loomis Watson, Clarence R. West, Leslie A. Wood, Jed C. Wilcoxen, James Winland, Homer C. Williams, Lewis James Watson and Clifford Edwin Zipf.

In addition to these several young women enlisted as "yeomanettes," proceeding to Norfolk, where they served the Government in various capacities. They were Garnet Edmonds, Ethel Smith Heilman, Bethel C. Riggs, Nellie Seckman, Estella Snyder and Martha Stanley.

The men were variously employed by the Government. Many of them were taken over sea and participated actively in the fighting; others were sent to the Northwest to get out lumber for the manufacture of airplanes, which had become a large factor in warfare, while still others were found qualified for mechanical and scientific occupations; but all, of course, were subject to an efficient and beneficial military training.

On June 27 came word that Dale Scott, serving in France, was killed by the enemy, the first victim of the war from Pleasants county. Then on August 27 came the news that Ola, son of James M. Weekly, had also been killed in battle, and not long after was received news of the deaths of Tom Johnson and Ingle Smith—the former slain on the field, the latter dying of illness. Two others who lost their lives in France were Alva, son of Randolph Hart, and Grover, son of John V. Seckman, while several were reported wounded.

A report was cabled to America on November 7 that Germany had agreed to an armistice, and there was great rejoicing throughout the country. It proved to be a false report. However, on November 11 came certain intelligence that an armistice had been signed that day, and a wave of wild enthusiasm spread over the nation. A great "Victory Parade" was held in St. Marys, participated in by people from all the surrounding country, and then came the anxious waiting for the return of the army. It seemed to take almost as long to withdraw the men as it took to prepare and send them over; but the delay was caused chiefly by arranging the details of peace, also, in the meantime, some of our men had been sent on to guard the shores of the Rhine while the treaty was being prepared. It was not until the 18th of June, 1919, that the first detachment returned. Six men, Roseman Skaggs, Owen L. Gregory, Olin S. Hissom, Ed Heilman, Floyd Abel and Ralph Core, were the first to come back, and were met at the station by a large crowd of people. Within the next week or two many others returned, and soon after all the Pleasants county survivors of the great World War were back home.

The war was ended, but the activities of the veterans of the war continued in service to their country through the organization of what is known as the American Legion. Founded somewhat after the manner of the Grand Army of the Republic, an outgrowth of the Civil War, the American Legion adopted still broader principles and more active work in the various communities in which their Posts were located. The prime object naturally was to help ex-service men, to seek out and aid those who needed assistance, but their attention was also given to the local needs of their communities.

Pleasants Post No. 79, American Legion, was organized February 22, 1920, and in the first year built up a membership of 52. In 1923 the membership fell down to only 28, but by earnest and persistent efforts it rose in 1925 to 177.

The attention of the members was called to the inefficiency of the fire fighting apparatus of the city of St. Marys, and in 1924 it was decided to make its improvement one of their objectives. They determined not only to purchase and equip a chemical fire truck but also to operate it. They commenced a series of "home talent" minstrel shows, besides of late years taking over the management of the annual county fairs. The citizens and business men of the community appreciated the motive and cheerfully co-operated, so that the Post not only purchased two fine chemical engines and motors but also was enabled to erect a two story concrete block building on Gallaher street in which to house the machines, while the second story furnished a suitable place in which to hold meetings.

On several occasions in the last three years the members of the Post, with their chemical engines, have been of great service to the city and surrounding communities, completely taking the place of the old City Fire Department, and with much greater efficiency.

THE NEW COURT HOUSE Williams, Photographer

217

CHAPTER XVI

RECENT IMPROVEMENTS

Although the population of Pleasants county has decreased about two thousand since the census of 1890, due to causes that have been related in a previous chapter, the prosperity of the people has increased materially. The truth of this is borne out by a comparison of the assessed valuation of this and neighboring counties.

Omitting the valuation of public utilities, which would really make a still better showing for this county, but which cannot be considered altogether a portion of the bona fide wealth of the people, it may be shown that the average per capita of real and personal property in Pleasants exceeds that of either Tyler or Wirt, and is only slightly inferior to that of Ritchie county; and if the personal property alone be considered, the average per capita of Pleasants is equal to that of Ritchie, somewhat greater than that of Tyler, and almost twice as great as that of Wirt.

The average inhabitant, man, woman and child, of Pleasants county is quoted on the assessor's books as possessing almost five hundred dollars in personal property, and it may be reasonably assumed that this is only a fraction of the average wealth, because of the inability to obtain complete returns and because of investments outside of the county. However, this may be taken as a fair indictaion of the general prosperity which obtains here.

Another index to the same purpose is found in the financial condition of the two local banks, each having started with a modest capital and gradually increasing, until now their combined assets amount to more than two million dollars; and the mercantile establishments afford still further proof in the fact that without a substantial citizenry they could not maintain such variety and quality of wares.

If a former resident of the county, after an absence of twenty-five or thirty years, should now return, he would find many alterations for the better, and he would appreciate the improvements more than we, who have scarcely noticed their steady growth.

He would remark upon the almost total disappearance of the many little groceries which once were strung along the highways at intervals of a few miles, supplying the needs of their immediate neighborhoods and affording convenient resting places for the slow-going travelers; their business is now taken care of by larger establishments, seated at greater distances, in which merchandise of greater varieties and better quality is handled.

He would find residents of the rural sections enjoying practically all the advantages of residing in a well organized community; more sanitary conditions in and about the houses, and a general use of telephones, whereby the people are kept in closer touch with each other and radios give them the news and amusements of the nation.

He would see a greater area of improved land, with much more attention to cultivation, with an increased air of comfortable conditions in the many outbuildings, neatly constructed and painted.

He would see children carried to school in automobiles, over roads which he avoided in his own school days because they were so rough and muddy that walking on them was difficult; and he would notice particularly that all the children are well-clad, and that the apparel of the older pupils is as modern as that of the largest population centers, in a most marked contrast to the garments worn by the preceding generation.

A large part of this change is due to better roads and the general use of automobiles, enabling the farmer and his family to travel in less than an hour the distance which formerly required a full day with the team. Thirty years ago comparatively few had ventured farther than Parkersburg or Wheeling, and one who had been at Pittsburgh or Cincinnati was regarded as a great traveler; but in these latter days motor vehicles carry increasing numbers to the most distant parts of the United States.

With this broadening of vision things are now done on a larger scale. The necessity of having good roads has become so apparent that people are no longer content with mending the mud holes of an old road with a few loads of coarse rock—they demand that the entire road be rebuilt and covered with a durable surface of cement or gravel. In October, 1925, the magisterial districts of McKim and Lafayette voted in favor of an increased levy to raise the sum of $5,000 a year for improving three sections of roads, and the county commissioners agreed to devote $10,000 a year out of the general county road fund for that purpose. The roads marked for improvement were that leading from the Ellenboro Pike down Turkey Run and up the Left Fork of French creek to the Wiley schoolhouse; that beginning at the Washington district line near the Shilling farm on Middle Island Creek and leading up McKim creek and Shawnee run, passing Pine Grove Church to Hebron; and the third section extending from the Pike at the head of Whiskey run through the village of Adlai, up Rock run and across McKim to intersect the second named road at Pine Grove Church. Much of these sections has been graded, and the creek road covered with gravel up to the mouth of Shawnee.

The road from State Road No. 2 up Cow Creek to Schultz has also been vastly improved. Formerly it followed the bed of the creek so closely that it crossed that stream at least a score of times within six miles, with not one bridge in the entire distance. Teaming was a great difficulty and motoring was often impossible. The commissioners took the road completely out of the creek, locating it on the northern side, and made a good grade all the way. Also the road up Triplett run passing the old sanitarium to Horseneck has been graded and coated with gravel.

Pleasants now has outlets on surfaced roads to the

North by way of Woodsfield and Ohio Road 8 to Cleveland; to the East over the Northwestern Pike, now known as U. S. Road 50; to the South over State Road 2, with No. 16, the Florida Short Route, nearing completion; and to the West by several roads leading out of Marietta and Parkersburg.

From the earliest times the passage of the river here has been effected by ferry. The first ferryman within our recollection was B. F. Pickens, who carried passengers over in a skiff and had a small flatboat, propelled with two oars, for wagons and cattle. For a time in the days of the greatest oil excitement a steam ferryboat was used, a typical boat of the shuttle style. The ferry rights were bought by Charles F. Ruttencutter, who made considerable improvement in the service, and finally passed into the hands of Hiram A. Carpenter, who greatly increased the capacity and service, also improving the landing on the Ohio shore, regrading and paving it and erecting a concrete retaining wall.

With better roads and many motor cars it became evident that no ferry service would be adequate to meet the new demands of traffic, and after careful consideration Mr. Carpenter was convinced that the time had arrived when a bridge was necessary. When he announced his intention of having a bridge built, the project was regarded by many with incredulity. There was already a bridge at Marietta, eighteen miles down the river, owned by the West Penn Electric Company, and another at Parkersburg, only twelve miles below that; and although both of these bridges were paying large dividends, it seemed hardly reasonable, to the doubting ones, that a third bridge, so near those two, would be a profitable investment.

But Mr. Carpenter had noticed the great increase in traffic over his ferry, and naturally concluded that if a ferry could draw traffic to such an extent the attraction of a substantial bridge would be much more effective, and he also reasoned that automobiles are getting more numerous every year. Men were stationed along the principal roads leading this way, enumerating the traffic and the "prospects," and their report was so encouraging that capital was easily interested. A bill permitting construction of the bridge was passed by Congress in February, 1927, but it was not until August that a commission of officials of the War department met at St. Marys to examine further into the feasibility of such an undertaking. The commission reported favorably to the head of the department at Washington, but the matter had to follow the regular slow routine of business so that the final approval was delayed until the first of October.

The company, incorporated as the Clarksburg-Columbus Bridge Company, was organized by electing H. A. Carpenter president and R. L. Griffin secretary. Plans of the bridge were drafted by the J. E. Greiner Company of Baltimore, being substantially the same as those of the bridge over the Ohio at Point Point Pleasant, which was then under construction. The resident engineer was J. W. Richardson of Baltimore, who had spent several years in South America on railroad construction and was engineer of the Point Pleasant bridge. The contract was let to the General Contracting Company of Pittsburgh, the work of erecting the piers being in charge of Harry Bogan; but the superstructure, or bridge proper, was let to the American Bridge Company, George Compson in charge.

Immediately material was ordered from Pittsburgh and shipped by boat, and on Sunday, November 6, the first actual work was done in excavating for the anchorage pier at the foot of George street. All through the Winter the work was carried on, although frequently interrupted by high water. The three piers and the two terminal or anchorage piers were completed in the Spring of 1928, and then the erection of the steel superstructure was begun.

Instead of using steel cables, eye-bars fifty feet long were used to suspend the bridge, this being the second structure of the kind in America, the first being the Point Pleasant bridge. The total length of the bridge including the approaches is 1902 feet; the length of the steel work is 1771 feet. The roadway is 27 feet wide, and at the highest part is 93 feet above the normal height of the river in the pool, and 40 feet above the 1913 flood. The length of the main span is 700 feet, affording ample space for the navigation of steamboats and large fleets of barges.

By reason of the enormous tensile strength of the eye-bars and the improved method of construction, this bridge is pronounced probably the strongest that spans the river. Coated with lustrous aluminum paint, when seen at a distance it bears a striking resemblance to the delicate arch of a spider's web; but its roadway, covered with two and one-half inches of amesite, feels as solid as if one were walking or riding over a hard surfaced street.

The bridge was completed in time for the opening celebration on October 25, in about two weeks less than a year from the time when work was begun, November 6, 1927, and on that occasion there gathered in St. Marys the largest assemblage ever held in this county. A count was made of the number of cars entering by the several roads, and they numbered 5,326. Estimating four persons to the car, there were more than twenty thousand visitors in attendance, besides the greater part of the people of St. Marys. People within a radius of one hundred miles showed their interest by attending, and it sorely taxed the abilities of the hotels, restaurants and church societies to feed the multitude.

There was a procession of the high school bands of New Martinsville, Marietta and St. Marys, with the Citizens Band; pageants showing the progress in methods of travel both on land and water; addresses by prominent men, their voices carried by microphones to loud speakers on both sides of the river. Twin children of Mr. Carpenter, only twenty-two months old, Mary Helen and Barbara Ann, loosened the bow-knot of a ribbon stretched across the bridge, and another daughter, Rebecca, broke a bottle and christened the structure the Short Route Bridge. The celebration was closed with a fine display of fireworks at the lower point of the island, which had been cleared of trees for that purpose.

The Short Route Bridge has been hailed as the connecting link of the nearest route from Cleveland to Florida, by way of Ohio Road 8 and West Virginia Road 16; also as the nearest route from Columbus to Washington, District of Columbia, via the Northwest Pike, now U. S. Road 50. In fact, the highway from Athens, Ohio, via

Barlow, Marietta and St. Marys to Ellenboro, has been designated as North U. S. 50.

A peculiar feature of the bridge is a ramp leading from the first pier down to Middle Island, thus connecting that valuable tract directly with the main land. While almost all the island is above ordinary high water, the southern part, opposite the city, is rather low, yet the surface can be raised, at a moderate expense, by building retaining walls and filling with dredges from the river, and it could then be used either as a city park or as a site for manufactures.

Next in vital importance to making good roads and the building of the bridge was the erection of a new court house, a matter, which, as we have seen, had been agitated for many years. In 1919 it was believed that the time was ripe to again submit the matter to a vote of the people. The great European war was just ended; the allied forces had effectually broken the power of Germany and Austria, and had compelled them to accept abject terms of peace; America, entering the war at a time when it seemed that France and Italy were about to be crushed, had turned the tide, and American boys led the hosts in driving the invaders back beyond the Rhine. Proud of their achievements, the whole country anxiously awaited their return from the field of victory, apparently desirous of honoring them in every possible manner.

It was a propitious moment to make an appeal for a memorial to their courage and ability, and in Pleasants it was thought that no more fitting testimonial to them could be offered than by building a new county capitol in which the names of all those from this county who participated in the war should be inscribed and perpetuated. The returning soldiers should be greeted with a vision of work actively begun on such a monument.

A petition, signed by 132 voters, was presented to the county court on January 4, 1919, asking for a special election at which to submit a bond issue for a memorial court house. On January 27 the court issued an order for such an election, to be held March 11, for an issue of bonds to the amount of $150,000. The project seemed to meet with a favorable reception, many urged it and few openly objected, but it failed of the three-fifths vote required by the law. A majority of 589 voted for it, while 521 voted against it.

For the first time a majority of the people favored a new building, so it was apparent that the sentiment of the people had changed from the vigorous opposition of previous years, yet no further attempt was made to secure a new county building until it was made absolutely necessary "by act of God," as the old chroniclers were wont to say.

In the course of a furious electric storm on the night of July 6, 1923, a bolt of lightning struck the cupola of the old court house, partly destroying it and so damaging the entire building that Homer B. Woods, judge of the circuit, held it to be unsafe. The commissioners were compelled to choose between holding an election for the issuance of bonds or to erect a new court house and jail piece-meal from the proceeds of an extraordinary levy.

Wisely they decided to submit the matter to the people; but it was feared that a proposal for $150,000 bonds would be rejected, so the amount suggested was $100,000, a sum utterly inadequate for the completion of an appropriate structure, yet sufficient to provide for the more immediate needs of the county. The election was held on August 14, and met with gratifying support, 1083 voting for it and only 215 against it. Only four precincts gave a negative majority.

In the meantime, the offices had been moved into other buildings. Those of the county and circuit clerks and of the assessor, with all their records, were installed in the Haddox building, in which the terms of court were also held, while the sheriff's office was established in the second floor of the Phillips building. In passing, it may be said that the convenience of having the county offices in the heart of the business section of the town was frequently commented on by people having business in them.

The square on which the old court house stood had been donated by A. H. Creel, providing a reversion to his heirs or assigns in case it should cease to be used for the county building, so the commissioners did not feel justified in abandoning that site. Besides, the place is far above the reach of the highest floods; it occupies a prominent position in the landscape, being visible for miles up and down the valley, and it is venerated by history and tradition. There the people had been accustomed for many years to gather on great public occasions; many notable men had addressed them there in the stirring days of the Civil War and in political contests. It was rich in old-time memories, albeit it was difficult of access; but this objection the commissioners removed as far as lay in their power.

They purchased the property on the east, thus extending the square to Barkwill street, and they also bought two small strips on either side of the approach up the hill. This additional ground enabled them to set the new court house farther from the brow of the hill and to make a very moderate grade from Third street up, with plenty of room for a separate jail and jailer's residence, and also for the parking of cars, a very needful provision in these days.

The plans selected were drawn by Holmboe & Pogue, architects of Clarksburg, and after meeting with some disappointment in awarding the contract for building, on May 20, 1924, the bid submitted by Putnam & Foreman of Marietta was accepted. The contract called for erecting and equipping the building, except the finishing of the basement and leaving the facade and cornices plain, for the sum of $99,983.

The tasks of demolishing the old building and erecting the new were begun almost simultaneously in August of that year, and on September 3 the cornerstone was laid with imposing Masonic ceremonies by Grand Master Fred C. Steinbecker of Wheeling. The orators of the occasion were Judge Homer B. Woods of Ritchie county and Clyde B. Johnson of Charleston, formerly a resident of Pleasants.

Work was pushed so rapidly through the Winter that in the following Spring the county officials moved into the new building, all completed except the basement. The wonder is that with labor and material so high, such a structure could have been made with the small sum at the disposal of the county commissioners. To the three men then serving, Wm. H. Steere, president, and A. W. Powell and H. S. Russell, great credit is due.

CHAPTER XVII

CITY CHARTER AND COUNTY POLITICS

Like the charters of most cities in West Virginia, that of St. Marys has been so amended and re-amended that nothing of the original remains. A large portion of the time of the Legislature is taken up in amending city charters, all of which could be easily avoided by enacting a uniform classification and granting wider powers to municipal corporations. In a presumed anxiety to protect the citizens of the community, the State has placed really unwarranted restrictions upon them in its general laws, but has left an opening for a majority of legislators, who know nothing about local conditions, to direct the citizens in what they may or may not do. Hence it happens that in the recent rapid growth of our cities conditions change so suddenly and frequently that every session of the Legislature is burdened with the task of enlarging city charters.

The first charter to the town had been granted by the Legislature in 1872, but upon petition it was repealed in 1876. Four years later a charter was obtained from the Circuit Court. This charter remained in effect until 1901, when it was amended by the Legislature, enlarging the corporate limits so as to include the Gallaher and Barkwill additions, also providing for an excise board with power to issue saloon license. In 1909 the charter was again amended by the Legislature, cutting out the excise board in a vain attempt to abolish the saloons. Then in 1921 came another and most sweeping amendment.

Under a provision of the bill a referendum was made, and at the election on May 5 it was adopted by a large majority, 651 votes being cast for it and 111 against it. Under this charter, which went into effect immediately, the boundaries of the city were greatly enlarged, extending from Tannery Hollow to Middle Island Creek, embracing the two lower glass plants, the refinery, the residence of Mrs. J. W. Barkwill, the Odd Fellows Cemetery, Williams' Park, Fairplains and Billsville and the B. & O. railroad. The low bottoms between the railroad and the Thoroughfare were excluded. By this act the population was probably increased to 2,500 or 3,000, and the city gained largely in property valuation.

Three wards were created, each represented by two councilmen chosen for a term of four years, while the mayor is elected every two years. The elections were made biennial. The permeating idea was to take the city out of the hands of political organizations, and this was supposed to be effected by nominating candidates at a non-partisan convention, at which only two candidates for each office may be named, and at the polls the voter is limited to a choice of these two only. Theoretically the plan is perhaps ideal, but practically this limitation of the suffrage makes it comparatively easy for any designing body of men to gain control.

The first non-partisan convention was held in the court house May 18, I. O. Ash being chairman and H. M. Locke secretary. W. C. Dotson was named for mayor and F. F. Morgan, H. C. Williams, W. P. Kerwood, O. C. Ogdin, B. A. Locke and A. H. Neyman for councilmen, without opposition.

Three days afterward a convention of the Citizens Party was held, nominating J. H. McBride for mayor and E. J. Edmunds, C. P. Newell, E. T. Weber, Victor Scott, S. D. Snyder and William Knight for councilmen. It was held that these names could not be printed on the ballot. The election was held June 14, and the nominees of the non-partisan convention were declared elected. The new council chose R. L. Griffin as recorder and Brady Meeks as city manager.

The real bone of contention had been the management of the city water works, which had never been a paying proposition, but rather had been running the community more and more into debt. The construction of the reservoir in 1914 had not helped materially, and there seemed to be a necessity for a new plant. A committee in 1921, composed of Ira Williams, O. C. Ogdin, J. D. Dinsmoor, A. N. Powers, J. B. Northrop and C. F. Ruttencutter, reported that the wells were capable of 1100 barrels a day. By making a few minor repairs they made a marked improvement.

In April, 1924, a bond issue for $60,000 to be used in improving the water system and in liquidating old debts was defeated, 141 for it and 299 against it. But by making considerable repairs to the machinery the output was largely increased and since then no serious trouble has arisen. In order to take care of old indebtedness a bill was passed by the Legislature of 1927 again amending the charter, so that an additional levy of fifteen cents on the hundred dollars may be laid, bringing the total city levy up to fifty cents. All parts of the city are now supplied with an ample quantity of pure well water, also with competent sewerage.

Politically Pleasants county has been very evenly divided. It has been rarely the case that all the county candidates of one political party only have been elected, and never, at any time since 1894, have all the county offices been in the hands of either party. In the election of 1916, as related in Chapter 14, the Democrats carried the county except for prosecuting attorney and surveyor, but in 1918 the Republicans were successful throughout. Joe Williams was elected to the Legislature, Guy C. MacTaggart as school superintendent, Wm. H. Steere commissioner for six years, Lafayette Pethtel commissioner for four years and S. K. Lamp commissioner for two years. That was the first time since the creation of the new county court that all three commissioners were chosen at one election.

In 1920, while the county gave Harding a plurality of 208, the Democrats won three important county offices: L. C. White to the Legislature, C. F. Ruttencutter sheriff and O. C. Childers assessor. On the Republican side James D. Dinsmoor was elected to the State Senate, Henry Russell commissioner, J. C. Powell prosecuting attorney, H. F. Simonton circuit clerk and R. L. Griffin county clerk. The last named had no opposition. At this election the State Road bond issue received 1904 votes to 762 against.

The county went entirely Democratic in 1922. J. R. Locke was elected to the Legislature, A. W. Powell commissioner and Ida P. Morris school superintendent. Two years later again the county went Democratic, electing Clarence T. McCullough to the Legislature, M. L. Barron prosecuting attarney, G. A. Smith sheriff, H. L. Sigler commissioner and O. C. Childers assessor. But in 1926 there was a change in the tide. Republican majorities were cast for C. E. Fogle for the Legislature, A. J. Underwood for commissioner for the short term, R. L. Griffin county clerk and H. F. Simonton circuit clerk. The Democrats elected C. C. Emrick commissioner for the long term and Ida P. Morris school superintendent.

A curious phase of this election was that Mr. Emrick, who received the largest vote cast for the office of county commissioner, and was a candidate for the long term, was elected from Washington district, while Mr. Underwood receiving the next largest vote, was candidate for the short term of commissioner from the same district, but the law specifies that no two commissioners may be elected from the same district. It was decided that Mr. Emrick, having received the largest vote, was legally entitled to the office, and therefore Mr. Underwood was ineligible. The candidate for the short term of commissioner receiving the next highest number of votes after Underwood was Sud Powell of McKim district, and he was declared to be the legally elected commissioner.

In the early days the Democrats possessed a large majority, dominating over the Whigs and Know Nothings, agreeing generally with the leading sentiment of the South. During the Civil War, notwithstanding a strong leaning towards Unionism, the Republican party had practically no following here.

The first Republican elected to a county office was William E. Bier, chosen sheriff in 1870, at a time when there was no Republican organization in the county, and in 1873 Archimedes W. Gorrell of the same political faith, was elected school superintendent. Mr. Bier held the office of sheriff six years, and was again made sheriff in 1879, holding the office a second time for a period of six years. Mr. Gorrell was again elected in 1877, 1881 and 1885, serving a term of two years each time. During all these years the other offices in the county were held by Democrats, and not until 1894 was a Republican elected as the nominee of his party.

The first county organization of the Republicans was effected in 1884, but all the nominees were defeated in in the election. When Mr. Gorrell was elected school superintendent in the following year he ran independently, in a three-cornered race. Despite these continual reverses, the Republicans maintained a party organization, and finally, is 1894, succeeded in electing a member of the Legislature, the circuit clerk, the school superintendent and the surveyor. Since that time party successes have varied, neither of the great national parties being entirely predominant. It would be saying too much to assert that fact as the cause of the excellent record of probity that has so highly distinguished official life in Pleasants, for the true reason is probably because the county has such a small population that the character of each candidate is pretty well known to all the people, and therefore as a rule only men of good repute were put in nomination.

From various causes the political complexion of the people has changed in several districts, but for many years Lafayette has been regarded as the banner Republican district, while McKim has held the same position in the Democratic ranks. In the old days it was common to jokingly paraphrase the well-known political adage about Maine, such as "as McKim goes, so goes the county," for it was noticed that generally the majority

given by McKim was the Democratic majority in the entire
county; but long ago that saying lost its prestige.

Grant and Union districts have generally been Republican, Jefferson somewhat Democratic, while Washington
has varied considerably. In Union the change to Republicanism has been brought about, it is said, by immigration
from the neighboring State of Ohio, but it has also been
largely influenced by its nearness to Lafayette and to
Tyler county; while in Washington the effect of a transient population has been largely felt, accounting for
fluctuations in politics.

Generally speaking, it may be said that the voters of
Pleasants are independent, especially in selecting local
officials; and the voting is so close that it is impossible
to forecast an election. In registering the voters in the
last election, that of November 6, 1928 it was ascertained
that the Republicans in the county numbered 1917 and the
Democrats 1893, a political difference of only twenty-four.

However, in that election the county went overwhelmingly Republican. The total vote polled was about 3100,
showing that at least 700 voters refrained from exercising their right. Of these it is estimated that 200 were
Republicans and 500 Democrats. Hoover, the Republican candidate for President, received 528 more votes
than Smith, while Hatfield, Republican candidate for
United States Senator, had a majority of only 185 over
Neely. The Republicans got all the county offices except
prosecuting attorney and the two-year term of county
commissioner, neither of which was contested.

But it may be thankfully said that generally the results
of an election in Pleasants are accepted without bitterness, for very seldom has an able and worthy candidate
been turned down for one who is unfit. That is one
of the blessings that accompany a small and compact
community, and may serve in a manner as a compensation.

COUNTY OFFICIALS

Sheriffs.—At the formation of the county, under the
Virginia law, a sheriff was to be appointed by the gov-

ernor, who selected Moses Williamson for the position. His appointment, however, did not come until July 15, 1851, and in the meantime, the county justices, sitting on the fifteenth day of May in that year, appointed Greenberry B. Riggs as crier, his duties being also to serve processes and to carry out the orders of the court. Mr. Riggs declining the office, on May 16 the court appointed Henry C. Creel as court crier and collector, so he may be considered as the first to serve as sheriff. Beginning July 15, 1851, the sheriffs were Moses Williamson; 1852, William Dils; 1854, Hugh L. Pickens; 1858, Nathan Morgan; 1861, Robert T. Parker was elected but declined to serve and Robert McKeag was appointed crier and Leonard C. Shingleton collector; Zachariah Cain was elected September 27, 1861, but declined to serve, and on December 10 Jacob Nine was appointed crier with the duties of sheriff, while James Patterson, on January 15, 1862, was appointed collector. James N. Hanlin, who had been elected sheriff December 27, 1861, qualified February 12, 1862; 1863, Thomas Gorrell; 1866, John Kester; 1871, William E. Bier; 1876, Robert T. Parker was elected but failed to qualify, and George S. Hammett was appointed February 5, 1877, resigning December 28, 1878; William E. Bier was elected for the unexpired term, but the court decided that he was ineligible and appointed Oliver Gorrell; the Supreme Court gave an opinion favoring Mr. Bier, and he took the office in 1879, being re-elected in 1880; 1885, Daniel W. Reynolds; 1889, Ralph H. Gorrell; 1893, Daniel W. Reynolds; 1897, Alonzo B. Core; 1900, Charles H. Ambler; 1901, B. F. Riggs; 1905, M. O. Swallow; 1909, W. E. Clovis; 1913, S. V. Riggs; 1917, O. C. Barkwill; 1921, Charles F. Ruttencutter; 1925, G. A. Smith; 1929, Mont L. Bonar.

Prosecuting Attorney.—1851, William L. Jackson; 1852, John E. Jackson; 1852, Jacob B. Jackson; 1861, John A. Hutchinson; 1869, Jacob B. Jackson; 1871, William W. Hall; 1884, Robert Patterson; 1885, Aug. M. Campbell; 1889, Joseph C. Noland; 1897, C. P. Craig; 1901, Robert E. Bills; 1905, M. L. Barron; 1909, Gilbert

D. Smith; 1913, M. L. Barron; 1917, J. C. Powell; 1925, M. L. Barron; 1927, F. J. Barron.

Circuit Clerks.—1851, Rodney Hickman; 1858, Hugn L. Pickens; 1863, Rodney Hickman; 1873, John L. Knight; 1893, Earl D. Knight; 1895, R. A. Flesher; 1909, W. R. Carson; 1921, Homer F. Simonton.

County Clerks.—1851, Rodney Hickman; 1858, Hugh L. Pickens; 1863, I. H. Henderson; 1865, Josiah Powell; 1869, John L. Knight; 1891, John W. Porter; 1896, W. E. Reed; 1896, W. C. Dotson; 1909, R. L. Griffin.

Presidents of County Court.—Beginning with the year in which the county commissioners served in a purely administrative capacity, 1881, J. Randolph Seckman; 1884, Leander B. Maxwell; 1887, John R. Shingleton; 1893, Job Smith; 1895, J. W. Morgan; 1897, B. F. Seckman; 1899, F. M. Triplett; 1901, W. N. Curtis; 1903. Jacob L. Varner; 1905, Daniel R. Dunn; 1907, Jacob F. Brammer; 1909, Lafayette Pethtel; 1911, John R. Shingleton; 1913, Marion Hart; 1917, J. W. Grimm; 1917, Friend Wagner; 1917, E. R. Smith; 1918, F. F. Morgan; 1918, William H. Steere; 1919, Samuel K. Lamp; 1921, Lafayette Pethtel; 1923, William H. Steere 1925, Henry S. Russell; 1927, Sud Powell, 1929. Luther Hanlin.

Assessors.—1851, John K. Prince; October, 1851, Henry Flesher; 1852, Hugh L. Pickens; 1857, John Watson; 1861, John W. Stout; 1862, John Kester; 1864, John M. Birkheimer; 1867, Thornton M. James; 1871, John Kester; 1873, William Kester; 1877, John R. Shingleton; 1881, William E. Hammett; 1889, G. D. Stout; 1893, Alonzo B. Core; 1897, J. T. Sullivan; 1905, Theodore R. Birkhimer; 1909, Ira E. Brammer; 1913, W. H. Myers; 1917, George A. Reed; 1921, Orlando C. Childers; 1929, Porter Cox.

School Superintendents.—1851, C. W. Core; 1852, Alexander H. Creel; 1855, Granville Keller; 1856, A. H. Creel; 1864, C. J. Wood; 1865, M. Williamson; 1867, Aaron DeLong; 1868, William N. Jones; 1872, Richard Towzey; 1873, A. W. Gorrell; 1875, Clinton C. Davis; 1877, Archimedes W. Gorrell; 1889, John F. Wayman; 1881, A. W. Gorrell; 1883, E. T. Fleming; 1885, A. W.

Gorrell; 1887, L. A. Ellis; 1891, Robert G. Anderson; 1893, Coleman L. Shingleton; 1895, R. L. Pemberton; 1899, Albert W. Locke; 1907. A. L. Baker; 1911, Charles S. Farnsworth; 1912, J. H. Fleming; 1913, Guy C. Mac-Taggart; 1923, Ida P. Morris.

Surveyors.—1851, Thomas Browse; 1852, Phineas P. Feeney; 1858, Thomas Browse; 1863, Thomas D. Gorrell; 1867, Francis M. Triplett; 1869, Thomas Browse; 1871, James M. Gallaher; 1881, F. M. Triplett; 1885, R. A. Gallaher; 1893, Clyde B. Johnson; 1895, S. D. Wells; 1897, J. M. Copenhaver; 1901, F. M. Triplett; 1909, John Triplett.

House of Delegates.—From the year when Pleasants was made a separate borough, 1882, Oliver Gorrell; 1884, John J. Poynter; 1886, Oliver Gorrell; 1888, Robert G. Hammett; 1890, W. G. H. Core; 1892, R. G. Hammett; 1894, Charles McKnight; 1896, George Kelsall; 1898, Ralph A. Gorrell; 1900, L. J. Murphy; 1902, Thomas C. Davis; 1904, C. P. Craig; 1908, E. C. Goodno; 1910. R. L. Pemberton; 1912, A. B. Flesher; 1914, J. R. McCollum; 1916, G. D. Smith; 1918, Joe Williams; 1920, Leonard C.White; 1922, J. R. Locke; 1924, Clarence T. McCullough; 1926, Charles E. Fogle.

During the period when Pleasants was united with Wood county to make a delegate district, this county was represented in the Legislature in 1864 by James W. Williamson; 1868, William S. Steere; 1870, J. R. M. Agnew; 1872, James M. Ruckman; 1877, Robert H. Browse; 1881, David Q Steere.

Mayors of St. Marys.—1876, Richard Towzey; 1880, Robert Patterson; 1886, J. B. Townsend; 1887, R. A. Gallaher; 1889, James Patterson; 1891, J. M. Imlay; 1892, J. F. Barron; 1893, George Lipf; 1894, George Kelsall; 1895, Robert Patterson; 1896, Andrew J. Porter; 1897, J. C. Noland; 1899, J. F. Barron; 1900, E. T. Martin; 1901, Tim C. Penwell; 1902, John D. Savell; 1903, A. H. Gregory; 1904, John D. Savell; 1905, Richard Bolard; 1907, E. M. Sellers; 1908, R. H. Triplett; 1910, George E. West; 1912, J. R. McCollum; 1913, Oran C. Ogdin; 1914, J. L. Brafford; 1915, Elmer J. Edmonds; 1916, J. Howard McBride; 1917, S. D.

Snyder; 1918, R. H. Triplett; 1919, W. L. Skaggs; 1920, G. Elwood Coen; 1921, William C. Dotson; 1923, Ira Williams; 1925, Charles Carroll.

Principals of St. Marys School.—1876, John F. Wayman; 1879, C. C. Davis; 1881, D. W. Reynolds; 1882, Nannie P.Hall; 1883, L. G. Brock; 1884, Homer McGregor; 1885, Robert S. Taggart; 1887, R. L. Pemberton; 1889, John R. Stanley; 1891, H. M. Flower; 1893, R. L. Pemberton; 1895, W. S. Powell; 1896, R. L. Pemberton; 1898, W. E. McKnight; 1899, John L. Hissom; 1902, D. Walter Dillon; 1903, Harry R. Bonner; 1907, W. H. Wayt; 1908, A. D. Givens; 1900, Charles N. Wagner; 1912, H. C. Humphreys; 1915, Dan B. Fleming; 1920, I. O. Ash; 1921, Jesse E. Riley; 1926, John D. Garrison; 1927, George W. Hogg; 1928, John D. Garrison.

WASHINGTON DISTRICT HIGH SCHOOL — Williams, Photographer

CHAPTER XVIII

NEWPORT

A history of Pleasants county would be incomplete without more than a passing allusion to the village or town of Newport, on the Ohio side of the river, directly opposite the old shipping port of Vaucluse. Although it is outside of the political limits of the county, yet it has had a great deal to do, directly and indirectly, with the development of the land on the West Virginia shore. For many years before Vaucluse was established the stores at Newport afforded facilities for commerce and were frequented by our people, and the old mill at that village was depended upon for the grinding of corn and wheat. I am indebted to Miss Eleanor F. Adkins of Newport for information concerning the early history of that place.

In the Spring of 1798, ten years after the first settlement was made at Marietta, the Dana family came from Massachusetts and made a new home on the broad bottom land which became the site of Newport. They were soon followed by the Greene family, coming from Rhode Island, and it was not long until a large clearing had been made in the forest and several rude but comfortable log cabins were erected. But such habitations were not satisfactory to these people from New England, who had been accustomed to more substantial homes, and in 1808 Daniel Greene built the first brick house, that now is occupied by the Greenwoods. The Adkins home, just above the town, was built in 1810 by Luther Dana, and was for many years conducted as an inn or tavern, the old sign, "Temperance House," even now resting in the attic. The old river road originally passed between this house and the river, and it was in this building that the first postoffice was located. It requires no great stretch of fancy to picture Temperance House as the temporary lodging of many eminent travelers, and one tradition is that William Henry Harrison campaigning for the Presidency in 1840, delivered an address in the shade of a large sycamore, whose stump still may be seen in the lawn. In 1815 William Dana built the third brick house near Milltown, and the fourth brick house, erected several years afterward, was that now occupied by the Greenes.

The famous old stone mill at Milltown was built about 1815. It is said that William Dana's sympathy was aroused for a number of Irish families who had been stranded here over the Winter, and in return for his kindness in providing them with food and shelter they dug and walled the mill race. This tradition reminds me of a similar one on the West Virginia side of the river. It has often been related that after the completion of the Baltimore and Ohio railroad to Parkersburg the Irish workmen who had been employed in its construction struck across the country to St. Marys for the purpose of embarking on a steamboat, but the river became closed with ice, and they were doomed to spend the Winter in this neighborhood. In return for housing and food, they are said to have erected the stone walls or fences which yet stand along the roads on either side of Middle Island creek about a mile from its mouth.

Near the old mill is the famous elm, a magnificent tree rising to the height of one hundred feet, and measuring twenty-nine feet around its trunk.

For many years the old brick building at the top of the Newport wharf has been a landmark. It was built probably along in the forties, and used as a store until the great flood of 1913, since when it has served as a town hall and a polling place.

Ebenezer Battelle is credited with building the first log house of considerable size, which in later years was covered with weather-boarding and is now occupied by the Gale sisters.

Other early settlers mentioned were the Newport, Bosworth, Ferguson, Little, Adkins, Greenwood, Reynolds, Edgell, Hayes and Gale families. It has been supposed by some that the town derived its name from the first of those families mentioned above, but the name was actually taken from the city in Rhode Island. It was not until 1839, more than forty years after the first settlement, that the town was platted into regular streets and lots by Ebenezer Battelle.

Caleb Greene conducted the first school in his own home in 1801, and three years later the first schoolhouse was erected, 26x36 feet in dimension, heated from a large open fireplace, and lighted through greased paper windows. It stood in the Haysville community, and was replaced with a brick structure. Later two grade schools were established, one at Milltown and the other at Newport, and also a high school at the latter place. The people of that vicinity have always born a high reputation for educational culture. A resident of Newport, Erastus Adkins, was a member of the second class graduated from Marietta College, in 1839, and since that time the community has produced many college and university graduates.

In the matter of religion, also, Newport has stood well in the front. As elsewhere, services were first held in private homes and in school houses, but when the first Methodist society was organized in 1825 with about twenty members, it was held necessary to have a building of their own, so four years later the first house of worship was erected. Forty years afterward a new and larger edifice was built, and the old structure was transformed into the township high school.

A Presbyterian society was formed in 1838, holding services in the school house, the ministers coming from Marietta, one being the Rev. Henry Smith, a former president of Marietta College. The society was not strong enough to build, and in 1869 it disbanded, the membership being transferred to the Marietta church of that denomination.

In the early days the Baptists formed part of the Little Muskingum organization, but meetings were held in the school house at Newport until 1841, when a church was built, which was dedicated in the following year, about twenty years after the first recorded meeting was held.

About twenty years ago the Church of Christ established an organization, which has been continued under the supervision of the denomination at St. Marys.

Newport has never possessed any large manufacturing industries. In the early days of oil production there were several cooper shops. Later a small cigar factory operated for a few years. After the old mill at Milltown ceased to function, another was built on the river bank, operated first by horse power and later by steam. This mill did a large business for several years, and for a time the company maintained a branch warehouse in St. Marys.

The village of about six hundred people is beautifully located on a broad river bottom that rises gently from the water edge to a considerable height above flood stage, the main street skirting the foot of the solitary hill described in a former chapter of this book as having once been probably circled by the Ohio river. The large area available gives plenty of space for detached residences, each surrounded by lawns or gardens, giving an air of ease and comfort. Like most of the towns on the Ohio side of the river, it has been known for many years as a "steamboat town," that is to say, many of the people have been and still are interested in river navigation. This is especially true of the Greene and Greenwood families, who have long been owners and navigators of steamboats.

Newport is also a "good roads" town, being on Ohio State Road 7. extending along the river from Cincinnati up to Pittsburgh, besides on North National Road 50, which crosses the river over the new bridge at St. Marys, affording easy and direct communication to all parts of the nation.

Many points of interest are in the vicinity, and the view from the "Lone Tree Hill" sometimes known as "Adkins Point," is famous for its great scope of vision up and down the Ohio. The well-kept cemetery attracts many visitors and its beautiful and orderly condition is a certain index of the thrift and culture of the people. The first burial in it was that of Nathaniel Little in 1808, and it contains the remains of most of the early settlers.

I recall that several years ago a resident of Newport pointed to a peculiar work on the side of one of the low sandy hills in the edge of the town, saying that it was an uncompleted race track. If so, the curious feature of the attempt was the inversion of the usual construction of such a course. Instead of having the track in an open arena, visible from the surrounding grounds, this peculiar track wound around on the outside of the hill, the spectators having their stand in the center and looking down upon the entire performance. Why the novel project was abandoned was not revealed.

But perhaps it could not be called so eccentric as the work of Benjamin W. Willard on Cow Creek in Pleasants county. He was an early settler, said to have been contemporary with Christian Schultz, and like the latter was evidently a well-read man, judging from the books in his library, an appraisement list of them being on record in the county clerk's office.

In the days "before the war," when Mr. Willard was getting up in years, he entertained an idea of constructing his sarcophagus out of a huge rock on the hillside just above the creek road. His house, a two storied structure with an upper veranda, stood a short distance above the old mill. Sitting on the veranda, where he had a plain view of the rock, he caused his slaves to work with pick and chisel, directing and urging them in their task.

For some reason, perhaps because of the emancipation of the slaves, the sepulchre was not finished; but a very neat, well shaped cavity, almost large enough to contain a casket, remains as a more lasting monument to his memory than a highly polished granite slab in a cemetery.

CHAPTER XIX

RELIGIOUS ACTIVITIES

It has been mentioned that the old log school houses were used as places of worship. If the tradition is true, that a Miss Nancy Dailey taught about a dozen pupils as early as the year 1808 in a little log cabin near the mouth of Middle Island creek, it is reasonably certain that religious services were also held in the same structure. Even then, it could not be averred that these were the first religious services held within the limits of the county. Before log cabins for school were built, itinerant preachers held services in private homes or out in the open.

It is unfortunate that no memoranda of the first traveling preachers are left; all we know is from rather dim tradition. From all accounts it seems that the first to penetrate the wilderness for the purpose of ministering to the spiritual welfare of the pioneers were Baptist missioners, Christians of the old school that welcomed hardships as a test of their faith. A reason assigned for the very early arrival of Baptist ministers is that they were driven out of the eastern part of Virginia by the Toleration Act, finding that the enforcement of that strenuous law was not carried into effect beyond the Blue Ridge. On the western side of that long range they could preach their doctrines, considered peculiar and odious in the east, to their heart's content and unquestionably to the comfort of many who would otherwise have been deprived of the undoubted blessings brought by religious worship. To the daring services of these men may be ascribed the fact that Baptists outnumber any other Protestant denomination in the United States.

But they were soon aided in their good work by preachers of the Methodist persuasion, with a few Episcopalian ministers in the more populated sections. But those who ventured into the wilderness were missionaries in the true sense of the word, having no permanent stations and very irregular circuits, journeying perhaps hundreds of miles on horseback or afoot, supporting themselves by hunting and fishing, occasionally being entertained with a pallet of corn husks and a meal of pone and bacon in the home of a settler.

If possible, they sent word in advance of their coming and arranged for a series of meetings in some clearing, to which families would come from far distances and camp about the pulpit in the forest. In a way these old camp-meetings served as joyous occasions for people who rarely saw each other to get together and interchange news and comment, and the preacher could always be depended on to bring them news of the outside world, for which they hungered almost as much as for the consolation of the Gospel. Readers of the novels of Edward Eggleston, himself an itinerant minister in comparatively early days, get vivid descriptions of these camp-meetings and of the men who conducted them.

Those preachers practiced muscular Christianity, helping at house-raisings and log-rollings, and not infrequently preserving order at their meetings with a ready fist. It required preachers of that rough and ready sort to instil a proper feeling of respect among the hardy and untamed sons of the wilderness. And the kind of preaching they gave was well suited to the character of their hearers— plain and blunt, delivered with the voice of authority.

If the Baptists were first to preach the Gospel in this section, it seems that the Methodists were first to organize. The date of the earliest organization of which we have record is 1829, when the Rev. Pardon Cook established a society of Methodists in the Beech Run neighborhood, among the members being Henry Flesher, Abner

Martin, James Allen, William Johnson, Elizabeth and Hannah Gorrell, Eli Wells and James Patterson. The minister, Mr. Cook, is said to have been born at Belpre, Ohio, in 1796, was licensed as a local preacher in 1825, admitted into the Pittsburgh Conference in 1827, and served as an itinerant minister forty years. Previous to that, but still at an uncertain date, the Rev. Reese Wolf of the Methodist Church is reported to have held services in what is now Grant district.

Probably the next society in that denomination was organized in 1838 in McKim district, under the pastorate of the Rev. Philip Green. The first members of this congregation were the families of Ralph Wilson, Job Locke, Thomas Locke, William Hart and Charles Wilson. Twelve years later, in 1850, this same minister is reported as having organized a society at Grape Island, building a meeting house called Bethesda Chapel, the first members being Jacob Hanes, W. V. Gill, Greenberry B. Riggs, John F. Taylor, B. W. Riggs and Phoebe Taylor. In 1881 a new church building was dedicated. but was destroyed by fire several years ago, and a third building was then erected near the schoolhouse. The congregation, however, dwindled until it was deemed advisable to sell the building, which was then torn down and removed.

In 1881 a Methodist Episcopal Society was formed at Raven Rock by the Rev. J. Engle, the congregation including the families of L. N. Coffield, A. S. Vance, J. W. Gardner and A. Kigans. In Jefferson district an organization was made at the Ruckman place on Cow Creek in 1851, under the leadership of the Rev. Mr. Guthrie, those joining being James Ruckman, Nancy Ruckman, William Howard, John and Jane Thornley and a Mr. Farley.

This denomination has spread to all parts of the county, several buildings being erected, but the slowest growth was apparently in the county town, where the first building was erected in 1885, as told elsewhere in this work. At first the pastorate was united with that of Sistersville, but in a few years the congregation was strong enough of itself to support a minister, for whose use a parsonage was built in 1900 on Upper Second street.

The first available record of the formation of a Baptist society is that by the Rev. W. C. Barrett on McKim creek in 1850, whose early members were Charles Seckman, John Coen, O. P. Shingleton, John R. Shingleton, John Lamp, Mrs. Margaret Wilson, Mrs. Martha Stout, Nancy Riggs, Christian McCardle, George S. Smith, Levi Gregg and William Medley. In 1857 another was organized on Gorrell's run in Union district, with the Rev. James Woods as pastor. Among the first members were Samuel B. Seckman, C. Hanes, Thomas and Ann Bonar, Mahlon Hanes, S. Speece, M. R. Crouse and Thomas Johnson. Outside of the city of St. Marys perhaps the strongest congregation at present is that of the Willow Island church, in Grant district, where the building occupies a beautiful site on the river road near the Cow creek bridge.

It is curious that almost every Protestant denomination established societies in the rural districts before entering St. Marys, and the Baptists were no exception to the rule. It was not until 1897 that an organization was effected in the city, but since that time the membership has greatly increased.

While the Episcopalians were early in the field, the growth of the church has been slow. From Bishop Peterkin's Records of the Episcopal Church we learn that the first services held by a minister of that denomination were at Willow Island in 1843, on the occasion of the funeral of Robert Triplett. The minister was the Rev. Thomas Smith of Parkersburg. who was accompanied by the late General John J. Jackson. After that occasional services were held in a building that was used jointly as a Methodist church and a school. In 1855 a parish known as St. John's was formed and a frame building erected on Cow creek, a few hundred yards up from the river road. The vestrymen were Burr Triplett, Samuel Triplett, Phineas P. Feeney, Giles Hammett, Frank Triplett, John W. Morris, James Irwin, David Garrett and John H. Rolston. The membership began to decline during the Civil War, and finally from lack of regular services and by reason of deaths and removals none was left. It continued, however, under the rules of the Church to be considered a parish until the last communicant had departed, the situation being similar to that of one of the United States, which must be considered as a State so long as enough citizens remain to conduct the business.

About the year 1859 the Rev. William L. Hyland of Parkersburg held Episcopal services in the Methodist Protestant Church at St. Marys, and was followed by the Rev. S. D. Tomkins. After an interval of several years the Rev. John F. Woods began holding monthly services in St. Marys, and was followed by the Rev. John Ambler from 1889 to 1892, when the Rev. Grant P. Somerville was located here as a deacon for two or three years, services being held in the Methodist Protestant and Methodist Episcopal churches, until, finding it necessary to have a home of their own, the little congregation met regularly in a large room over George Kelsall's store, where a sewing machine, properly draped, answered the purpose of a pulpit. On July 16. 1894, Bishop G. W. Peterkin confirmed a class of five, the first class in the new congregation, this service being conducted in the Methodist Episcopal church.

In 1895 the congregation bought the old mill lot on the bank of the Thoroughfare from George Leonard of Ravenswood. This had been the site of the first grist mill in the town, and was also the place where John Suck later built his planing mill, which had burned down a few years before it was bought by the Episcopalians. The building was practically completed in 1898, at a cost of $4,500, but not being clear of debt was not consecrated until 1905, when the ceremony was done by Bishop Peterkin, the presentation being made by the Rev. Paca Kennedy on behalf of the vestry, composed of George Kelsall, Robert Henry Browse, Edward A. Sayre, Joseph C. Noland and Robert L. Pemberton.

Succeeding Mr. Somerville the ministers of this church have been J. A. Hiatt, 1895-1901, C. M. Smith, 1901, George C. Shaw, 1901-04, Paca Kennedy, 1904-07, C. A. Dowell, 1907-08, N. P. McDonald, 1908-10, John L. Fish, 1910-12, Harold Jenkins, 1912-13, W. E. Merington, 1914-15, James H. Clark, 1915-16, G. H. Crook, 1916-21, J. H. Gehri, 1921, S. Scollay Moore, 1922-24, Morris W. Derr, 1926, and George Wood, 1928. The present vestrymen are Robert L. Pemberton, Dr. J. Riley McCollum, Robert W. Russell, Elgin Adkins, Dan B. Fleming, Julius A. Schauwecker, John McComas, Charles Carroll and R. A. Hall.

The Rev. I. A. Barnes, one time a minister of the Methodist Protestant Church in St. Marys, has written a history of that denomination in West Virginia. He states that a society was organized in the location of the present city of St. Marys some time before 1850, and that a quarterly conference of the Tyler circuit was held here in that year. He adds that William Rymer, who had come from Harrison county, was probably the first member of that church in this section.

A great meeting was held in St. Marys in 1858, probably at what had been called the Union Schoolhouse, on the Silas Gallaher farm. This meeting was conducted by the Rev. Isaac Holland, a preacher of great force, and immediately afterward a meeting house was erected on the corner of Second and Washington streets, the lot having been purchased from A. H. Creel for fifty dollars. The first trustees were David Gregg, P. H. Hudkins and William T. Sharp. But before this, according to Mr. Barnes, there was an organization at Sylvan Mills on Middle Island creek, which he declares the oldest and strongest Methodist Protestant society in the county, but he does not give the date of its formation.

At Hebron a society was formed in the early sixties and a building erected in 1869-70. The Hebron and Bethel churches were combined into the Maple Lane church in 1924, about a mile below Hebron on McKim creek. John McGregor, William Pyles, John Wrick and John Odell and their families were among the first members of the Hebron church. Valley Chapel is also mentioned among the McKim appointments organized between 1860 and 1865, and Bibbee Chapel near Shiloh is another of the older societies. The Nine Mile church was organized in 1866 by the Rev. H. A. J. Francis, then pastor at St. Marys, the first members being Job Locke and wife, Thomas Locke and wife, H. C. Poynter and wife, J. J. Poynter and wife, Maria Stanley and William C. Locke. After using the schoolhouse several years, a log church was built under the pastorate of the Rev. John M. Conaway, and was dedicated in 1878, the sermon being delivered by the Rev. Peter T. Conaway. The present building was erected in 1901. From this society two prominent ministers of the Church have emanated— the Rev. John J. Poynter and the Rev. J. H. Mossburg, each serving as President of the West Virginia Conference. The former, for many years superannuated, was one of the best pulpit orators I have heard, and still resides at Cloverdale, near the scene of his first labors.

The Rev. H. A. J. Francis also organized a society on Cow Creek in 1866, the members being Miss Ellen Sharp, William Kester and wife, David Hawkins and wife, and the Ruckman, Feeney and Cornell families. The church building was erected in 1885 under the supervision of the Rev. Joseph Dunn. David Hawkins for many years officiated as a local minister.

In 1898 the Rev. J. J. Mason organized a class at Belmont with the families of William Kester, and Greenberry Ruttencutter and Ellen Sharp and Mary Hammett as charter members. While the neat building in that town belongs to the Methodist Protestant Church, there is a provision in the deed that when not used by that church it may be used for services by the Methodist Episcopal Church South. This Belmont church is a part of the Friendly circuit.

Near Cloverdale a society was formed about 1878, services being held in the schoolhouse until Dunn Chapel was built under the pastorate of the Rev. Joseph Dunn. At the head of Shawnee Run stands the Mount Pleasant church, which, Mr. Barnes states, succeeded the old Wagner Chapel, owned jointly by the Methodist Protestant and the Methodist Episcopal Churches.

As heretofore related, the first church building in St. Marys was that of the Methodist Episcopal Church South, erected in the year of the county's formation, 1851. The congregation has never been large and has never been able to support a resident minister, services having been held intermittently, sometimes regularly. A few years ago it was generally supposed that the two Methodist Episcopal denominations would unite, and services in the South church were discontinued until recently. So far as we know, the only other societies of this denomination in the county are at Sugar Valley and Eureka, the latter place of worship being the neat brick edifice built in 1910.

The Church of Christ, or the Christian Church, is represented in the county in several communities, that at Pine Grove near Hebron being probably the first. It was formed in 1847, Daniel Sweeney being the first minister, and the early members were the families of Samuel Maxwell, Smiley Maxwell, A. S. Gorrell and Susannah Lamp. In 1880 Samuel Albright organized a society at Cloverdale with Salathiel and Catherine Hart, Eugenius and Hester Newbrough, Marion and Martha Hart and William and Matilda Hart. In Union district the same minister organized a society at Mount Nebo, among the original members being the families of Henry Beagle, Lloyd Barnhart, James N. Hanlin and David M. Barnhart. This denomination put up a building in the city in 1907 and a few years afterwards built a handsome parsonage for the resident minister.

A United Brethren society was formed by the Rev. M. D. Altice in the upper end of Union district in 1875 and a meeting house built on Point Lookout, a very commanding situation. For a time there was an organization in St. Marys and a church was built, but the congregation fell off and the building was sold to the Roman Catholics.

The only Presbyterian church in the county, we believe, is that in St. Marys, established in 1904, since when the society has grown rapidly, so that it has its resident minister. The first was W. D. Harrell, who was succeeded in 1907 by J. P. McDonald.

Since its organization the following ministers have officiated: W. D. Harrell, J. P. McDonald, S. E. Foote, Rev. Ramsey, Rev. Kiskadden, Charles J. Callier, Thomas B. Sheldon, D. C. Marshall, W. H. Chase and Joseph G. Kane.

The present Elders of the church are P. S. Tarbox, R. W. Douglass, A. H. Neyman, R. L. Griffin and E. L. Burk.

When I first came to Pleasants county there were frequent allusions to the Quaker settlement on Bull creek. Very little was known here of this peculiar sect; yet while many regarded the Quakers with suspicious curiosity, it was the universal opinion that they were strictly honest and dependable in any business dealings. At that time the church was in a flourishing condition, but within a few years the congregation fell off and the building they had erected has been used by other denominations. It still stands at the mouth of Rawson's Run, often erroneously called Horseneck Run. I am indebted to Mr. Elisha B. Steere for a brief history of this settlement of the Friends or Quakers.

William H. Steere, his younger brother, had been chosen to manage the oil production of a company composed of Quakers of Mount Pleasant, Ohio, of which place the Steeres were then residents. The property was known as the Greer Oil Lease, located on Horseneck, and he took charge in August, 1865. In a few months he returned to his old home and married, bringing his bride then into this new territory. Presumably seeing opportunities in the neighborhood for improvement, and also desiring more kindred company, he persuaded his father and mother, Joseph and Deborah H. Steere, to move to that locality, and also there came Dr. D. Q. Steere and his family.

Mrs. Joseph Steere induced her husband and son to buy several hundred acres along Rawson's Run, including three farms and residences. Many years before a number of families named Johnson, of Quaker descent, had moved in from Greene county, Pennsylvania, buying land on both sides of Bull Creek. Mrs Steere at once formed their acquaintance, organized them, and they cleaned up an old church building in which Sunday school and Church services were held. From the Mount Pleasant quarterly meeting they obtained authority to establish a Quaker Church, subject to the Mount Pleasant meeting.

The new meeting increased in membership rapidly. Mrs. Steere was very punctual in attendance, preaching every "First Day" after Sunday school, and always to goodly gatherings. When it was deemed necessary to erect a new meeting house, the deed was soon accomplished. At the close of a revival the membership had increased to one hundred.

Soon after the Rev. Jesse Lloyd, a Quaker from near Mount Pleasant, moved to the settlement with his family, and he and Mrs. Steere held meetings in various places in the neighborhood. The church seemed to be well established; but death made inroads, several prominent members moved away, among them Mr. Lloyd, and in April, 1892, Mrs. Steere passed "from works to rewards." The crippled society hobbled along for a time thereafter, but finally services were altogether abandoned.

CHAPTER XX

THE OLDER FAMILIES

Although most of the early settlers came to Pleasants county as late as the beginning of the last century, I find that records of them are rapidly dying out, so soon are our ancestors forgotten. A few persons have voluntarily assisted in gathering materials for the following brief family sketches, but for most of them I am indebted to Hardesty's book of the year 1882, and have tried to correct, so far as possible, some of the inaccuracies found in that work.

A noticeable fact, of especial interest to students of sociology, is that in the colonizing period, when luxuries were few and life generally was a continual rugged combat, the families were almost invariably large, the number of children ranging from six to twelve or more. In many instances, notwithstanding the rough life and the rarity of medical attendance, eight or ten children have grown to maturity.

LARUE.—LaRues were undoubtedly the first permanent settlers. In regard to the manner in which Jacob and Isaac became possessed of land in this county I am enabled now to correct a slight misstatement made on page 11 of this book.

The brothers were descendants of Abraham LaRue, a French Huguenot or Protestant who escaped from France during the year 1680, at the time of the great religious persecution. He seems to have first gone to Holland, and from there to this country, where he settled in New Jersey and acquired considerable property. His son, Peter, became a large landholder in Berks county, Pennsylvania, and the same thrifty qualities seem to have been inherited by Peter's son Isaac, who settled in Virginia and purchased large tracts of wild land in what are now Kentucky and West Virginia. His home was near Berryville, in Clark county. A compiler of the history of the LaRues estimates that his descendants now number more than ten thousand, scattered all over the Union.

His daughter, Elizabeth, married a cousin, Peter LaRue, and to four of her sons Isaac devised his land at the mouth of Middle Island creek—300 acres on the island and 2,000 acres on the main land. This is the land which Jacob and Isaac came to settle upon in 1790. Isaac, the oldest, was married to Elizabeth Hughes of Pennsylvania before coming here. One of their eight children, Sarah, married Daniel Reynolds. After the death of his first wife in 1837, Isaac married Mrs. Elizabeth Roby, the widowed mother of Isaac and Godfrey Roby.

Jacob LaRue married a sister of Daniel Reynolds, and died before 1824. Of their children Mary Ann married James Chambers; Nancy married Isaac Riggs; Eliza married William Medley, Jr., and a son, Perry, married Rebecca, a daughter of William Bills. Perry resided at the mouth of Broad Run, and was the father of Lansford W. LaRue, whose family is the only one left of that name in the county.

MAXWELL.—Samuel S. Maxwell, born 1805, moved from Brooke county in 1842, established the postoffice of Hebron in 1844. His wife was Eliza Lowery. Their son was Dr. Leander B. Maxwell, whose first wife was Josina, daughter of John and Frances (Hawkins) Hammond; their children were Samuel L., James F., Leslie M., Albert R. and Edmund H. Samuel Maxwell's parents were Scotch, immigrating to America in 1800.

FEENEY.—Prominent in the early history of the county was Phineas P. Feeney, school teacher and surveyor, and who competed with Rodney Hickman for the honor of being the first recorder of the county, ranking high both in scholarship and penmanship.

Phineas P. Feeney and his wife, Sarah, were born in Ireland, and came to America early in a sailing vessel which was six weeks in making the crossing. It was a leaky ship; the passengers were forced to work the pumps, and on her return trip the vessel foundered.

The Feeneys located on Cow creek, about three miles from the river, and the old log house he built still stands on its original location, though now weatherboarded. As a surveyor he established many original land marks and at the same time taught school successfully. They had four sons and four daughters—Thomas A., George W., William J., Benjamin W., Eleanor A., Mary Jane, Maria and Frances. The family was noted for hospitality, the door being always open to the wayfaring and especially to ministers of the Gospel. Of the children only Thomas A. and Benjamin W. are living, but there are many of the third and fourth generations.

IRWIN.—William Irwin, of Belfast, Ireland, came to this country in 1809; in 1819 he married Euphremia Murray, born in Paisley, Scotland; moved to Pleasants in 1830; William died 1851, his wife died 1865. There were ten children, of whom James, born in Maryland 1820, was the oldest; he married Alvira, daughter of Ruel and Elizabeth (Leap) Johnson, who was born in Greene county. Pa., 1823.

ROLSTON.—William Rolston settled in Grant district in 1804, coming from Pennsylvania, where he had participated in the Whiskey insurrection. His wife was Mary Hopkins. Their son Nathan was born in Rockingham county, Virginia in 1794, and married Sarah, daughter of Solomon and Kate (Stump) Harness, who was born in Hardy county in 1797. Their children were Archibald Rufus, born 1818; Mary Catherine (Thornley), born 1820; George Wilson, born 1823; Granville Harness, born 1825; David Compton, born 1827; Eliza

Alcinda (Ingraham) born 1830; Solomon William, born 1833; John Tyler, born 1836. George W. Rolston married Elizabeth, daughter of Lloyd and Frances Biddle.

Nathaniel Rolston served under Harrison in the war of 1812.

REYNOLDS.—From what I can learn the progenitor of the Reynolds family in this section was a certain Noah Reynolds, an Englishman, who came to America sometime in the eighteenth cenaury. His son, Thomas, settled at Rea's Run, and was a soldier in the war of 1812. He bought forty acres on Middle Island and built his home there. His son, Daniel, married Sarah, a daughter of Isaac LaRue.

The children of Daniel Reynolds were Rodney, who married a daughter of James Benson; Drusy, married William Cooper; Lucy, married James Stephens; Dorcas Medora, married A. H. Cole; Robert, married a Miss DeLong; Joseph, married Ann Pethtel; Amanda, married William Shannon, and Isaac, married Cassie Bills.

Other descendants of Noah and Thomas Reynolds here were George Reynolds and his children, Thomas H. Reynolds, Mrs. George W. Riggs and Mrs. B. F. Pickens. Thomas H. had more names than any other man I have met. He gave me the list one day as we were walking up the Pike hill, and I here reproduce them: Thomas Henry Coswell Crawford Richard Robinson Dixon Dotson Reynolds, and he gave me the derivation of most of the names from old English families.

WAGNER—Many years ago a gentleman who was canvassing the upper section of the county told me that it was peopled by Wagners and Williamsons, and his statement was very nearly true. Christopher and Catherine (Musser) Wagner, of Pennsylvania Dutch families, immigrated from that State in 1820 and took up land on Sugar creek. One of their sons, Joseph, born in 1810, married Nancy Williamson, and their children were Catherine Hays, William, Calvin, Margaret Bullman, James, John R., Thomas J. and Asa F. Another son, David, married Margaret, daughter of James and Margaret (Ball) Williamson, and their children were Isaac,

John, Joshua, Elizabeth Weekley, Christopher J., Joseph, Amos, Friend, Elroy and Sarah Q. Lamp.

SMITH.—What time William and Susan Gorrell Smith came to this county is not given, but it was very early in the last century. I find records of three of their children. Elza, born in 1816, married Eleanor Robinson, their surviving children being Mary J. and Mansfield. Squire, married Priscilla, daughter of Eli and Hannah (Gorrell) Wells; their children were Amos, Martin L., Susan J. Wagner, Sylvester, Sheridan and Dorothy. Cyrus P., married Mary E., daughter of Asa and Margaret Taylor Allen; their children were Landora A., William A., Maggie F. and Hattie O.

WILLIAMSON.—There are many of this name in the county, but the records given me are few and disconnected. Captain James W. Williamson was a son of William and Sarah (Fuget) Williamson; was born in 1816 and married Susannah, daughter of John Adams. He was active in early affairs, was frequently mentioned in the Browse diary, and served in the State Legislature. James and Margaret (Ball) Williamson, early settlers, had a son, John, who married Margaret, daughter of Christopher and Catherine Wagner, and their children were Christopher J., Martha M., Margaret C. Birkheimer, George M., Charles W., Mary J. Flesher, Sidney C., Sarah A. Weekley and Chester.

WATSON.—The Watsons settled in Lafayette district about Rock Run. John and Rosanna Watson moved to Pleasants in 1844, and later he moved to St. Marys, serving as constable for many years. His father's name was George. John's children were A. Jackson, who married Charlotte, sister of W. G. H. Core; Dr. Joseph Barnett Watson, who married Mary, daughter of William and Catherine Carroll, and Christina, married to Abraham Ruttencutter. Ada, a sister of John, married Harvey Locke.

HARNESS.—John and Solomon Harness came from Virginia in 1809 and settled on the river bottom near

Bull Creek. Solomon married Catherine Stump, and their son, John L., married Elizabeth A., daughter of William and Euphremia (Murray) Irwin.

PETHTEL.—The Pethtels may properly be considered as old settlers. The progenitor, Henry Pethtel, immigrated at an early date from Germany to Greene county, Pennsylvania. In 1855 his son James moved to this county, having a rough journey down Fishing creek to New Martinsville, thence down the river. He bought land on the Ellenboro Pike, building a home near the house later built by Erve Grandon, and afterwards erected a more substantial home at the forks of Broad Run.

He left six sons and five daughters—Isaac, Solomon, William, Zadock, Lafayette, Joseph, Mrs. Emmeline Robinson, Mrs. Ann Reynolds, Mrs. Eliza DeLong, Mrs. Rebecca Delong anl Mrs. Nancy Cornell. Lafayette has been distinguished by being twice elected county commissioner.

COCHRAN.—The Cochrans were among the very earliest comers. The original Thomas Cochran came from Ireland in the eighteenth century and took part in the Indian wars around Fort Henry, where Wheeling stands now, served in the Revolution, was captured by the Indians, who wished to adopt him, but was killed while endeavoring to escape. His son, Thomas, also fought in the Indian wars. He married Elizabeth Morris, and was the father of eleven children. They moved to Tyler county, where his son Friend was born in 1809. At one time he owned Grape Island and other land near by. He sold the island to James Bailey in 1811 for $90.00. Friend Cochran married Catherine. daughter of William and Elizabeth (Taylor) Johnson. and also became the father of eleven children, of whom Joseph Cochran is the sole survivor residing in this county.

KESTER.—The Kester family has been prominent in local affairs for nearly one hundred years. Adam Kester and wife, Sarah Devol, were natives of Maryland, and he served as a soldier in the war of 1812. They crossed the mountains about 1819, settling first in Harrison county, and about 1830 removed to the Ohio valley, for ten years residing on the Parker farm, just below the present village of Belmont, and then he bought one hundred acres in Grant district, on which he resided until his death. They had four sons and three daughters.

JOSEPH WILLIAM AND JOHN KESTER

John, the eldest son, was elected sheriff of the county in 1866, and at the expiration of his term served two years as assessor, or commissioner of revenue, as the office was then called. His first wife was Nancy Oliver, and his second wife Mary Elizabeth Bailey, who was one of the first teachers under the free school system of the sixties. Some time in the seventies they moved to Jackson county.

William, the second son, was born in Harrison county on May 9, 1824. He succeeded his brother as assessor, and later was elected a member of the county court. In 1849 he married Ann E., daughter of G. A. and Drusilla W. (Jamison) Sharp, their children being Thomas S., Minerva J., Rufus W., James Buchanan, John Breckinridge, Cassius Clay (these three being tripletts), Charles H., Sophia D. and Mary Ella. Rufus moved to Washington, but the others remained in Grant district.

Joseph married Hannah Joy, and they took up their residence at Reno, Ohio, with many children.

Peter married a Miss McGee, and moved to Schultz, where his descendants still reside.

Of the daughters of Adam Kester, Catherine married William Carroll, Sophia married a Mr. Hill of Kansas, and Mary Ann married J. F. Ruttencutter.

SMITH.—Gilbert D. Smith, a leading member of the bar, may also claim to belong to one of the older families, his father, Ambrose, having moved here in 1847 and following his trade as carpenter and builder assisted in constructing the Cain House and the first court house, afterwards moving back to his former home near Middlebourne, in Tyler county.

PATTERSON.—Robert Patterson, frequently mentioned in the Browse journal, was born in Jefferson county, Ohio, in 1816, his father being Robert Patterson formerly of Ireland and his mother Sarah VanMeter Patterson.

In 1837 the son married Jane, daughter of John and Massey (Wilson) Patterson, the mother of James, John and Robert H. Patterson. In 1855 he married his second wife, Mrs. Simpson, their daughter being Mrs. Sallie V. King, and in 1882 he married his third wife, Mrs. Emma J. Raider Clifford. He was an able lawyer, served a term as county commissioner and also two years as State Senator.

SHINGLETON.—The Shingletons came from Virginia, and the original name, I am told, was Singleton, which leads one to suspect that they might be connected with the family of John Singleton Mosby, a celebrated colonel in the Confederate army who lived east of the mountains.

The ancestor, William Shingleton, came from England and settled in Hampshire county, but moved to Harrison county in 1812. He was a soldier in the Revolution and a member of Washington's body guard, also serving with three of his sons in the war of 1812. A fourth son, Alexander, was the father of John R. and Leonard C. Shingleton. The latter was a merchant and postmaster at Hebron for many years, and the former was ordained as a minister in the Baptist Church, also actively engaged in business and was prominent in political affairs, serving as county commissioner and in other offices. Other brothers were Oliver Perry, James, William Jasper and George Washington Shingleton.

MORGAN.—Most of the Morgans of Pleasants county are descendants of Jacob Morgan, who immigrated from Britain to North Carolina about 1732, where he married a McCoy. Jacob, his oldest son, married Nancy Ann Smith in North Carolina and about 1790 moved to Greene county, Pennsylvania, and thence to Fishing Creek in Wetzel county, where he died in 1863 lacking only fourteen days of completing one hundred years, and leaving six sons and three daughters.

Of his daughters, Elizabeth married William Shreaves and moved to Minnesota; Jane married William Odell of Hebron, and raised ten children; and Margaret married Abraham Copenhaver, their sons being John and Jacob M.

Richard, the oldest son, married and died in Kentucky.

Huey (probably Hugh) married Rachel Snodgrass, and settled at Hebron. Three of his sons, James, Jacob M. and Charles, served in the Civil War.

James married a Thorn, and lived in Wetzel county.

Nathan, born in 1810, married Melinda Odell of Hebron, raising six sons and four daughters; John Wesley, married to Oella Maxwell, served a term as member of the county court, and his son, Faran F., also served on the same court. Eli H., a younger son of Nathan, married Jacqueline, daughter of Thomas D. Gorrell.

Isaiah Dain Morgan married Lydia, daughter of Moses and Nancy Ball Williamson, resided in Mason county. His oldest daughter, Nancy, married Godfrey C. Roby.

Jacob, the youngest grandson of the first immigrant, married Jennie, sister of Abraham Copenhaver, and lived in Wetzel county.

CARROLL.—William Carroll came from Harford county, Maryland, on the shore of Chesapeake Bay in the third decade of the last century. He was a son of William Carroll, and presumably a member of the family that furnished the last survivor of the men who signed the Declaration of Independence.

After coming here he married Catherine, daughter of Adam and Sarah Devol Kester. They resided for several years at Vaucluse, where Mr. Carroll kept a woodyard, furnishing fuel to the steamboats, which then burned wood, and after the founding of St. Marys moved to the county seat, engaging in the mercantile business and also serving as postmaster from the close of the war until his death in 1880.

Their children were George, married to Georgiana Marr of Kentucky; William, married Ella, daughter of Aaron Barker; James, married Eva, also daughter of Aaron Barker; Thomas J., married Sarah Knight; Elizabeth, married George Kelsall; Mary, married Dr. Joseph B. Watson, and Anne M., married R. A. Gallaher.

ROBY—The Robys, probably originating in the Pennsylvania Dutch families of southeastern Pennsylvania, came West from near Harper's Ferry or Hagerstown. Otha Owen Roby was married twice. By his first wife he had a son named William Hare Roby, born 1813, who came West early and settled at Ravenswood, having three sons, Isaac, Frank and William. For his second wife Otha Owen married Elizabeth Cramer, widow of a German named Dittmer, daughter of Godfrey and Rebecca Cramer, of Pigeon Cove. Pennsylvania. He died in 1837. and by the persuasion of William Hare Roby the widow and her six children ventured in the Fall of that year to cross the mountains. Four of her husband's sisters had married and gone to the Ohio Valley. namely: Elsie. married to a man named Engle. living above Raven Rock; Elizabeth, married to Edmond Riggs; Mary, married to Bazil Riggs, and Susanna. married to John Witten, residing just above New Martinsville in the house built by Edward Doolin, who was killed by the Indians on the brook that bears his name.

The family stopped that first Winter with the Wittens, and then moved to the Wells farm at Bens Run. then called Thomas Run. Her children were Isaac. born 1825; Otha Owen, born 1829; Godfrey Cramer, born 1833; Susanna, born 1827; Ann Elizabeth, born 1831, and Ellen, born 1837. Isaac worked on the farm for fifty cents a day, but in a few years Mrs. Roby married Isaac LaRue, and they moved into the brick house near the mouth of Middle Island Creek where young Isaac Roby kept the ferry.

In 1856 Isaac married Sarah Jane Hudkins. and in 1869 moved to a farm he bought on the Ellenboro Pike. He was a member of the Home Guards during the Civil War. His wife died in 1901 and in 1907 Isaac died. Their children were Godfrey C.. William. Mrs. Lizzie Jones of Ridgeville, Indiana. and Mrs. Carrie Pryor and Mrs. N. Smith Locke, both of Belmont.

Godfrey Cramer Roby married Nancy Ann, daughter of Isaiah D. and Lydia Williamson Morgan in 1859. He enlisted in Company A, 11th Virginia Infantry, in 1863, and served through the war. In the Fall of 1866 he settled on a farm on Middle Island Creek, where he died in April. 1908. Their children were Ellen, Otha O., Isaiah M., Lydia, Godfrey Cramer, Jr., Mrs. Della Cornell, Everett E., Mrs. Capitolia Wilhelm, Mrs. Ida Hemsworth, George K., Vance R., Earnest Earl, Ralph S. and Pearl, the last deceased.

Susanna Roby married Enoch Vincent of White Oak.

Ellen Roby married Jonathan Burge of Douglass Run.

TRIPLETT.—The Tripletts established themselves in this neighborhood sometime prior to 1799. A Mr. Triplett is mentioned in the early annals as having been slain by Indians in 1792 on the Little Kanawha, near the mouth of Burning Springs Run. He was with Daniel Rowell. a son-in-law of Captain James Neal, and Henry, the latter's son. They were hunting, and lured by the appar ent call of turkeys on the south bank of the river, paddled across. Reaching the shore, they were fired on by Indians. and Neal and Triplett were killed, their bodies falling into the water while Roswell leaped overboard and swam in safety to the northern shore.

Next we hear of a Robert Triplett being appointed surveyor of Wood county at its formation in 1799. He proceeded to William and Mary College and passed an examination. receiving a certificate that he was "able to execute the office and fulfill the duties of a surveyor of a county." This diploma was signed by James Madison. president of the college and afterward President of the United States. Armed with that document, he secured a commission signed by the Governor of Virginia, James Monroe, who also later became President of the United States.

He served as surveyor of Wood county from that time until 1831. His son. Robert S. Triplett, was also a surveyor. his grandson, Francis M. Triplett, served many years as official surveyor of Pleasants county, and his great-grandson, John, now occupies the same position. and has in his possession the compass and Jacob-staff used by the first surveyor of Wood county.

Of Robert Triplett's two sons Burr married Effie Butcher. and their children were Elizabeth Ann Sarber, Columbia Cox, Peyton. America Patterson, William. Robert Harry, Mary Ella Steere and Catherine. Of these the only survivor is Mrs. Steere of St. Marys.

Robert S. Triplett married Rebecca Maria Robinson, and their son, Francis M. Tiplett, married Isabella, daughter of John and Isabella Arnott of Marietta. Their children were Charles A., Isabella, Maggie, Elizabeth, Robert S.. John. Ida May and Francis M.

CRAIG.—James Craig was born in Greene county, Pennsylvania, in 1816, moved to Pleasants and married Edith, daughter of John and Abigail (Childers) Gatrell. Their son is Commodore P. Craig, who has served this county as prosecuting attorney, member of the House of Delegates and State Senator.

The father of James Craig was named John, a native of old Virginia who moved to Greene county, Pennsylvania, early in the last century, and in 1826 came to

Shiloh on the Pleasants county line, buying a farm of about 400 acres. His sons were John, James and Thomas. John was a merchant in St. Marys about the time of the Civil War and James served as postmaster in the same town, succeeding his cousin, Robert Harvey, while Thomas lived on the Browse farm at Grape Island.

McCULLOUGH.—Daniel and Rachel Kelley McCullough came from Pennsylvania, settling at Pine Grove in 1854. He was a farmer and a blacksmith.

Three sons, George, James and William, were soldiers in the Union army, the latter losing his life at Massa Wooten Mountain. George married Rebecca Clovis. James married Sarah Gatrell and lived at Pine Grove. Their children were Maxie, John and William.

Daniel married Susan Lamp and resides at Rock Run. Their children are Emma, married to Frant Lamp; Allen, married Emma Jones; Clarence, married Allie Mae Dillon; George, married Zora Elder; Coleman, married Racie Hartman, and John married Delphia Whaley.

HANES.—William and Deborah Wells Hanes moved from Middlebourne to McKim creek, half a mile above Jonestown, in March, 1840, with their ten children, Betty, Sarah, Abigail, Mary, Agnes, Margaret, Ralph, William, John and Matilda.

Sarah married John Lamp and Abigail married George Lamp, brothers of the Susanna Lamp family, Mary married Abra Lamp of the Joseph Lamp stock.

Margaret married John Locke and lived on the home place, rearing two sons, J. Ralph and Okey J. J. Ralph married Sophia Martin, and to them were born ten children; Okey married Blanche Rice, and three children were born to them.

Ralph married Christina, daughter of Joseph Lamp.

William married Hannah Griggs, settling on Bull Creek, and were parents of eight children.

SMITH.—Alfred and Mary Lapping Smith came from Pennsylvania in 1848. Their son, Job, was born in 1838, married Barbara, daughter of Joseph and Joanna (Ambler) Hubbs. He lived on Broad Run and served ably as a county commissioner six years.

LOCKE.—This family has played an important part in local affairs, Andrew was the first of the name to come to America, settling in either New Jersey or Delaware. His son Andrew came west and located near Uniontown in Pennsylvania, where he raised a family of four sons and one daughter—Thomas, John, Job, Isaac and Maria. About the year 1840 they moved to Pleasants county in McKim and Lafayette districts.

Thomas built a hewed long house on Middle Island Creek near the present home of Charles Fetty. In Pennsylvania he had married Elizabeth Kerwood. Their six sons were Abia, Daniel, Charles, William Butler, George A. and Thomas, Jr., and their daughters were Nancy and Mary.

Abia enlisted in Stonewall Jackson's regiment and served the Confederacy till the close of the war, afterwards settling in Indiana.

Daniel joined the Union forces in the Civil War, and then settled near Middlebourne, the father of two children, Frank and Nancy.

Charles was a farmer and ordained minister and married Lavina Ankrom. They lived on a farm above Sylvan Mills with their five children, Harlan P., John B., Sina, Mary and Florence. Harlan married Martha Ella Amos and practiced law; John married Ella Kester and after her death married Minnie Douglass; Sina married Jacob L. Varner; Mary married Albert Jones and Florence married George W. Feeney.

William Butler Locke married Rebecca Wrick. Their children were Albert W., who was twice elected county school superintendent, John T., Forrest Brady, George T. and Ida B.

George A. Locke married Christina Locke and died in 1919, and is well remembered as having been a barber here for many years.

Thomas, the youngest son, was killed in youth by being thrown from a horse.

Nancy married William Fetty, five of their many children are still living: Abia, Charles, Herbert, Okey and Mrs. Grace Schultz.

Mary married William Reed, their only surviving child being George A. Reed, now of Parkersburg.

HOLDREN.—Joseph, the first Holdren of whom there seems to be record was a farmer and shoemaker, residing in Holland. Coming to America he settled in Greene county, Pennsylvania, and in 1801 moved to the settlement at Newport, Ohio, later making a home just below Ferguson's Landing, where he died in 1824. His wife was Grace, daughter of Thomas Coleman of Trenton, New Jersey. Their children were Mrs. Nancy Gilke, Mrs. Betsy McVay, Matthias, Joseph, Mrs. Ruth Knowlton, Mrs. Polly Racer, Mrs. Grace Ferguson, Mrs. Susan Racer and Coleman.

Joseph Holdren, Jr., was married to Ruth Coleman, their three children being Mrs. Grace Parker, Thomas and George. He was a resident of Grandview, having gone there in 1803, and died in 1872.

His first son, Thomas, married Mary Ann, daughter of Edmund and Elizabeth Roby Riggs, and they raised eight children: Calvin, who married Catherine Bell; Irvin, married Mary Martin; Edmund, married Mary E. Browse; George Henry, married Harriett Weber; Allen; Josiah, married first Ella, daughter of John William Morgan, second Julia, daughter of Martin Rea, and third, Emma, daughter of Selmon Wells; Mary M. C., married Lafayette Ellis, and Eliza Jane, married James Moore.

Of these the only survivors are Edmund and Josiah, the former living on his farm near Grape Island and the latter residing at Belpre, Ohio.

CORE.—William G. H. and Adelia (Barrack) Core were natives of Harrison county, and after their marriage moved to Newport, Ohio, and then to St. Marys, following his trade as a tailor. This was about the time of the formation of Pleasants county. He became an active man of business and took a very prominent part in the affairs of the county, serving as constable, county commissioner and member of the Legislature.

HAMMETT.—There are two or three branches of the Hammett family in this county, all tracing their ancestry back to a Hammett of Virginia who was a sea captain in the Revolution, and whose son, George, also served in that war. George married Sarah Tillett, and their son,

Samuel. took part in the war of 1812. His first wife, married in 1811, was Winifred Howell, and his second wife, married in 1832, was Ellen Gale, who became the mother of Mary Ellen, George S., John E., James W., Samuel C., Thomas C. and Robert G. Hammett. The last named served as member of the Legislature for Pleasants.

COLE.—Alexander Hamilton Cole. a veteran of the Civil War, and who married Dorcas, daughter of Daniel Reynolds, traced his ancestry back through eight generations to James Cole. who was born in England about 1600 and settled at Plymouth, Massachusetts, in 1633 Ichabod, the fifth in line from James, was a soldier in the Revolution, and his son, Benjamin, crossed the mountains and settled at Powhatan. where William C.. the father of A. H. Cole. was born.

KELSALL.—George Kelsall. son of George and Elizabeth Rundle Kelsall, was born in Baltimore in 1828. and after roving around the West came to St. Marys in 1851; where he opened a cabinet making shop. He married Elizabeth, oldest daughter of William and Catherine Carroll, dying without issue.

OUTWARD.—William Outward's parents came from England in 1825 and settled first on Bull creek. where he was born. In 1846 he married Judith Ingram. Their children were Catherine, married Granville Ingram; Rhoda, married Aaron Ruckman; Belle, married John R. Bills, and Stephen.

BOLTON.—John W. W. Bolton, a distinguished minister of the Methodist Episcopal Church, was born at Hebron in 1834, the son of John and Elizabeth Hanlin Bolton. He served as chaplain in the Civil War, and was celebrated for his learning and eloquence.

STOUT.—Another old family is that of the Stouts. Elias D. and Martha Hathorne Stout were natives of Harrison county, and moved here before the organization of Pleasants. They were the parents of John W., Granville, Sarah A., B. M. and George D. Stout. The last named married, in 1864, Ann M. Pickens, and their nine children were named India R., Granville, Herbert L., George D., John W., Mary Urania, Okey E., Grover C. and Clyde H. He was second major of the militia four years and served a term as assessor.

SEEVERS.—The Seevers family is said to be descended from the old French family of Xaviers, that settled in the Carolinas about two or three hundred years ago. Anyhow, they were early residents of Pleasants. David and Hannah Britton Seevers had a son George Wilson Seevers, who married Lucy C., a daughter of Hiram J. and Mary A. (Medley) Curtis.

LAMP.—Two families of this name settled well up on McKim creek in 1835, both of the same ancestry. They have been traced back to Belmont county, Ohio, and had probably migrated there from Pennsylvania.

Joseph and Martha (Hessen) Lamp settled at the mouth of Cave Run, where he built a saw and grist mill. His wife is said to have descended from the Hessians who had been brought from Germany to aid King George in the Revolution. Nine of their ten children grew to maturity and married. They were Abram, married to Mary Hanes; David, to Hannah Moore; Isaac, to Martha Ward; Serena, to Greenberry Jones; Jane, to John Morgan; Rebecca, to Daniel Fetty; Elizabeth, to Simeon Jones; Christina, to Ralph Hanes, and Jacob, to Nancy Odell.

Joseph Lamp had a brother, Jacob, whose wife was named Susanna. She was born near Harrisburg, Pennsylvania, in 1794, and died in 1891, at the age of 97. With her ten children she moved from Captina creek to McKim in 1835. Her children were John, married to Sarah Hanes; George, to Abigail Hanes; Abram, to Elizabeth Varner; Henry, to a Miss Ward; Joshua, to Lottie Virden; Sarah, to a Milhoan; Margaret, to Joseph Varner; Catherine, to Seth Ward; Caroline, to Eli Wilson.

George, the second son, was a wood worker, making wagons, furniture, spinning wheels, etc. He made the window frames and sashes for the old Cain House in St. Marys. Eli and Caroline Wilson built the log house on McKim, now used for the Four-H Camp.

ISRAEL.—Reuben and Julia Shipley Israel left Frederick, Marpland, in 1838, and after residing in Belmont county, Ohio, two years, settled on Rock Run, building a brush house near where Mount Zion church now stands, and later erected a grist mill near the forks of the run. Their children were Harriett, married to Joseph Hughes; John, to Margaret Davis; Elizabeth, to Louis Davis; Rachel, to Jacob May; Jeannette, to A. Jackson Riggs, and Saran, to Isaac Riggs.

BAILEY.—James and Elsie Bailey came from eastern Virginia about the beginning of the last century and settled in what was then Ohio county but later became Tyler, where their son Jonathan Daniel Bailey was born in 1807. Daniel married Maria, daughter of John Hill, who had come from Pennsylvania and settled in Ohio on the Muskingum river while that section was still a wilderness. Mr. Hill had been a soldier in the war of 1812.

James Bailey served as justice of the peace in Tyler county, and established the postoffice of Grape Island, the first in the county, and also kept an inn or tavern, as then called, to accommodate travelers.

Theodore J., a son of J. Daniel Bailey, was born March 11, 1840, and still resides on the old home farm, where he has served as postmaster. He was married to Eliza, a daughter of Ralph and Rachel Wagner Gorrell.

RUTTENCUTTER.—Daniel and Mary (Pacracy) Ruttencutter were natives of Germany and immigrated to America on the same vessel, not then knowing each other, but afterwards met and were married, settling at Sistersville early in the last century. They raised a family of eight children: J. Frederick, married Mary Ann, daughter of Adam Kester; Eliza, married Greenberry Riggs; William; Rosina, married John Taylor; Joshua; Louisa, married a Robinson; Abraham, married Christina Watson; and Elizabeth, married Joseph Porter.

BROWSE.—Thomas and Eliza Browse left Devonshire, England, in 1830 and settled at Grape Island. He was an active and energetic citizen, served many years as surveyor and justice of the peace, and died while serving as president of the county court in 1880. Of their children, Eliza J. married Henry Clay Creel, son of Alexander H. Creel, and moved to Missouri, where she died in 1863. It was at the home of his son in the same State that Alexander H. Creel, the founder of St Marys, died in 1872, at the age of 85. The son of Thomas Browse, Robert Henry, married Sarah A. Browse in England in 1868, and Mary E., the younger daughter, married Edmund Holdren.

TAYLOR.—Joseph Taylor came from Loudoun county, Virginia, and married Phoebe Cochran. Their son, John F., born June 1, 1820, married Rosina, daughter of Daniel Ruttencutter, making their home at Grape Island, where their eleven children were born: Mary E., died in infancy; Phoebe C. Knight, Harriett R. Flesher, Zachary T., Eliza C., Joseph William, Thomas Jefferson, Maggie M. Bailey, Ella L., Frank Marion and Alice B.

PICKENS.—Samuel and Cyrus H. Pickens, twins, are given as the founders of the several branches of that family in this vicinity. They were born in 1801, natives of North Carolina, came north and first settled in Richland, county, Ohio, later moving to this section, where they bought the Creel land, on which the city of St. Marys now stands. After a few years they sold a portion of this back to Alexander H. Creel, and the remaining parts were bought by Samuel Barkwill, Silas Gallaher and William Bills.

RIGGS.—Soon after the first colony was established in Massachusetts, there came to this country four brothers named Riggs, men of Essex, England. They were shipbuilders, but as England then did not permit the building of ships in the colonies, they brought with them a box or two of oats, in which their tools were hidden. They settled in one of the Bay State colonies, and their descendants scattered out all over the country.

One branch settled in Maryland, and there James Riggs was born in 1745. He married and with his two small sons, Basil and Edmund, came to the Ohio Valley in 1797, making his home below what is now New Matamoras. He died in 1818 and was buried in the cemetery there.

Basil Riggs crossed the river and made a home in the bottoms above the Raven Rock Narrows, marrying Mary Roby. Their children were Isaac, Squire, Hezekiah, Edmund, William, Greenberry, Harriett and Adaline. Isaac married Nancy, daughter of Jacob LaRue, and was the father of Elting, George H., Arthur and Stephen M. Riggs. Squire's children were B. Frank, Scott, Joseph, William, Asbury and Walter S. Edmund's children were Mrs Harriett Hibbs, Mrs Elizabeth Dye, Basil, Martin, George W., Zachariah, James, Mrs Mary Ann Smith and John.

Edmund, the other son of the pioneer James Riggs, married Elizabeth Roby, and their children were Owen, Calvin, Josiah, Mrs. Mary Ann Holdren, Betsy, Maria and Caroline. Owen and Calvin went to Missouri.

Almost every page of Thomas Browse's journal contains some reference to the Riggs family, invariably indicating a strong friendship.

SECKMAN.—The Seckmans came from Berks county, Pennsylvania. Two brothers, Charles and Samuel, left families closely connected with the history of Pleasants.

Charles was born in 1807, married Mary Custer, also of Berks, moved first to Fayette county, then Greene, then to the State of Ohio, and finally to Pleasants, in the Rock Run neighborhood. His children were Margaret, John Randolph, Ann Elizabeth, Andrew Jackson and Mary Ellen.

Margaret's first husband was John Wilson, and their children were F. A. Wilson and Laura, wife of John A. Riggs. Her second husband was David Dillon, and their children were Ida, wife of William Sheets, Edna S., D. Walter and Allie, wife of C. T. McCullough.

John Randolph married Harriett Locke and served with distinction on the county court. He moved to Nebraska and then to Idaho, where he died. His sons are Charles Seckman of Twin Falls, Idaho, and John V. Seckman of Belmont.

Ann Elizabeth married James C. Locke in 1854, and moved to Idaho. Their children were William Jackson, Mrs. Martha Ellen Tuttle, Mary Elizabeth, Mrs. Edith Deerfield and John.

Andrew Jackson married Olive Curtis. Their children are Tyree Alton Seckman of Nebraska and J. Brady Seckman of Roane county.

Mary Ellen married Rev. James P. Varner in 1872. Their children are Walter Forrest and Winifred W., of Akron, Ohio, and Mrs. Catherine Jenkins of Kingsville, Texas.

Samuel the brother of the first Charles Seckman, settled first in Tyler county, then in Pleasants, where his son, Benjamin Franklin Seckman, served as member of the county court, and was married to Sarah Jane Coen, their home being in the Adlai neighborhood. Their children are Mrs. Belle Satterfield of Weston, Mrs. Florence Jones, Mrs. Mattie Clovis (wife of Thomas E. Clovis), Mrs. Josephine Gorrell of Wood county, S. A. Seckman of Belmont and K. R. Seckman of Brooke county.

ADDENDUM

Mention has been made on page 176 of the establishing of a Roman Catholic Church here, but a note on the development of the society was omitted in the chapter of Religious Activities.

The society is in the nature of a mission, under the supervision of the church at Parkersburg, and consequently there are no resident officials in the way of a vestry. From its organization in 1913 the following priests of Parkersburg have officiated: Fathers Balz, Hanrahan, Flynn and McGlone, and the membership numbers about sixty.

FULLNAME INDEX

----, Nicholas 43
ABEL, F C 164 Floyd 214 Floyd C 209
ADAMS, 113 John 256 John Quincy 212 Moses 212 R U 206 Susannah 256 William E 212
ADKINS, 237 239 Elgin 247 Erastus 239 W F 193 William F 168
AGNEW, J R M 100 234 John R M 89
ALBRIGHT, Samuel 249
ALLEN, Asa 256 Asa P 61 James 244 Margaret Taylor 256 Mary E 256 W S 162 165
ALTICE, M D 249
AMBLER, Charles H 232 Joanna 264 John 246
AMOS, Martha Ella 265
ANDERS, Charles 211
ANDERSON, 116 177 C Claude 195 P H 176 R A 138 Robert 148 Robert G 204 234
ANKROM, 171 Clarence 212 Lavina 265 S 164-165 Saul 131 138 148 164
ARBUTHNOT, Dr 182
ARMSTRONG, Robert A 148
ARN, 8 John 74
ARNOTT, Isabella 263 John 263
ARTHUR, T S 100
ASH, I O 227 235
ASHLEY, Nina L 186
ATKINSON, Harry 212
ATWATER, Caleb 15
BAILEY, 33 43 C M 185 Clifford R 212 Daniel 89 Eliza 269 Elsie 269 Frank M 211

BAILEY (cont.)
Harry C 209 Herbert T 208 J Daniel 269 James 44 69 89 257 269 James L 89 Jeff 206 John 42 John D 89 John W 211 Jonathan Daniel 269 Latimer 124 Lloyd 147 183 Maggie M 270 Maria 269 Mary E 89 Mary Elizabeth 258 R G 89 Samuel F 212 Theodore J 269 Wesley D 209
BAKER, A L 182 234 Elisha 103
BALDWIN, J W 89
BALL, Margaret 255-256
BALLARD, L H 151
BALZ, Father 272
BARKER, Aaron 261 C Perry 147 Earl B 212 Ella 261 Eva 261 James 72 Joseph 43
BARKWILL, 33 42 66 170 189 226 Earl K 212 J W 227 O C 197 199 207 232 Oliver C 199 Samuel 59 63 69 90 112 152 158 165 199 270
BARNES, I A 247
BARNHART, Brady B 212 David M 249 George B 211 Lloyd 249
BARNSDALL, 136 141 145 149 151 T N 86 139 149
BARRACK, Adelia 266
BARRETT, W C 245
BARRICK, Wm O 89
BARRON, Alonzo G 212 C L 144 F J 233 Frank J 201 212 J F 139 164-165 234 234 John Franklin 204 M L 148 178 189 229 232-233
BARTLETT, 173

BARTRUG, George 153
BATTELLE, Ebenezer 238-239
BAYLAN, D K 89
BEAGLE, Henry 249
BECKLEY, John 145
BEESON, Jesse C 56-57
BELL, 70 Catherine 266 Robert H 212
BENEDUM, 173
BENNETT, Wm 89
BENNINGER, 173
BENSON, James 255 W H 89
BERK, 89
BERRY, Dode 97 James D 189 Selby 97
BETTMAN, 151
BIDDLE, Bolden 89 Elizabeth 255 Frances 255 Lloyd 255
BIELDZ, John 44
BIER, 143 George 50 W E 88 134 William E 88 230 232 Wm E 88-89
BILLS, 161 171 197 Belle 267 C W 162 Cassie 255 Charles 63 89 Charles W 140 147 Charles Ward 204 F K 175 James 187 John R 267 Joseph 59 168 R E 169 Rebecca 253 Robert E 232 Solomon 63 89 187 William 43-44 54 253 270
BIRKHEIMER, John M 233 Margaret C 256
BIRKHIMER, T R 178 204 Theodore R 233 Thomas J 74
BLACK, E V 178 George 212 Samuel 176
BLAIR, 81 Jacob B 56 80
BLENNERHASSETT, Herman 36
BLOUIR, David J 212
BOGAN, Harry 221
BOLARD, Richard 234
BOLEN, John 31

BOLEY, Andrew 66 Anthony 89 D D 89 David 89 Everett S 212 Harrison 211 John 89 151 183
BOLLES, R E 203
BOLTON, Elizabeth Hanlin 267 John 267 John W W 267
BONAR, Abel 74 Ann 245 Mont L 232 Thomas 245
BONNER, Claude M 211 Harry R 235
BOOKMAN, Annie 146 H M 139 153 Hugh M 131 135 Joseph 74 89
BOOTH, C S 182
BOREMAN, Arthur I 56 56 102 155 William I 56
BOSS, D W 175 George W 86 146 T N 131 141
BOSWORTH, 79 239
BOTTOM, Dr 68
BOUQUET, Col 19
BOWMAN, 203
BOYD, 141 H P 168 R H 139 Robert H 139 146
BOYERS, Edgar 73
BOYLEN, 73
BOYNTON, Paul O 134
BRADDOCK, 19
BRADEN, 89 152
BRADFORD, James A 211
BRADY, Walter 89
BRAFFORD, J L 234
BRAFORD, P S 100
BRAMEL, Thomas 59
BRAMMER, Clyde 212 I E 184 Ira E 233 J F 134 175 Jacob F 233 Lawrence 212
BRANDIS, B 54
BRECKENRIDGE, 70
BREWER, 89 Pearle 212 Samuel J 209 Thomas E 211
BROADHURST, Banks W 89
BROCK, L G 106 235 Thomas 211

275

BROCKUNIER, 8 139
BROOKS, E A 178 Mary 198
BROWN, 37 54 122 164 Frank
   M 85-86 George W 134
   Joseph 74 Joseph C 174 Rev
   175 William 151 Wm 89 Wm
   A 89
BROWSE, 37-40 42-43 45-47 50
   56 61 72-74 140 173 256 259
   264 Eliza 269 Eliza J 270
   Mary E 266 270 Nicholas 37
   40 R H 118 124 128 143 157
   159 165 R T 172 174 Robert
   H 72 107 130 175 234
   Robert Henry 61 246 270
   Sarah A 270 Thomas 33 36
   41-42 48 53-61 63 65 72 89
   194 234 269 271
BRYAN, 155 William Jennings
   168
BRYSON, John 74 89
BUCHANAN, Okey S 211
BULLMAN, John 59
BURGA, Noah 209
BURGE, Ellen 262 Jonathan
   262
BURK, E L 199 250 Evert L 189
BURR, Aaron 36
BUSHFIELD, J M 89
BUTCHER, Effie 263 Pearle
   Raymond 212 William C 207
BUTLER, David A 209
BYNUM, Congressman 169
CADWALADER, 173
CAIN, 66 106 259 268 C T H 160
   Zachariah 89 232 Zachary
   60
CALDWELL, Charles T 169 R G
   141 144 R P 88-89
CALEB, J M 183
CALLIER, Charles J 249
CAMDEN, Johnson N 107
CAMP, Henry 49
CAMPBELL, 33 A M 144 Aug M
   143 145 232 August M

CAMPBELL (cont.)
   119 158 Calvin 74 Henry W
   212 John L 212 L S 186 T F
   165
CAREY, 109
CARLISLE, John 14
CARNEY, James 74
CARPENTER, 222 Barbara Ann
   222 H A 66 193 221 Hiram A
   220 L V 201 Mary Helen 222
   Rebecca 222 Roy Dewey 212
CARROLL, Anne M 261
   Catherine 256 259 261 267
   Charles 235 247 Elizabeth
   261 267 Ella 261 Eva 261
   Fern 212 George 261
   Georgiana 261 H Eugene
   212 Herman 212 James 261
   Jesse 82 Mary 256 261
   Postmaster 98 Sarah 261
   Thomas J 261 William 46 96
   135 256 259 261 261 267
   Wm 89
CARSON, 196 C Allen 212 W R
   184 192 195 233
CARTER, Dr 158
CECIL, Isaac 59
CELERON, 13-16 Louis 14
CHALMERS, Harvey 184
CHAMBERS, James 253
   Maryann 253
CHAPMAN, Nathaniel 14
CHASE, W H 249
CHILDERS, 83 Abigail 263
   Basil 82 O C 82 160 169 201
   229 229 Orlando C 233
CLARK, Frank S 164 Frank
   Wells 178 185 James H 247
CLARKE, George R 201
CLENDENING, R W 174
CLEVELAND, Grover 119 132
   145
CLIFFORD, Emma J Raider
   259
CLINTON, Dewitt 15

CLOVIS, 175 Mattie 272
   Rebecca 264 Theodore 135
   159 Thomas E 272 W E 162
   180 184 193 202 232
COBURN, Jonathan 30
COCHRAN, 78 121-122 134 136
   Catherine 257 Elizabeth 257
   Friend 71 257 Joseph 257
   Joseph E 164 Marion 74
   Phoebe 270 Thomas 257
COEN, G Elwood 235 John 245
   Sarah Jane 272
COFER, Harvey 158
COFFIELD, L N 244
COHAGAN, Fanny 89 Timothy
   89
COLE, A H 138-139 158 164 176
   255 267 Alexander
   Hamilton 267 Alfred H 208
   Benjamin 267 Dorcas 267
   Dorcas Medora 255 Ichabod
   267 James 267 Postmaster
   162 William C 267
COLEMAN, Grace 266 Ruth
   266 Thomas 266
COLLARD, John M 89
COLVIN, Charles H 212
COMPSON, George 221
CONAWAY, John M 248 Peter
   T 248
CONGLETON, Moses 43
CONLEY, 81 Thomas S 80
COOK, 244 Pardon 243
COOKE, 89 E N 88-89 89 130
   Martha 89
COOPER, Drusy 255 I J 89
   John 89 102 202 William
   102 255 William H 183
COPEN, C E 155
COPENHAVER, Abraham 260-
   261 J M 234 Jacob M 155
   260 Jennie 261 John 260
   Margaret 260
CORBIN, Daniel 74
CORBITT, 47 R 125 R M 157

CORE, 68 81 203 A B 138 145
   155 A S 80 Adelia 266
   Alexander 43 Alonzo B 232-
   233 C W 233 Charlotte 256
   Donald 208 212 Opal 186
   Ralph 209 214 Thomas H
   158 W G H 99 139 169 234
   256 William G H 266
   William L 208 Wm G H 89
CORNELL, 248 Della 262
   George E 212 J W H 160
   James E 212 Nancy 257
   William 59
CORNWELL, John J 207
COST, J F 158
COTTON, J C 171 Lillian 186
COWEN, 42
COX, F V 123 George C 211 H C
   175 Isaac B 74 Porter 233
CRAIG, C P 155 178 182 232
   234 Commondore P 263
   Edith 263 James 263-264
   John 263-264 Mary 135
   Thomas 264
CRAMBLETT, Charles A 211
   Frank 212 Fred M 212
CRAMER, Elizabeth 261
   Godfrey 261 R A 71 Rebecca
   261
CRANFORD, 37
CRAWFORD, H T 189 Wm 30
CREEL, 56 64 67 69 73 A H 55-
   58 66 90 138 224 233 247
   Alexander 54 66 Alexander
   H 45 53 55 62-64 115 233
   270 Eliza J 270 Henry C 57
   232 Henry Clay 270
CRESAP, Col 14 Daniel 14
CROGHAN, George 16
CRONIN, Bruce 211 John T 211
CROOK, G H 247
CROSS, Leroy 212 William A
   212
CROUSE, M R 245 Willis Park
   203

CROW, H B 175
CRUMMETT, S P 182
CUMBLIDGE, Benjamin 212
CUNNINGHAM, Clyde M 211
    David 74 George W 209
    James F 212 Samuel 171
CURTIS, Guild 169 Harry K
    209 Hiram 59 Hiram J 268
    Lucy C 268 Olive 272 W M
    155 W N 233 William 167
    William M 194
CUSTER, 122 John 121 Mary
    271
CUTLER, 171
DAILEY, Nancy 242
DALY, Marcel 177
DANA, 237 Luther 237 William
    238
DAUGHERTY, James A 125
DAVIS, C C 235 Clinton C 92 99
    233 Elizabeth 269 Henry M
    209 James L 202 Louis 269
    Margaret 269 Mike 106 T A
    171 Thomas C 119 138 175
    234
DAWKINS, Harold V 209
DAWSON, Harry H 164
DAY, H P 167
DEAN, R C 152
DEARTH, Henry 212 Howard
    M 212 Jacob 74 Jacob W 89
    Maxwell 89
DEBIENVILLE, Celeron 12
DECKER, 49 Elias 89
DEEMS, Chester A 211
DEERFIELD, Edith 271
DEFIBAUGH, Bernard Wayne
    212
DELAGALISSONIERE,
    Marquis 12 15
DELAVAN, Catherine S 89
    Nancy 36
DELONG, 255 Aaron 91 233
    Eliza 257 Fred 212 Paran
    212 Rebecca 257

DENNIS, John Henry 212
DERR, Morris W 247
DESPARD, 115 C S 114
DEVOL, Sarah 257
DEWEY, Adm 161
DICKENS, Charles 92
DIEHL, Patricia S 13
DILLON, Allie 271 Allie Mae
    264 Capt 106 D W 131 175
    D Walter 235 271 David 271
    Edna S 271 Ida 271
    Margaret 271
DILS, 68 89 James 59 William
    57 60 232 Wm 90
DINSMOOR, 173 177 186
    George W 183 194 J D 228
    James D 177 180 192 229
    John C 177 180 L D 177
    Lyell E 177
DINWIDDIE, Gov 19
DITTMER, 261 Elizabeth 261
DOAN, J H 135 146 175
DODDRIDGE, Joseph 38
DONAHUE, Bishop 176
DOOLIN, Edward 30 262
DORNAN, Harry 125
DOTSON, Beryl A 206 Floyd L
    212 Glenna 186 Harry G
    212 Martin L 194 W C 154-
    155 159 164 172 174-175 182
    192 201 227 233 William C
    159 207 235 Wm C Jr 212
DOTY, Bernie Wesley 212 Roy
    212
DOUGLAS, 33 70 William 71
DOUGLASS, C L 199 Minnie
    265 R W 178 189 250
DOUTT, Aaron 66 76 Aaron R
    121
DOWELL, C A 182 246
DRAKE, 79
DUFF, Parker J 95 99
DUFFY, John 166
DULIN, C R 164 168
DUNN, D R 169 Daniel R

DUNN (cont.)
  233 Joseph 117 248
  Lawrence E 212
DUTY, A W 59
DYE, 89 Elizabeth 271 John 89
  Wm H 89
EDDY, Arlando 159 169
  Michael 204 Michael L 212
EDGELL, 239
EDMONDS, Elmer J 234
  Garnet 213
EDMUNDS, 181 E J 227
EDWARDS, John 39 W S 173
  William Seymour 175
EGGLESTON, Edward 243
ELDER, Zora 264
ELIZABETH, Queen 28
ELLIFRITZ, 42
ELLIOTT, John O 211
ELLIS, Benjamin 212 Brooks F
  212 L A 159 234 Lafayette
  266 Leander A 135 203
  Mary M C 266
ELLSWORTH, Joseph H 173-
  174
EMRICK, C C 229
ENGLE, Christian 58 Elsie 261
  J 244
EVERLY, M E 145
EXLINE, Rev 139
FAIRFAX, George 14
FARLEY, 244
FARNSWORTH, C L 185
  Charles S 234
FARREN, James W 209
FARSON, James Wm 212
FAUSS, Ernest J 209 Leroy C
  212
FEARING, Paul 15
FEENEY, 248 Benjamin W 254
  Eleanor A 254 Florence 265
  Frances 254 George W 254
  265 Maria 254 Mary Jane
  254 P P 60 Phineas P 56-57
  234 245 254 Thomas A 254

FEENEY (cont.)
  William H 211 William J
  254
FELLER, H G 165
FELLERS, E D 183
FENNEY, Sarah 254
FERGUSON, 239 Grace 266
  Rachel 89
FETTY, Abia 265 Charles 265
  265 Daniel 268 Grace 265
  Herbert 265 John 61 Nancy
  265 Okey 265 Rebecca 268
  William 265
FISH, John L 246
FITCH, E L 128
FLADING, H J Chalky 172
FLEMING, 24 A B 133 Dan B
  186 196 206 235 247 E T 120
  125 233 J H 234 T E 146
FLESHER, A B 189 234
  Crayton 74 Ervin V 212
  Ethel 186 Harriett R 270
  Henry 57 233 243 Mary J
  256 R A 144 151 155 174-
  175 233
FLINN, 24-25
FLINT, Harriett 89
FLOWER, H M 235
FLOWERS, Hobart 211 Leo E
  212
FLOYD, Gov 58 John B 55
FLYNN, Father 272 J P 189
FOGLE, C E 229 Charles E 234
FOOTE, S E 249
FORBES, Gen 19
FOREMAN, 191 225
FRANCHOT, 173
FRANCIS, D R 178 H A J 247-
  248
FREMONT, John C 61
FRIED, 173-174
FRINK, Edward W 181
FUGET, Sarah 256
FULLERTON, J A 135
FURBEE, A 127

GABBERT, Frederick 164 H B 144
GAINER, Scott 168
GALBRAITH, J H 14
GALE, 238-239 Catherine A 89 Ellen 267 George 157 George W 89
GALLAHER, 58 65 73 155 162 165-166 170 177 183 226 Anne M 261 Edith 186 James M 234 Kate 148 R A 66 89 99 104 152 154 234 234 261 R Alexander 119 Robert Alexander 187 S 106 131 Silas 44 63 89 89 92 95 116 138 187 247 270 Silas A 145 W S 104
GALLAHUE, Rev 47
GALLOWAY, J Emory 138
GAMBLE, Mac 97
GANO, P 92
GARD, Herbert L 212
GARDNER, J W 244 Kenney Ross 212 Ralph 209 Truman M 212
GARRETT, David 245
GARRISON, John D 235 Wm 212
GARRITY, J H 160
GARVEY, 109
GATRELL, Abigail 263 Edith 263 Glenn 212 John 263 John W 74 89 Sarah 264
GEHRI, J H 247
GEORGE, John 171 King 268
GEOTGELUCK, Leon 177
GERBER, 164
GIBBONEY, Lewis 74
GIBBS, Dennis M 210
GIESE, R S 197
GILFILLAN, 81-82 John 80
GILKE, Nancy 266
GILL, U V 58 Uriah V 56 W V 244
GILMORE, Jonathan F 211

GIST, Christopher 14 16 19
GIVENS, 152 A D 235 W M 185
GOERDER, Robert 147
GOETGELUCK, Oscar 170
GOFF, Gen 134
GOLDSTEIN, Joe 164
GOODNO, E C 184 234
GORRELL, 32 56 91 A C 176 A S 249 A W 8 119 125 233-234 Abraham S 55 Archimedes W 91 230 233 Effie 186 Eliza 269 Elizabeth 244 Hannah 244 256 Jacqueline 260 John W 162 Joseph 57 Josephine 272 M L 138 Moses 176 Oliver 117 138 169 190 232 234 R A 132 134 157 162 Rachel Wagner 269 Ralph 269 Ralph A 133 234 Ralph H 232 Thomas 60 232 234 Thomas D 260
GRAHAM, 33 164 Hattie 186
GRANDON, Erve 257
GRANT, Pres 56
GRAVER, Roland 212 Willard L 212
GREEN, Philip 244
GREENBERRY, 43
GREENE, 237 240 Caleb 239 Daniel 237
GREENWALT, Harley 212 Truman 212
GREENWOOD, 239-240
GREGG, David 74 247 Levi 245 Roy M 212
GREGORY, A H 234 O L 209 Owen L 214 T B 189
GREINER, J E 221
GRIFFIN, 196 R L 184 195 207 221 228-229 229 233 250
GRIFFITH, 173 Alfred O 209 Henry C 212 John A 175
GRIGGS, Hannah 264
GRIMM, A S 157 182

GRIMM (cont.)
  Frank 164-165 Homer W
  209 J W 190 233
GUFFEY, 122 J M 121
GUTH, W H 164 198
GUTHRIE, Rev Mr 244
GYLES, Jacob 14
HADDOX, 167 Charles 172 E S
  90 George 212 Green 136
  Greenberry 194 Ray 172
HADLEY, Loman D 209
HAGUE, Wm H 198
HAINES, 98 201 Ralph 78
HALL, 113 C 172 C W 212 E M
  203 John S 95 99 104 164
  195 204 John Sebastian C
  204 Jonn S 178 Leonard S
  56 56 Nannie P 195 235 P
  172 R A 247 Rachel 95 204
  Samuel 204 W A 212 W W
  108 William W 98-99 120
  195 232
HALLECK, 109 112
HALLETT, Benjamin 59
HAMILTON, S C A 82
HAMMETT, 56 80 Arch B 201
  Ed 182 Ellen 267 George
  266 George S 74 232 267
  Giles 59 122 245 James 152
  James M 198 203 James W
  267 John 72 136 John E 267
  Mary 248 Mary Ellen 267 R
  G 234 Robert G 134 145 196
  234 267 Russ 134 140 142
  Russell 85 Samuel 55 267
  Samuel C 74 267 Sarah 266
  T C 7 Thomas C 267
  William E 119 176 198 233
  Winifred 267
HAMMOND, Frances 253 John
  253 Josina 253 Thomas 89
  William 48 Wm 54 89
HANES, Abigail 264 268 Agnes
  264 Betty 264 C 245
  Christina 264 268

HANES (cont.)
  Deborah Wells 264 Hannah
  264 Jacob 244 John 264 L
  Cecil 209 Leander C 138
  Mahlon 61 245 Mahlon D
  133 Margaret 264 Mary 264
  268 Matilda 264 Ralph 264
  268 Sarah 264 268 Theodore
  W 201 Thodore W 135
  William 57 264 William K 59
HANLIN, James L 61 James N
  232 249 Luther 233
  Tarleton 161
HANNA, 142
HANNEN, A D 160
HANRAHAN, Father 272
HARDESTY, 252
HARDING, 229
HARMON, Adam 20
HARNESS, 32 47 Catherine 257
  Elizabeth A 257 John 59 256
  John L 257 Kate 254 Sarah
  254 Solomon 254 256-257
HARPER, Donald H 212
HARRELL, W D 178 249
HARRIS, 54 John 38 136 144
  Tice 211
HARRISON, 255 Benjamin 135
  William Henry 42 238
HART, Alva 214 Alva T 212
  Catherine 249 James 33
  John F 74 Marion 185 233
  249 Martha 249 Matilda 249
  Randolph 214 Slathiel 249
  Thomas H 74 198 William
  33 244 249
HARTMAN, Racie 264
HARVEY, Robert 89 264
HASHMAN, George 212
HATFIELD, 231
HAWKINS, David 248 248
  Frances 253 Okey J 211
HAYES, 239 Frank H 209
HEDLESTON, M L 175
HEILMAN, Ed 202 214

HEILMAN cont.)
  Ethel Smith 213
HELMICK, M D 176
HEMSWORTH, Ida 262
HENDERSHOT, 81-82 Harvey 74 Jacob 80-81
HENDERSON, 30-31 Alexander 30 I H 233 J G 30
HENDRICKSON, 171
HENRY, Patrick 26 62-63
HESCHT, Herbert Clyde 212
HESS, Henry 89
HESSEN, Martha 268
HIATT, J A 246
HIBBS, Harriett 271 Samuel M 59
HICKMAN, Rodney 55-56 60 89 233 254
HIGGINS, Martin L 211
HIGHLEY, Peter W 212
HILL, John 269 Maria 269 Sophia 259
HINES, Benjamin H 212 John 89
HISSOM, 194 J L 160 192 John L 104 175 193 235 Olin S 209 214
HOBBS, E F 154
HODGINS, I N 89
HOGG, George W 235
HOLDREN, Allen 266 Betsy 266 Calvin 266 Catherine 266 Coleman 266 Edmund 39 117-118 270 Eliza Jane 266 Ella 266 George 266 George Henry 266 Grace 266 Harriett 266 Irvin 266 Joseph 266 266 Joseph Jr 266 Josiah 266 Julia 266 Mary 266 Mary Ann 266 271 Mary E 266 270 Mary M C 266 Matthias 266 Nancy 266 Polly 266 Ruth 266 Susan 266 Thomas 266
HOLLAND, Isaac 74 247
HOLMBOE, 225
HOLMES, Mary J 100
HOLT, John H 168
HOOPER, Thornton 66
HOOVER, 231
HOPKINS, 57 68 89 Mary 254
HORNBROOK, Thomas 50
HORNER, John W 56 William E 212
HOUSER, D A 89 David 72
HOWARD, 164 William 244
HOWE, Lieut 73
HOWELL, Floyd C 211 Henry 182 Winifred 267
HOY, Albert P 212
HOYT, E W 121 W E 127 William E 113
HUBBARD, 116
HUBBS, 73 Barbara 264 Joanna 264 Joseph 63 71 89 96 100 264
HUDKINS, Eli 89 G H 135 P H 247 Sarah Jane 262
HUGGINS, A J 147
HUGHES, Ed D 211 Elizabeth 253 Harriett 269 Harry Dean 212 Joseph 269 William 66
HULBERT, Prof 12 24
HUMPHREY, Edgar 195
HUMPHREYS, H C 196 235
HUNTSMAN, Thomas 96
HUPP, Howard E 212
HUTCHINSON, John A 232
HYLAND, William L 246
IDONISE, Jacob 74
IMLAY, A C 143 176 202 Annie 143 J M 66 234 Kenneth P 213
INGLES, Mary 21
INGRAHAM, 33 Abraham 212 Charles F 96 Clyde T 211 Eliza Alcinda 255 Howard 212 James W 212
INGRAM, Catherine 267

INGRAM (cont.)
  Granville 267 Judith 267
IRWIN, Alvira 254 Elizabeth A
  257 Euphremia 254 257
  Francis M 74 James 245 254
  William 43 254 257
ISNER, C A 182
ISRAEL, Elizabeth 269 Harriett
  269 Jeannette 269 John 269
  Julia Shipley 269 Margaret
  269 Rachel 269 Reuben 269
  Sarah 269
JACKSON, 42 172 Benjamin W
  56 J B 89 J H 185 J L 95
  Jacob B 61 232 James M 56
  John E 232 John H 72 John
  J 56 245 John J Jr 56 John
  T 43 Stonewall 198 265 W L
  59 61 William L 56 90 232
JAMES, King 28 Thornton M
  233
JAMISON, Drusilla W 259
JANES, Brady 212 Mary A 126
JARVIS, William 89
JENKINS, Catherine 272
  Harold 246
JERARD, Amanda 89
JOHNSON, 24-25 139 142 153
  250 A L 151 Alvira 254 Bert
  125 C B 148 165 Catherine
  257 Clyde B 145 185 225
  234 Edward Sr 90 Edward
  W 57 Elizabeth 254 257 J
  172 L 172 Ruel 254 Thomas
  245 Tom 213 Tom J 211 W F
  150 William 129 136 244 257
JOHNSTON, William 149
JONES, 98 201 Albert 265
  Elizabeth 268 Emma 264
  Florence 272 Gen 79-80 190
  Greenberry 268 Lizzie 262
  Mary 265 Serena 268
  Simeon 268 Simpson 78
  William 91 William N 91
  233

JORDAN, James B 213
JOSEPH, George M 209
JOY, Abram 74
JUNKINS, Bartholomew 29
JUSTICE, John 89
KAMINSKY, 136
KANE, Joseph G 249
KECKALINE, George 74
KELCH, 42-43
KELLER, Granville 90 233
KELLEY, 60 153 John 74 W W
  135 William C 209
KELLY, John 89
KELSALL, 60 117 Elizabeth
  261 Elizabeth Rundle 267
  George 66 89 95 102 131 135
  144 155 157 171 196 234 246
  261 267
KEMP, 44
KENDALL, Elias 129
KENNEDY, 173 Paca 246
KERNS, Charles Edwin 213
KERWOOD, Elizabeth 265
  James 89 Richard 89 W P
  227
KESTER, 33 Adam 257 259 261
  269 Ann E 259 Cassius Clay
  259 Catherine 259 261
  Charles H 259 Ella 365
  Ernest 213 Hannah Joy 259
  James Buchanan 259 John
  61 232-233 258 John
  Breckinridge 259 Joseph
  259 Joseph H 74 Mary Ann
  259 269 Mary Elizabeth 258
  Mary Ella 259 Minerva J
  259 Nancy 258 Peter 259
  Robert E 212 Rufus W 259
  Sarah 257 Sarah Devol 261
  Sophia D 259 Thomas S 259
  William 74 119 233 248 248
  259
KIESTER, Arthur M 213
KIGANS, A 244 J B 127
KIGER, M F 182

KIGGINS, Joseph 183
KIMBALL, Catherine 89
KING, 68 H P F 129 135 L D 116 Paul 74 Rev 117 Sallie V 259 Samuel 147
KINNARD, 120 S 119
KISKADDEN, Rev 249
KLINZING, Ella 175
KLYNE, S S 183
KNIGHT, Aaron 89 Earl D 150 161 233 J L 139 John L 92 99 119 127 145-146 150 233 Phoebe C 270 Sarah 261 William 227 Zadock 89
KNOWLTON, Ruth 266
KOHLER, Leroy 206
KUNTZ, V J 197
KURTZ, Peter J 209
LAMP, 33 A G 175 Abigail 268 Abra 264 Abram 268 Caroline 268 Christina 264 268 David 268 Elizabeth 268 Emma 264 Frant 264 George 268 Hannah 268 Henry 268 Isaac 268 Jacob 268 Jane 268 John 245 264 268 Joseph 264 268 Joshua 74 268 Lottie 268 Margaret 268 Martha 268 268 Mary 264 268 Nancy 268 Rebecca 268 S K 228 Samuel K 233 Sarah 264 268 Serena 268 Susan 264 Susanna 264 268 Susannah 249
LANCASTER, Clyde 211
LANE, George 211
LARIMORE, Washington 90 Wm 90
LARUE, 30 63 252 Abraham 252 Eliza 253 Elizabeth 253 Isaac 11 29 43 54 90 131 252-253 255 262 Jacob 11 29 32 39 252-253 271 L W 39 Lansford W 253 Maryann 253 Nancy 253 271

LARUE (cont.) Perry 54 77 253 Peter 253 Rebecca 89 253 Sarah 32 131 198 253 255
LASALLE, 12 15
LAWRENCE, 173
LAWSON, Alonzo 76
LEAP, Elizabeth 254
LEBARON, Amos C 158
LEE, J M 146
LEMASTER, Brady 74
LEMLEY, Jacob 74
LEONARD, George 246
LETCHER, Gov 70
LEWIS, 20 Virgil A 5
LINCOLN, 195 Abraham 70
LINDSAY, 22
LITTLE, 60 239 Lawrence 211 Nathaniel 241 Richard 211 Robert B 211
LLOYD, E 125 Jesse 251
LOCKE, 18 A W 162 175 Abia 265 Ada 256 Albert W 234 265 Andrew 265 Ann Elizabeth 271 B A 227 Blanche 264 Charles 209 265 Charles E 74 Charles W 213 Christina 265 Daniel 265 Dennis A 211 Edith 271 Elizabeth 271 Ella 265 Florence 265 Forrest Brady 265 Frank 265 George A 199 265 George T 265 H M 227 Harlan P 265 Harriett 271 Harvey 90 256 Ida B 265 Isaac 265 J R 199 229 234 J Ralph 264 James C 271 Job 33 244 247 265 John 264-265 271 John B 196 265 John T 265 Lavina 265 Margaret 264 Maria 265 Martha Ella 265 Martha Ellen 271 Mary 265 Mary Elizabeth 271 Minnie 265 Nancy 265 Okey J 264

LOCKE (cont.)
  Rebecca 265 Sina 265
  Sophia 264 T 60 Thomas
  244 248 265 Thomas Jr 265
  William 74 William Butler
  265 William C 248 William
  Jackson 271 William T 139
  William T(?) 204
LOGAN, 57 66 68 95 John 56 90
  S 60 Samuel 90
LORILLARD, 124
LOUIS, Xv King Of France 15
LOWERY, Eliza 253
MACKEY, 152
MACTAGGART, G C 195 Guy C
  190 228 234
MADISON, James 263
MAHAN, 152
MALLORY, 149 151 159 166
  177 197 E W 196 John F 165
  171 S T 152 Sid T 154
MALONE, 60 Michael R 212
  William 74
MARKLEY, Dan C 212
MARLIN, Jacob 20
MARR, Georgiana 261
MARSH, Harold V 160
MARSHALL, D C 249
MARTIN, 22 56 Abner 55-57 59-
  60 63 244 Alfred W 213
  August 183 E T 165 171 234
  J W 159 Mary 266 Sophia
  264
MASON, J J 248 J R 184 John R
  202 Joseph 74 90
MASSIE, Edward 174
MASTON, Harvey 213
MATHENY, Charles N 146 164
  William C 212
MAXWELL, Albert R 253
  Edmund H 253 Eliza 253
  James F 253 Josina 253
  Leander B 132 233 253
  Leslie M 253 Oella 260
  Samuel 249 Samuel L 253

MAXWELL (cont.)
  Samuel S 253 Smiley 249
MAY, 25 George 59 Jacob 269
  John 24 Rachel 269
MCBRIDE, J H 227 J Howard
  234
MCCALLY, John G 90
MCCARDLE, Christian 245
MCCLELLAN, T W 129 Thomas
  W 127
MCCLURE, 68
MCCOLLUM, J R 195 207 234
  234 J Riley 247
MCCOMAS, David 59 John 198
  247
MCCONNELL, Maj 108
MCCORMICK, 168
MCCOY, 260
MCCULLOGH, Clarence T 229
MCCULLOUGH, 140 Allen 264
  Allie 271 Allie Mae 264 C T
  183 271 Clarence 264
  Clarence T 182 234
  Coleman 264 D M 5 Daniel
  264 Delphia 264 Emma 264
  George 264 James 264
  James H 212 John 264
  Maxie 264 Rachel Kelley
  264 Racie 264 Rebecca 264
  Sarah 264 Susan 264
  William 264 Zora 264
MCCUNE, Jeremiah 74 Jerry
  203 John 90
MCDONALD, J P 182 249 N P
  246
MCDONALDSON, John 38
MCFADDEN, George A 213
MCFARLAND, 33
MCGEE, 259
MCGILLIS, Dan A 154
MCGLONE, Father 272
MCGREGOR, 33 Homer 235 J
  C 159 John 247 W B 164-
  165 W Burns 164
MCGUFFEY, 159

MCINTIRE, G B 195
MCKEAG, Robert 232
MCKINLEY, 45 William 168
MCKINNEY, 65 J M 159 Wm P 90
MCKNIGHT, 31 Charles 151 213 234 Okey O 213 W E 235
MCLAUGHLIN, J C 106
MCLERRY, William 62
MCMAHON, J R 175 Rolla 164
MCVAY, Betsy 266 Epsie 175
MEANOR, George W 176 182 202
MEDLEY, Eliza 253 Mary A 268 William 245 William Jr 253 Wm 54
MEEKS, Brady 228
MEISENHELDER, Phillip 90
MERCER, Albert C 212 Frank 213 George N 211 Paul 209
MERINGTON, W E 247
MESSER, S G 189
MESSERLY, Charles M 101 John 101
MEWBROUGH, Hester 249
MEYER, Raymond M 212
MEYERS, Ervin D 57
MIDDAUGH, I S 195
MILES, French L 195 Rev 129
MILHOAN, Sarah 268
MILLER, S 189 W F 189
MILLICENT, 173
MINTER, Fred A 201 209
MONROE, James 263
MOOR, Elinor 90
MOORE, 136 Alva B 133 Eliza Jane 266 Hannah 268 James 266 Joseph C 56 S Scollay 247 W H 182
MOREHEAD, J T 176 Wm 90
MORGAN, 33 73 Ap Morgan 20 197 Arja 209 Brady 97 Charles 260 Charles Wesley 203 Eli H 260 Elizabeth 260

MORGAN (cont.)
Ella 266 F F 227 233 Faran F 260 Francis H 204 Harry H 213 Huey 260 Hugh 260 Isaiah D 262 Isiah Dain 260 J W 166 233 Jacob 260-261 Jacqueline 260 James 260 Jane 260 268 Jennie 261 John 268 John S 74 John W 139 John Wesley 197 260 John William 266 Lieut 30 Lydia 260 Lydia Williamson 262 Margaret 260 Melinda 260 Nancy 261 Nancy Ann 260 262 Nathan 232 260 Oella 260 Rachel 260 Richard 20 260
MORRELL, Charles H 212
MORRIS, Elizabeth 257 Emory B 211 Ida P 229 234 John W 245 William R 213 William W 143
MORRISON, 154 173 Ed H 153 Rev 47
MORROW, Col 177
MOSBY, John Shingleton 260
MOSSBURG, J H 248
MOTT, Isaac H 202 Isom H 201
MURPHY, Francis 150-151 Joseph M 201 L J 169 172 234 William 150
MURRAY, Euphremia 254 257
MUSSER, Catherine 255
MYERS, 60 68-69 Capt 72 I B 176 I D 90 Ira 211 Kencil 213 W H 190 233
NEAL, 263 Henry 262 James 262
NEELY, 173 231
NELLIS, Edward 198
NESBITT, Judge 186
NEWBROUGH, Eugenius 249
NEWELL, C P 227
NEWPORT, 238
NEYMAN, A H 227 250

NICHOLS, Arch 194
NIMMO, William 14
NINE, Jacob 232
NOLAND, Harry 213 J C 66 145
  234 Joseph C 232 246
  Willard E 209
NOLE, E P 160
NORRIS, John W 74
NORTHCRAFT, Clarence 211
NORTHROP, J B 228 J Bruce
  189
NYE, 90
O'BRIEN, 109
ODELL, Jane 260 John 247
  Melinda 260 Nancy 268
  William 260
ODENWELDER, Peter 90
OGDIN, 171 N 147 157 N A 172
  Newton 131 134-135 139
  143 146 157 168 O C 168
  171 199 227-228 Oran C 199
  234
OLDFIELD, James A 133 169
  179 John B 183 Thaddeus
  182 William J 211
OLIVER, Alva B 212 Nancy 258
OLMSTEAD, Barney 121
OUTWARD, 33 Belle 267
  Catherine 267 Judith 267
  Rhoda 267 Richard V 213
  Robert H 213 S E 209
  Stephen 267 Stephen E 213
  William 74 176 267
OWENBY, A W 152
OWENS, Corda 213
PACRACY, Mary 269
PARFIT, Lieut 161
PARK, E B 123
PARKER, 258 Grace 266 R T
  89-90 Robert 59 Robert T 57
  71 123 232
PATTERSON, 73 Bert 213
  Emma J 259 James 54 58 90
  143 201 232 234 244 259
  Jane 259 Jenny 143

PATTERSON (cont.)
  John 259 Massey 259
  Robert 70 99 120 201 232
  234 234 259 Robert H 259
  Robert J 125 Robert Jr 90
  Robert W 161 172 Sallie V
  259 Sarah Vanmeter 259
PAYTON, Friend 31
PEDEN, 31
PEMBERTON, R L 135 146 151
  192 234 234-235 Robert L
  185 246-247 Robt L 104 206
PENWELL, Tim C 234
PERCIVAL, F C 165
PERSHING, I C 117
PETERKIN, Bishop 245 G W
  246
PETHEL, Hobart 212 Lafayette
  178
PETHTEL, 73 Ann 255 257
  Eliza 257 Emmeline 257
  Henry 257 Isaac 257 James
  257 James Arthur 213
  Joseph 257 Lafayette 228
  233 257 Nancy 257 Rebecca
  257 Richard 213 Solomon
  257 William 257 Zadock 192
  257
PEYTON, 31
PHILIPS, 22
PHILLIPS, 202 Charles M 81
  George B 180 199 Thomas
  W 81
PICKENS, 44 Ann M 267 B F
  90 220 255 Cyrus H 270 H L
  46 61 H Lee 60 Helen 90
  Hugh L 64 90 232-233
  Narcissa 90 Samuel 54 270
  Samuel W 90
PIERSOL, B K 90 Ben K 89 92
PLEASANTS, James 55
POGUE, 225
POLLARD, Homer E 211
POMEROY, 171
PORTER, Andrew J 234

PORTER (cont.)
 Elizabeth 269 F R 166 J W
 139 John W 114 133 148 154
 233 Joseph 96 131 139 269
POWELL, A W 226 229 Arza W
 206 C J 197 Isaac A 90 J C
 209 229 233 Jonathan 198
 Joseph 72 Josiah 90 233 Sud
 229 233 W S 235
POWERS, A N 228 Jack 90
POYNTER, Dewitt 211 Earl E
 213 H C 248 J J 128 175 248
 John J 104 119 126 234 248
 Reese Asa 213
PRETTYMAN, M P 104 113
 Minos P 104
PRICE, C T 119
PRINCE, 56 Benjamin 59 John
 K 55-57 233
PRUNTY, Jacob 90
PRYOR, Carrie 262
PUTNAM, 191 225
PYLES, William 247
RACER, Polly 266 Susan 266
RAMAGE, S Y 173
RAMSEY, Rev 249
RATHBONE, 79-80
RAWSON, David 74
REA, Julia 266 Martin 266
REED, C S 125 Earl 161 G A
 197 George A 233 265
 Henry 176 L A 189 Mary
 265 Sarah 90 W E 171 233
 William 265 William E 146
 William Edwin 204 Wm E
 154 157
REESE, William 149
REYNOLDS, 17 146 161 239
 Amanda 255 Ann 255 257 D
 54 D W 145 147 157 164 169
 235 Daniel 32 53 58 58-59
 90 131 198 253 255 267
 Daniel W 70 119 232 Daniel
 Webster 58 Dorcas 267
 Dorcas Medora 255

REYNOLDS (cont.)
 Drusy 255 Geo W Jr 74
 George 255 George W 90
 Henning R 212 I O 139 157
 172 Isaac 58 66 96 255 Isaac
 O 134 157 James 70 James
 E 74 Joseph 74 255 Lucy
 255 Lynden E 213 Noah 255
 Robert 255 Rodney 74 90
 158 165 198 255 Sarah 32
 131 198 253 255 T H C 90
 Thomas 32 255 Thomas H
 255 Thomas Henry Coswell
 Crawford Richard Robinson
 Dixon Dotson 255
RICE, Blanche 264 Joseph 74
RICHARDSON, Gen 99 J W 221
 James L 99 121
RICHEY, John 154
RICKEY, T P 182
RIFE, Ralph 209 Ralph A 213
RIGGLE, H L 183
RIGGS, 40 56 142 171 194 A
 Jackson 269 A P 152
 Adaline 271 Andrew Gale
 213 Arthur 271 Arthur P
 145 Asbury 271 B F 169 232
 B Frank 271 B W 244 Basil
 30 39 43 270-271 Bazil 261
 Bethel C 213 Betsy 271
 Calvin 271 Caroline 271
 Donald B 211 Edmond 261
 Edmond Jr 30 Edmund 42-
 43 53-55 57 59 63 266 270-
 271 271 Edmund Jr 63 65 90
 Eliza 269 Elizabeth 261 271
 Elizabeth Roby 266 Elmer E
 213 Elting 271 Ferris 213
 Frederick W 213 G W 90
 George 17 George H 271
 George P 31 George W 95
 255 271 Greenberry 56 59
 269 271 Greenberry B 57 61
 232 244 Harriett 271
 Hezekiah 271 Howard C 213

RIGGS (cont.)
    Isaac 43 54 59 90 194 253 269 271 J D 138 James 270-271 Jeannette 269 John 271 John A 271 John W 74 Joseph 271 Josiah 42 54 271 Josiah D 134 Laura 271 Maria 271 Martin 90 206 271 Mary 261 271 Mary Ann 266 271 Mary F 90 Nancy 90 245 253 271 Owen 42 271 S M 90 S V 160 189 202 232 Sarah 269 Scott 271 Squire 271 Squire D 42-43 Stephen M 175 193 271 Walter S 271 William 271 Z T 172 Zachariah 271

RILEY, Jesse E 235 John W 212

ROBERTS, D A 83 George F Jr 213

ROBEY, H H 174 201

ROBINSON, Charles 74 Eleanor 256 Emmeline 257 Harry 171 James E 74 201 Louisa 269 Rebecca Maria 263 Thomas A 209 Walter Otha 213 William F 74

ROBY, Ann Elizabeth 262 Capitolia 262 Carrie 262 Della 262 Earnest Earl 262 Elizabeth 253 261 271 Ellen 262 Elsie 261 Everett E 262 Frank 261 G K 161 George K 262 Godfrey 253 Godfrey C 261-262 Godfrey Cramer 262 Godfrey Cramer Jr 262 Harry M 213 Ida 262 Ira C 212 Isaac 68 90 253 261-262 Isaiah M 262 Lizzie 262 Lydia 262 Mary 261 271 N Smith Locke 262 Nancy 261 Nancy Ann 262 Otha O 262 Otha Owen 261-262 Pearl 262 Ralph S 262 Sarah Jane 262 Susanna 262

ROBY (cont.)
    Vance R 262 William 261-262 William Hare 261

RODGERS, Everett H 211

RODICK, Bernard 108

ROE, Will 139

ROGERS, 22 Arthur 213 R H 178

ROLSTON, Archibald 254 David Compton 254 Eliza Alcinda 255 Elizabeth 255 George W 255 George Wilson 254 Granville Harness 254 John H 203 245 John Tyler 255 Mary 254 Mary Catherine 254 Nathan 32 254 Nathaniel 255 R 125 Sarah 254 Solomon William 255 William 254

ROOSEVELT, Col 169 Theodore 168 190

ROSENBERG, 171

ROSS, C P 125 Lieut 72

ROSWELL, 263

ROWELL, Daniel 262

RUCKMAN, 248 Aaron 267 J C 160 James 58 72 244 James M 194 234 M A 169 Moses 59 143 Nancy 244 Rhoda 267

RUSSELL, Alexander 179 Frank E 209 H S 226 Henry 229 Henry S 233 Kenneth C 211 Robert W 247

RUTTENCUTTER, 32 47 164 Abraham 74 134 256 269 Abraham R 206 C F 228-229 Charles F 196 199 220 232 Christina 256 269 Daniel 194 269-270 Eliza 269 Elizabeth 269 Frederick 194 Green 129 146 Greenberry 93 248 J F 90 259 J Frederick 93 269

RUTTENCUTTER (cont.)
    Joseph A 161 Joshua 90 269
    Joshua R 74 Louisa 269
    Mary 269 Mary Ann 259 269
    Rosina 269-270 William 269
    William C 74
‹ RYAN, Daniel Lester 213
RYMER, H H 90 Mary 90
    Thomas 57 90 William 57
    176 247 Wm 90
SAMBERSON, Abe B 212
    Abraham 201 Abram 90 Ode
    J 211
SAPP, 172
SARBER, Ben 125 Burr 125
    Elizabeth Ann 263
SATTERFIELD, Belle 272 Elias
    J 74
SAVELL, John D 234
SAYRE, E A 189 Edward A 157
    203 246
SCADDEN, Daniel P 211 John I
    211
SCHAUWECKER, 181 C C 157
    John 103 112 157 172 175
    199 Julius A 247
SCHLEGEL, 173-174
SCHMIDT, Hamilton 90
    Washington 90
SCHULTZ, 34 181 Christian 33
    35-36 241 Grace 265
    Lawrence 213 Nancy 35-36
SCOTT, Dale 209 213 E P 176
    Esau P 183 199 Victor 227
    W S 146
SCRIBNER, Elijah 90
SECKMAN, Andrew Jackson
    271-272 Andrew M 74 Ann
    Elizabeth 271 B F 145 233
    Belle 272 Benjamin F 74
    Benjamin Franklin 272
    Charles 245 271-272
    Florence 272 Grover 214
    Grover C 209 Harriett 271 J
    Brady 272 J Randolph 233

SECKMAN (cont.)
    John 271 John Randolph
    213 John V 214 271
    Josephine 272 K R 272
    Margaret 271 Mary 271
    Mary Ellen 271-272 Mattie
    272 Nellie 213 Olive 272
    Randolph 271 Roy C 211 S
    A 272 Samuel 60 271-272
    Samuel B 61 245 Sarah
    Jane 272 Thomas 72 Tyree
    Alton 272
SEEVERS, David 60 268
    Ephraim W 204 George
    Wilson 268 Hannah Britton
    268 Lucy C 268 Mary A 268
    William M 74
SELLERS, E M 177 234
SEWELL, Stephen 20
SHAFER, Frederick 74
SHAI, George 90
SHANNON, Amanda 255
    William 255
SHARP, 33 Ann E 259 Drusilla
    W 259 Ellen 248 G A 259
    George 58 William T 247
SHAW, George C 246
SHEETS, F 125 Ida 271 W H
    143 William 271
SHELDON, Thomas B 249
SHEPHERDSON, Francis 90
    William R 183
SHINGLETON, 33 142 259
    Alexander 260 Coleman L
    148 234 Earl 211 George
    Washington 260 James 260
    John R 117 132 185 199 233
    245 260 Leonard C 232 260
    O P 245 Oliver Perry 260
    William 260 William C 211
    William H 202 William
    Jasper 260
SHRAKE, P Q 165
SHREAVES, Elizabeth 260
    William 260

289

SIGLER, H L 229
SIMMONS, 179 Holly 171 198
SIMONTON, H F 229 229
  Homer F 233 Wm H 213
SIMPSON, 259 Rev 117
SIMS, J L 128 Rev 176
SIPE, Conrad A 125
SKAGGS, Roseman 214
  Roseman L 209 W L 135 235
SKIDMORE, C 179 182
SKILES, 24-25
SLATER, 170 John 171
SLEMAKER, C E 91
SLOAN, Wiley 211
SMITH, 7 32 60 203 231 A T 165
  Absalom 90 136 Agnes 90
  Alfred 264 Ambrose 57 57
  259 Amos 138 159 177 256
  Annie 175 Asa C 211
  Barbara 264 C M 246 C W
  71 Clark 61 Cyrus P 256
  Dorothy 256 Dudley 119 E
  R 106 153 159 177 192-193
  197 202 233 Eleanor 256
  Elza 59 256 Emanuel 74 G
  A 229 232 G D 184 186 197
  234 George S 245 Gilbert D
  233 259 Hattie O 256 Henry
  239 Homer B 212 I Bud 198
  Ida P 134 Ingle 213 Ingle S
  213 Israel B 74 J G 152
  James S 175 Job 74 90 134
  151 233 264 Landora A 256
  Maggie F 256 Mansfield 256
  Martin L 256 Mary Ann 271
  Mary E 256 Mary J 256
  Mary Lapping 264 Nancy
  Ann 260 Priscilla 256 Rev
  47 Sheridan 256 Squire 256
  Susan Gorrell 256 Susan J
  Wagner 256 Sylvester 256
  Thomas 245 Thomas A 90
  William 256 William A 256
  Wm H 175
SNIVELY, J M 146 176

SNODGRASS, Rachel 260
SNYDER, Estella 213 S D 227
  235
SOMERVILLE, G P 152 Grant
  P 246
SOUTHWORTH, E D E N 100
SPARKS, Thomas 211 W S 182
SPEECE, Jacob 74 S 245
SPENCE, J H 182 Rev 117
SPENCER, Joseph 56 59
  Meredith 90
STACY, Lucy 186
STAFFORD, John 60
STANCLIFF, 173
STANDIFORD, B F 164 B
  Franklin 206
STANLEY, 42 159 171 177 A H
  183 Allen H 168 George 144
  George C 153 John R 144
  153 172 182 235 Maria 248
  Martha 213 Robert 74
STEALEY, James 131
STEELE, Elijah 128 Henry 146
  176
STEERE, 251 D Q 250 David Q
  196 234 Deborah H 250 E B
  80 138-139 Elisha B 250
  Joseph 250 Joseph B 213
  Mary Ella 263 William H
  193 233 250 William S 234
  Wm H 226 228
STEINBECKER, Fred C 225
STEPHENS, A A 90 Albert A 74
  James 255 Lucy 255
STEWART, 56 166 177 Bishop
  212 John 55-58
STICKNEY, 159
STORY, Joseph 136
STOUT, Ann M 267 B M 267
  Clyde H 268 Elias D 267 G
  D 134 158 233 George D 74
  198 267-268 Granville 59
  267 Grover C 268 Herbert L
  268 India R 268 John 233
  John W 267-268 Martha 245

STOUT (cont.)
    Martha Hathorne 267 Mary
    Urania 268 Okey E 268
    Sarah A 267
STRICKLER, Will A 126
STRICKLING, 171 Joseph 138
STROBEL, John M 88 90 96 102
    131
STROUS, 60
STUMP, Catherine 257 J S 158
    Kate 254
SUCK, John 124 143 246 O H
    155 172 174
SULLIVAN, J T 155 169 233
SUMMERS, 31 George 30
    Lewis 30
SUNDERMAN, James C 211
    Raymond L 209
SWALLOW, M O 178 182 232
SWEENEY, August O C 194
    Daniel 249 Howard T 213 O
    C 153 202
TAFT, W H 190 William H 184
TAGGART, 127 H Mac 125 P L
    129 Robert S 126 235
TARBOX, Leon Albert 213 P S
    189 250
TAVENNER, L N 126 176
    Lewis N 155
TAYLOR, 32 127 142 Alice B
    270 Alpha 211 Amlin 44
    Charles 44 Eliza C 270
    Elizabeth 257 Ella L 270 F
    C 90 Frank Marion 270
    Harriett R 270 John 42 44
    59 269 John F 89-90 244 270
    Jos 54 Joseph 47 57-59 90
    270 Joseph William 270
    Maggie M 270 Mary E 270
    Phoebe 244 270 Phoebe C
    270 Rosina 269-270 Roswell
    44 T J 192 Thomas 90
    Thomas Jefferson 270 Zach
    154 Zachary T 270
TERRY, O J 125

THOMAS, Henry 62
THOMPSON, Lizzie 164 W P
    107
THORN, 260
THORNE, O E 176
THORNLEY, Jane 244 John
    244 Mary Catherine 254
THORNTON, William 14
THURMAN, Allen G 133
TICE, Franklin Luther 213
TILLETT, Sarah 266
TIPLETT, Francis M 263
    Isabella 263
TOLER, 90
TOMKINS, S D 246
TOWNSEND, J B 90 234 John
    B 99
TOWZEY, Richard 68-69 90-91
    100 233-234 W J 168
TRAUGH, C A 168
TRAUTMAN, Howard L 213
TREES, 173 Joseph C 167 174
TREMBLEY, John William 212
TRENT, William 19
TRIPLETT, 262-263 America
    Patterson 263 Burr 245 263
    Catherine 263 Charles A
    263 Columbia Cox 263
    Dollie 175 Donald 212 Effie
    263 Elizabeth 263 Elizabeth
    Ann 263 F M 90 146 151 162
    167 169 178 184 233-234
    Francis 59 Francis M 30 190
    263 Frank 182 245 Frank M
    134 Guy 193 H C 193 Harry
    193 Ida May 263 John 30
    190 197 234 263 263 Maggie
    263 Mary Ella Steere 263
    Peyton 263 R H 180 193
    234-235 Ralph 193 Rebecca
    Maria 263 Robert 30 59 245
    263 Robert Harry 263
    Robert S 263 Samuel 245
    William 263
TURNER, E M 176

TUTTLE, Martha Ellen 271
TYGART, 11
UNDERWOOD, A J 63 229 Earl 213 Ernest 212
VANBUREN, Martin 42
VANCE, A S 128 244
VANVALEY, G Wallace 213 George R 180 Lyle 209
VARNER, Catherine 272 Elizabeth 268 J L 167 J P 175 Jacob L 162 233 265 James P 272 Joseph 268 L S 183 Margaret 268 Mary Ellen 272 Sina 265 Walter Forrest 272 Winifred W 272
VERBEKE, Charles 177
VINCENT, Dustin 213 Enoch 262 Susanna 262
VIRDEN, A C 176 Abner C 183 John 74 Lottie 268 William 60
VIRGIN, 161
VOGEL, 32
W, L Neely 66
WAGNER, 175 255 Amos 201 256 Asa 161 Asa F 255 Bernard L 211 C N 186 Calvin 255 Catherine 255-256 Catherine Hays 255 Charles N 235 Christopher 33 255-256 Christopher J 256 David 255 Elizabeth Weekley 256 Elroy 174 256 Friend 195 233 256 G A 177 Isaac 138 255 James 18 255 John 256 John R 255 Joseph 255-256 Joshua 256 Margaret 256 Margaret Bullman 255 Nancy 255 Sarah Q Lamp 256 Susan J 256 Thomas J 255 William 255
WALKER, L P 165 189 Ronald R 213
WALTON, W N 124

WARD, 268 Catherine 268 Martha 268 R B 152 Seth 268
WARE, Bruce R 208
WARREN, Rev 47
WASHINGTON, 6 29 260 Augustus 14 George 11 19 21 Lawrence 14
WATSON, 68 151 A Jackson 95 256 Ada 256 Charlotte 256 Christina 256 269 George 256 Isaac 90 J B 90 John 61 128 233 256 John B 159 John Loomis 213 Joseph B 128 157 198 261 Joseph Barnett 256 Lewis James 213 Mary 261 Rosanna 256
WATTS, Ella 179
WAUMAN, John F 235
WAXELBAUM, 154
WAYMAN, John F 93 233
WAYNE, Gen 21
WAYT, W H 235
WEAVER, Michael 90
WEBER, E T 227 Harriett 266 Michael 90
WEEKLEY, Susan A 256
WEEKLY, James M 213 Ola 211 213
WELLS, 79 262 Austin G 74 Charles 31 Chas 31 Daniel 43 Eli 244 256 Emma 266 Hannah 256 J M 129 Jacob 211 James 43 James M 127 145 147 158 Lee 212 M M 139 Nicholas 43 72 Priscilla 256 Ross 210 S D 234 Selmon 266
WENTZ, George W 172
WERNECKE, Arland D 209 C A 179 196
WEST, Clarence R 213 George E 202 234 Stephen 62-63
WETZEL, Lewis 21
WHALEY, Delphia 264

WHERRY, Ed 125 William E 211
WHITE, H S 121 John 160 L C 229 Leonard C 234 Samuel 183 197 Samuel Ray 213
WIDDERFIELD, John 57 John W 56
WIGNER, John G 74
WILCOXEN, Jed C 213
WILDING, George C 116
WILEY, Arza E 213 Daniel W 203 James P 213
WILHELM, Capitolia 262
WILLARD, Benjamin W 241
WILLIAMS, 31 Charles E 212 H C 96 227 Homer C 213 Ira 228 235 Isaac 12 29 James 42 Joe 155 179 228 234 Susannah 256 W Mack 144 William 43
WILLIAMSON, 32 255 Charles W 256 Chester 256 Christopher J 256 E W 160 F 60 George M 135 204 256 H J 164 171 194 Isaac 55-56 James 61 255-256 James W 71 177 234 256 John 59 256 Lydia 260 M 233 Margaret 255-256 Margaret C 256 Martha 256 Mary J 256 Moses 55-56 58 232 260 N J 179 Nancy 255 Nancy Ball 260 Sarah 256 Sarah A 256 Sidney C 256 W D 201 Wayland F 211 Wiley M 212 William 256
WILLIS, Edward 90
WILSON, 73 Caroline 268 Charles 244 E J 162 Eli 268
WILSON (cont.) F A 271 G I 178 J B 185 John 271 John E 212 Laura 271 Margaret 245 271 Massey 259 Newman 74 Otha 211 Pres 197 207 Ralph 33 244 Sylvester 74 W A 185 192 William 74 Woodrow 190
WINER, 136
WINLAND, Ben A 212 James 213
WINSTANLEY, Rev 47
WISE, Ernest Lee 212
WISEMAN, George F 74
WITTEN, John 262 Susanna 262
WOLFE, Reese 244
WOOD, C J 233 Charles I 74 George 247 John F 129 Leslie A 213 Rev 47
WOODBRIDGE, George 43
WOODROP, James 14
WOODS, Francis 90 Homer B 183 186 224-225 J F 168 James 245 John F 246
WRICK, John 247 Rebecca 265
WRIGHT, Freeman 211 Jesse 213 Joseph 203 Reuben 74 Wm R 212
WYANT, 172
XAVIERS, 268
YATES, 103 F M 94-95
ZAHNISER, M L 177
ZAHNIZER, 173 M L 173
ZIKA, John W 202
ZIPF, Clifford Edwin 213 George 202 234

www.ingramcontent.com/pod-product-compliance
Lightning Source LLC
Chambersburg PA
CBHW071449250426
43671CB00042B/1902